WITHERBY'S
DICTIONARY OF INSURANCE

Witherby's
Dictionary of Insurance

by
Hugh Cockerell
O.B.E., B.A., F.C.I.I., Barrister

LONDON

WITHERBY & CO. LTD.
32–36 Aylesbury Street
London EC1R 0ET

Published 1980
1st Edition
2nd Edition 1987

ISBN 0 948691 21 2

Printed in Great Britain by
Witherby & Co Ltd
32–36 Aylesbury Street
London EC1R 0ET

Contents

Preface
to the First Edition

This dictionary is intended to help people who practise insurance or who need to read about it, to understand the terms and abbreviations they may encounter. It is not encyclopaedic. The aim is to give the reader in a few words the meaning of each term defined, without going into great detail.

The main problem in compiling the vocabulary has been to decide where to draw the line. For example, there are a great many technical American terms but only a selection of them has been included. Many others are to be found in Lewis E. Davids' Dictionary of Insurance. Again, the marine insurer will need to know the vocabulary of ships and ship construction. For this it would be necessary to go to R.H. Brown's Dictionary of Marine Insurance and Terms. Actuarial science has a vocabulary of its own which the dictionary has not attempted to cover. The aim has been to provide for the general practitioner in any class of insurance rather than for the highly specialised.

To make the book more useful I have included not only abbreviations and definitions but short notes on the principal institutions of insurance in the United Kingdom.

Commercial usage is constantly changing and the book will need updating from time to time. Suggestions for improvements will be welcome. Meanwhile I hope that users of the dictionary will find it of some service.

Hugh Cockerell

Preface
to the Second Edition

Insurance does not stand still. For this new edition I have added over 300 terms and abbreviations without removing many obsolete ones as they may still be encountered in some places. About 200 additional terms have been defined and the notes on insurance institutions have been updated.

I am grateful to correspondents for suggestions and corrections. I hope readers will continue to write to me so that the utility of the book can be further increased.

Hugh Cockerell
Visiting Professor in Insurance Studies
City University Business School
Frobisher Crescent
Barbican
London EC2Y 8HB

Abbreviations

NOTE Practice varies in the use of capitals, full stops, and strokes between letters. There is no uniformity. In this list full stops have been used as a rule but there is a growing and welcome tendency to print abbreviations, especially acronyms, without stops.

A

@	At
a.a.	After arrival. Always afloat
A.A.I.	Alliance of American Insurers
A.A.R.(D)	Accounting and auditing review department (Lloyd's)
A.B. or A.B.S.	American Bureau of Shipping
A.B.I.	Association of British Insurers
A.B.I.S.	Association of Burglary Insurance Surveyors
A/C	Account current
A/c	Account
Acc.	Accident
A.C.I.I.	Associate of the Chartered Insurance Institute
A.C.I.L.A.	Associate of the Chartered Institute of Loss Adjusters
ACOG	Aircraft on ground
ACT	Advance corporation tax
A.C.V.	Air cushion vehicle (hovercraft)
A.D.	Accidental damage
Ad. val.	Ad valorem

1

A.F.I.A.	American Foreign Insurance Association
A.F.I.I.	Associate of the Federation of Insurance Institutes (India)
A.H.F.	American Hull Form
A.H.I.S.	American Hull Insurance Syndicate
A.I.A.	Associate of the Institute of Actuaries. American Insurance Association
A.I.B.	Authorised inspection body
A.I.D.A.	Association Internationale du Droit de l'Assurance (International Association for Insurance Law)
A.I.I.C.	Associate of the Insurance Institute of Canada
A.I.I.E.	Australian International Insurance Exchange
A.I.M.U.	American Institute of Marine Underwriters
A.I.O.A.	Aviation Insurance Offices Association
AIRMIC	Association of Risk Managers in Industry and Commerce
A.I.S.A.M.	International Association of Mutual Insurance Societies
A.L.I.A.	Associate of the Life Insurance Association
All E.R.	All-England Law Reports
A.L.M.	Association of Lloyd's Members
A.M.L.	Absolute maximum loss
A.N.L.	Above-normal loss
A/o	Account of
A.O.A.	Accident Offices' Association
a.o.a.	Any one accident
A.O.A.(O)	Accident Offices' Association (Overseas)
a.o.b.	Any one bottom
A.O.C.	All other contents
a.o.e.	Any one event
a.o.l.	Any one loss
a.o.o.	Any one occurrence
A.O.T.C.	Associated Offices Technical Committee
a.o.v.	Any one vessel
a.o.voy.	Any one voyage
A.P.	Additional premium. Annual premium. Agricultural produce
APEX	Association of Professional, Executive, Clerical and Computer Staff
a.p.l.	As per list
A.P.M.I.	Associate of the Pensions Management Institute

A.P.P.	Adjustable premium policy
Appd	Approved
A.P.T.	Association of Pensioneer Trustees
A.R.	All risks
A.R.P.	Accrued rights premium
Arr. T.L.	Arranged total loss
A.S.G.	Advanced study group
ASIR	Advanced Simulation of Insurance and Reinsurance Operations
A.S.L.O.	Associated Scottish Life Offices
ASTIN	Actuarial Studies in Non-Life Insurance
ASTMS	Association of Scientific, Technical and Managerial Staffs
A.T.L.	Actual total loss. (Sometimes wrongly used for Arranged total loss.)
A.T.O.L.	Air Travel Organiser's Licence
att.	Attached
Auto P.A.	Automatic personal accident (aviation insurance)
AUTO P.A.	Automatic personal accident (aviation insurance)
A.V.C.	Additional voluntary contribution
Av.	Average

B

B.B. Clause	Both to blame collision clause
Bd.	Bond
B.D.I.	Both days inclusive
B.D.S.	Broker's daily statement
B/E	Bill of exchange
b.f.s.l.	Being fully signed line
b.f.w.l.	Being fully written line
B/G	Bonded goods
B/H	Bordeaux/Hamburg limits
B.I.	Business interruption. Bodily injury
B.I.A.	British Insurance Association
B.I.B.A.	British Insurance Brokers' Association
B.I.E.C.	British Insurers' European Committee
B.I.F.U.	Banking, Insurance and Finance Union
B.I.G.	British Insurance Group
B.I.I.C.	British Insurers' International Committee
B.I.L.A.	British Insurance Law Association

3

B.I.P.A.R.	Bureau International des Producteurs d'Assurance et de Réassurance (International Association of Insurance and Reinsurance Brokers and Agents)
B/L	Bill of lading
BLAT	British Life Assurance Trust for Health Education
Bls.	Bales. Barrels
B.M.U.A.	British Marine Underwriters' Associations
B.N.A.	British North America
BORD or bord	Bordereau
B.R.	Builders' risks (marine)
Brok.	Brokerage
B.S.	Boiler survey. British Standard
B.S.I.	British Standards Institution
bsst	Brick or stone built, slated or tiled
B.S.T.	British Summer Time
B.T.U.	British Thermal Unit
B.V.	Bureau Veritas

C

C.A.A.	Civil Aviation Authority
C.A.D.	Cash against documents
C.A.P.A.	Comité d'Action pour la Productivité dans l'Assurance (Committee for promoting Productivity in Insurance)
C.A.R.	Contractors' all risks. Constructors' all risks.
c. & f.	Cost and freight
c. & i.	Cost and insurance
C.C.	Civil commotions. Cancellation clause. Collecting commission
C/D	Country damage
C.E.A.	Comité Européen d'Assurances (European Insurance Committee)
C.E.I.S.S.	Conference of European Insurance Supervisory Services
C.E.O.C.	Colloque Européen des Organismes de Contrôle (European Colloquium of Inspecting Organisations)
C.E.P.	Contributions equivalent premium
c.f.i.	Cost, freight and insurance
c.g.a.	Cargo's proportion of general average
CGT	Capital gains tax
C.I.E.	Canadian Insurance Exchange

4

C.I.F.A.	Corporation of Insurance and Financial Advisors
c.i.f.	Cost, insurance and freight
c.i.f. & e.	Cost, insurance, freight and exchange
c.i.f. & i.	Cost, insurance, freight and interest
c.i.f.c. & i.	Cost, insurance, freight, commission and interest
CIFT	Committee on Invisibles and Finance relating to Trade
C.I.I.	Chartered Insurance Institute
C.I.L.A.	Chartered Institute of Loss Adjusters
C.I.R.T.A.	Convertible increasable renewable term assurance
C.I.T.U.	Confederation of Insurance Trade Unions
Cl.	Clause
C.L.C.	Consequential Loss Committee
CLORA	Consequential loss rating adjustment
C.L.U.	Chartered Life Underwriter (U.S.)
C.M.B.	Corporation of Mortgage Brokers and Life Assurance Consultants
C.M.I.	Comité Maritime International (International Maritime Committee)
C.M.R.	Convention on the Contract for the International Carriage of Goods by Road
C/N	Cover note. Credit note
C.O.D.	Cash on delivery
COINTRA	Coopération Internationale pour les Assurances des Risques Aggravés (life insurance)
CONFIMA	Confederation of Insurance Managers' Associations
Cont: B/H	Continent between Bordeaux and Hamburg inclusive
C.P.A.	Claims payable abroad. Contractors Plant Association
C.P.C.	Component parts clause
C.P.C.U.	Chartered Property and Casualty Underwriter (U.S.)
C.P.I.C.	Company Pensions Information Centre
C.R.	Current rate
CRISTAL	Contract Regarding an Interim Supplement to Tanker Liability for Oil Pollution
C.R.O.	Cancelling returns only
CSC	(International) Convention for Safe Containers

C.T.C.	Corn Trade Clauses
C.T.L.	Constructive total loss
C.T.L.O.	Constructive total loss only
C.T.O.	Capital Taxes Office
CTT	Capital Transfer Tax
C.V.	Commercial vehicle. Curriculum vitae
c.w.o.	Cash with order
CY	Currency

D

D	Delivery. Delivered
D/A	Deductible average
D. and O.	Directors and Officers
DANDO	Directors' and Officers' liability (U.S.)
D.C.	Direct costs
D/C	Deviation clause
D.C.I.	Difference in conditions insurance
Dd.	Delivered
D/D	Damage done
Deb.	Debenture
Def.	Deferred
D.F.D.	Double fire break door
D.H.S.S.	Department of Health and Social Security
D.I.B.	Double indemnity (accident) benefit
D.I.C.	Difference in conditions
D.I.P.	Difference in perils
D-I-S	Death in service
D/N	Debit note
D.N.O.	Debit note only
D.O.B.	Date of birth
D.O.L.	Dock owner's liability
D.R.C.	Damage received in collision
D.S.I.	Daily sum insured
D.S.D.	Documentary sight draft
D.T.A.	Deferred term assurance
D.T.B.A.	Date to be advised
D.Tp.	Department of Transport
D.T.R.	Double taxation relief
D.V.	Declared value
D/V	Dual valuation
D/w	Deadweight

E

E.A.I.C.	East Asian Insurance Congress
E.A.R.	Engineering all risks

e. & e.a.	Each and every accident
e. & e.l.	Each and every loss
e. & e.o.	Each and every occurrence
E. & O.E.	Errors and omissions excepted
E. & S.	Excess and surplus (lines) (U.S.)
EC	European Community
E.C.G.	Electro-cardiogram
E.C.G.D.	Export Credits Guarantee Department
E.C.O.	Extra-contractual obligations
ECU	European currency unit
E.D.P.	Electronic data processing
E.E.	Errors excepted
E.E.C.	European Economic Community
E.E.G.	Electro-encephalogram
E.F.T.A.	European Free Trade Association
E.I.C.	European Insurance Committee
E.L.T.	English life tables
E.M.L.	Estimated maximum loss
E.M.P.L.	Estimated maximum probable loss
e.o.h.p.	Except as otherwise herein provided
E.P.	Equal proportions
E.P.B.	Equivalent pension benefits
E.P.F.	Excepted provident fund
E.P.I.	Earned premium income. Estimated premium income
E.P.P.	Executive pension plan
E.R.I.S.A.	Employee Retirement Income Security Act 1974 (U.S.)
E.S.A.	Early Signings Account
E.T.A.	Estimated time of arrival
	F
F/A	Fire and accident (insurance)
f.a.a.	Free of all average
Fac./Oblig.	Facultative/Obligatory
F.A.F.R.	Fatal accident frequency rate
F.A.I.I.	Fellow of the Australian Insurance Institute
F.A.I.R.	Federation of Afro-Asian Insurers and Reinsurers
FAP	Future annual premium
F.A.R.	Free of accident reported
F.A.S.	Free alongside ship
FASS	Federation of Associations of Specialists and Sub-Contractors

F. & A.P.	Fire and allied perils
F.C.A.R.	Free of claim for accident reported
F.C. & S.	Free of capture and seizure
F.C.E.C.	Federation of Civil Engineering Contractors
fch.	Franchise
F.C.I.I.	Fellow of the Chartered Insurance Institute
F.C.I.L.A.	Fellow of the Chartered Institute of Loss Adjusters
F.C.O.D.	Fire, collision, overturning and derailment
F.C.R.	Forwarding agents' certificate of receipt
F.C.S.R.C.C.	Free of capture, seizure, riots and civil commotions
F.C.S.S.R.C.C.	Free of capture, seizure, strikes, riots and civil commotions
F.C.T.	Forwarding agents' certificate of transport
F.C.V.	Full contract value. Full completed value
F.D.	Fire break door
F.D.D.	Freight, demurrage and defence
F.D.O.	For declaration purposes only
F.E.A.	Fire extinguishing appliances
F.F.A.	Fellow of the Faculty of Actuaries in Scotland
F.F.I.I.	Fellow of the Federation of Insurance Institutes (of India)
F.G.	Fidelity guarantee
F.G.U.	From the ground up
F.G.A.	Foreign general average. Free of general average
F.I.A.	Fellow of the Institute of Actuaries. Federal Insurance Administration (U.S.)
f.i.a.	Full interest admitted
F.I.I.C.	Fellow of the Insurance Institute of Canada
F.I.L.	Foreign insurance legislation
FIMBRA	Financial Intermediaries, Managers and Brokers Regulatory Association
F.I.R.T.O.	Fire Insurers' Research and Testing Organisation
F.L.E.	Fire, lightning and explosion
F.L.I.A.	Fellow of the Life Insurance Association
F.L.M.I.	Fellow of the Life Management Institute (U.S.)
F.M.	Factory Mutuals
f.o.b.	Free on board
F.O.C.	Fire Offices' Committee. Free of claims. Free of charge. Free of cost. Flag of convenience

F.O.C.(F.)	Fire Offices' Committee (Foreign)
F.O.D.abs.	Free of damage absolutely
F.O.M.	Flag, ownership or management
F.P.	Floating policy. Fully paid. Fire plug
F.P.A.	Free of particular average
F.P.A.abs.	Free of particular average absolutely
F.P.A.u.c.b.	Free of particular average unless caused by
F.P.A.unless	Free of particular average unless
F.P.I.L.(P.I.A.)	Full premium if lost (from a peril insured against)
F.P.M.I.	Fellow of the Pensions Management Institute
F.R.C.	Free of reported casualty. Fire resisting construction
F.R.C.C.	Free of riots and civil commotions
F.R.O.	Fire risk only
f.r.o.f.	Fire risk on freight
f.s.l.	Full signed line
F.S.R. & C.C.	Free of strikes, riots and civil commotion
F.S.S.U.	Federated Superannuation Scheme for Universities
f.t.	Full terms
FUEDI	Fédération des Unions Professionnelles d'Experts en Dommages après Incendie at Risques Divers dans le cadre de la C.E.E. (Federation of Professional Assocations of Adjusters of fire and other losses in the E.E.C.)
f.w.d.	Fresh water damage
f.w.l.	Full written line

G

G.A. or G/A	General average
G.A.D.	General average deposit. Government Actuary's Department
G.A.D.V.	Gross arrived damaged value
G.A.L.	General average loss
G.A.S.V.	Gross arrived sound value
G.B.	General (non-life) business. General branch. Great Britain
G.b.o.	Goods in bad order
G.D.D.I.	Guaranteed direct-dealing intermediary (Lloyd's)
G.E.P.	Gross earned premiums
g.f.a.	Good fair average

G.G.B.	Guaranteed growth bond
G.I.B.	Guaranteed income bond
G.I.T.	Goods in transit
G.L.	Germanischer Lloyd
G.m.b.	Good merchantable brand
G.M.P.	Guaranteed minimum pension
G.m.q.	Good merchantable quality
G.M.T.	Greenwich mean time
G.O.R.	Gross original rate
G.P.	General practitioner
G.R.O.	Ground risks only
G.R.R.	Good record returns
G.T.P.	General third party (liability insurance)
G.W.P.	Gross written premiums

H

HASAWA	Health and Safety at Work etc. Act 1974
H.&M.	Hull and Machinery
H.C.	Held covered
H.G.V.	heavy goods vehicle
H.M. etc.	Hull and machinery etc.
H.M.G.	Her Majesty's Government
H.M.S.O.	Her Majesty's Stationery Office
H.N.S.	Hazardous and noxious substances
H.O.	Head Office. Home Office (U.S.)
H.P.	Horse-power
H.P.R.	Highly protected risk (U.S.)
H.P.H.W.	High pressure hot water
H.S.C.	Health and Safety Commission
H.S.E.	Health and Safety Executive
H.W.D.	Heavy-weather damage

I

I.A.A.	Insurance Adjusters' Association
I.A.H.	International Association of Hail Insurers
I.A.R.	Industrial all risks
IATA	International Civil Air Transport Association
I.B.	Industrial (life) business. Industrial (life) branch
I.B.A.	Insurance broking account
I.B.C.	Institute Builders Risk Clauses (marine)
I.B.N.R.	(losses) incurred but not reported
I.B.N.P.R.	Incurred but not properly reported

I.B.R.C.	Insurance Brokers Regisration Council
I.C.A.O.	International Civil Aviation Organisation
I.C.C.	Institute Cargo Clauses. International Chamber of Commerce
I.C.D.	International Classification of Diseases
I.C.E.	Institution of Civil Engineers
ICW	Increased cost of working
I.E.I.C.	Independent Engineering Insurers' Committee
I.F.C.	Institute Freight Clauses
I.H.P.	Indicated horse power
IHT	Inheritance Tax
I.I.A.	Insurance Institute of America (U.S.). Irish Insurance Association
I.I.A.A.	Independent Insurance Agents of America (U.S.)
I.I.C.	Insurance Institute of Canada. Independent Insurance Conference (U.S.). Institute of Insurance Consultants
I.I.F.	Irish Insurance Federation
I.I.I.	Insurance Information Institute (U.S.)
I.I.L.	Insurance Institute of London
I.I.R.	Institute of Insurance Research (U.S.)
I.I.T.C.	Insurance Industry Training Council
I.L.O.	International Labour Organization
I.L.O.A.	Industrial Life Offices' Association
I.L.U.	Institute of London Underwriters
I.M.C.O.	Inter-Governmental Maritime Consultative Organization
I.M.I.A.	International Machinery Insurers' Association
I.M.I.U.	International Marine Insurance Union
I.M.O.	International Marine Organization
INMARSAT	International maritime satellite system
Inst.	Institute of London Underwriters
I.O.B.	Insurance Ombudsman Bureau
I.O.I.	International Oil Insurers
i.o.p.	Irrespective of percentage
I.P.A.	Individual (or independent) pension arrangement
I.P.R.C.	Institute Port Risk Clauses
I.R.	Inland Revenue
I.R.I.	Industrial Risk Insurers (U.S.)
I.S.C.A.P.	Institute for Study and Investigation of Central American and Panamanian Insurance

I.S.O.	Insurance Services Office (U.S.)
I.S.S.A.	International Social Security Association
I.T.C.	Institute Time Clauses (Hulls)
I.U.A.I.	International Union of Aviation Insurers
I.V. or I/V	Increased value. Insured value. Invoice value
I.Y.C.	Institute Yacht Clauses

J

J.	Mr Justice
J. & W.O.	Jettison and washing overboard
J.C.T.	Joint Contracts Tribunal for Standard Forms of Building Contracts
J.H.C.	Joint Hulls Committee
J.I.A.	Journal of the Institute of Actuaries
J.S.A.	Job safety analysis
J.S.P.	Job safe practice

K

K&R	Kidnap and ransom (insurance)
K.K.	Knock-for-knock
K.O.	Keep off (do not insure)

L

L/A	Lloyd's Agent
LACC	Lloyd's Aviation Claims Centre
L.A.D.	Lloyd's Aviation Department
L.A.D.(A.)	Lloyd's Agency Department (Aviation)
L. & P.	Life and Pensions
L.A.P.R.	Life assurance premium relief
L.A.S.C.	Life assurance salesman's certificate
L.A.T.F.	Lloyd's American Trust Fund
L.A.U.A.	Lloyd's Aviation Underwriters' Association
LAUTRO	Life Assurance and Unit Trust Regulatory Organisation
L/C	Leading company (companies)
L.C.A.	Lloyd's Central Accounting
L.C.J.	Lord Chief Justice
L.C.T.A.	London Corn Trade Association
L.C.T.F.	Lloyd's Canadian Trust Fund
L.D.P.I.	Latent defects protection insurance
L.E.L.	Lower earnings limit
L.H.A.R.	London, Hull, Antwerp or Rotterdam
L.I.A.	Life Insurance Association
L.I.B.C.	Lloyd's Insurance Brokers' Committee
LIBRA	Life Insurance Brokers' Association

L.I.M.R.A.	Life Insurance Marketing Research Association (U.S.)
L.I.P.	Life insurance policy
L.J.	Lord Justice
Ll. & Cos.	Lloyd's and companies
L.L.A.G.	Linked Life Assurance Group
Ll.L.R.	Lloyd's List Law Reports (former designation of Lloyd's Law Reports)
Lloyd's Rep.	Lloyd's Law Reports
L.M.I.	Life Management Institute (U.S.)
LMX	London Market Excess-of-loss
l.n.y.d.	Liability not yet determined
L.O.A.	Life Offices' Association
L.O.A.I.	Life Offices' Association of Ireland
L.O.C.	Letter of credit
L.O.M.A.	Life Office Management Association (U.S.)
LOP	Loss of profits
L.P.C.	Loss Prevention Council
L.P.C.B.	Loss Prevention Certification Board
L.P.I.	Legal protection insurance
L.P.O.	Lloyd's Policy Office
L.P.S.O.	Lloyd's Policy Signing Office
L.P.T.C.	Loss Prevention Technical Centre
L.R.	Lloyd's Register
L.R.M.C.	Lloyd's refrigeration machinery certificate
L.R.P.	Limited revaluation premium
L.S.	Livestock. Locus sigilli (place for seal)
L.S.R.	Line, syndicate and reference (Lloyd's)
L.S.S.D.	Lloyd's Syndicates Survey Department
L.T.A.	Long term agreement
L.T.D.	Long term discount
L/U	Leading underwriter. Laid up
L.U.A.	Liverpool Underwriters' Association. Lloyd's Underwriters' Association
L.U.A.A.	Lloyd's Underwriting Agents' Association
L.U.A.M.C.	(To be governed by) Leading Underwriters' Agreement Marine Cargo
L.U.A.M.H.	(To be governed by) Leading Underwriters' Agreement Marine Hull
LUCRO	Lloyd's Underwriters' Claims and Recoveries Office
LUNCO	Lloyd's Underwriters' Non-Marine Claims Office
L.U.T.C.	Life Underwriter Training Council (U.S.)

M

MALIC	Market Liaison Committee for Reinsurance Education and Training
MAR	Medical attendant's report
MARPOL	Marine pollution
M.A.S.	Maximum amount subject
M. & W.	Marine and war risks
M.B.D.	Machinery breakdown
M.D.	Malicious damage
ME	Medical examination
M.E.R.	Medical examiner's report
M.F.L.	Maximum foreseeable loss
M.I.A.	Marine Insurance Act 1906
M.I.B.	Motor Insurers' Bureau
M.I.P.	Marine insurance policy, Maximum investment plan
MIRAS	Mortgage interest relief at source
M.L.E.	Maximum loss expectancy
M.L.I.	Market level indicator
M.P.C.U.	Marine Pollution Control Unit
M.R.	Master of the Rolls
M.R.S.B.	Motor Risks Statistics Bureau
M.S.V.	Main stop valve
M.T.E.	Monthly total of entries
M.T.O.	Multi-model transport operator
M.V.	Motor vessel
M.W.P.A.	Married Women's Property Act

N

N.A.	Net absolutely. Not available. Not applicable
N.A.P.F.	National Association of Pension Funds
n.b.	New business. Next birthday
N.C.A.D.	Notice of cancellation at anniversary date
N.C.A.R.	No claim for accident reported
N.C.B.	No-claim bonus
N.C.B.O.R.	No-claim bonus on renewal
N.C.C.	No collecting commission
N.C.D.	No-claim discount
N.C.V.	No commercial value
N.D. or N/D	No discount. Non-delivery
N.D.O.	Number and date only
N.E.	Not entered
N/E or n.e.	Not exceeding
N.E.P.	Net earned premiums

14

N.F.B.T.E.	National Federation of Building Trades Employers
N.F.I.A.	National Flood Insurers Association (U.S.)
N.G.A.D.	Notice given arrival date
N.G.O.	Non-governmental organisation
N.H.B.C.	National House-Building Council
N.H.S.	National Health Service
N.I.B.A.	National Insurance Brokers' Association (Ireland)
N.L.O.W.	Not a line or warranty
N.L.U.R.	No laying up return
N.M.	Non-marine
NMA	(Lloyd's Underwriters) Non-Marine Association
N.O.R.	Net original rate
No S.I.	No short interest
N.P.	Non-proportional
N/P	Net proceeds
N.P.I.	Net premium insurance
N.R.	No risk. No return
n.r.a.d.	No risk after discharge
n.r.a.l.	No risk after landing
n.r.a.s.	No risk after shipment
N.R.B.	Net retained brokerage
N.R.D.	Normal retirement date
N.R.T.	Net registered tonnage
n.r.t.b.	No risk until on board
n.r.t.o.r.	No risk until on rail
n.r.t.w.b.	No risk until waterborne
N.R.V.	Notional reinstatement value
N.S.C.I.A.	National Supervisory Council for Intruder Alarms
N.S.L.	Non-selection limit
n.s.p.f.	Not specially provided for
N.T.U.	Not taken up
N.U.I.W.	National Union of Insurance Workers
N.U.R.	Not under repair
N.W.P.	Net written premiums
N.Y.I.E.	New York Insurance Exchange

O

O.B.	Ordinary (life) business. Ordinary (life) branch

15

o/b	On or before
O.B.A.	Overseas broker — claims payable abroad
O.B.C.L.	Overseas broker — claims payable in London
O.C.	Open cover
o/c	Open cover. Off cover
O.C.A.	Outstanding claims advance
Occ	Occurrence
O.D.	Own damage
O/D	On deck
O.D.I.C.	Owners' difference in conditions
OECD	Organisation for Economic and Cooperative Development
O.F.T.	Office of Fair Trading
O.G.	On gross
O.G.P.	Original gross premium
O.G.P.I.	Original gross premium income
O.G.R.	Original gross rate
O.L.T.	Ordinary long term
O.M.P.A.	One man pension arrangement
o.n.	On net
O.N.P.	Original net premium
O.N.R.	Original net rate
O.N.R.P.I.	Original net retained premium income
O.N.R. to H.O.	Original net rate to head office
O.P.	Open policy. On plan
O.P.A.S.	Occupational Pensions Advisory Service
O.P.B.	Occupational Pensions Board
O.P.O.L.	Off Shore Pollution Liability
O.R.	Owner's risk
O/R	Overrider
Orig.	Conditions as per original policy
Ors.	Others
O/S	Outstanding
OSHA	Occupational Safety and Health Act 1971 (U.S.)
o.s.l.	On signed lines

P

P.A.	Personal accident. Particular average
p.a.	Per annum
P.A. &/or G.A.L.	Particular average and/or general average loss
P.A.N.	Premium advice note
Pax	Passengers (Aviation)

16

PAYE	Pay as you earn
PAYG	Pay as you go
P. & I.	Protection and indemnity
P. & L.	Profit and loss
P.C.	Private car
P/C	Particular charges. Profit commission. Property and casualty (insurance) (U.S.)
P.D.	Property damage. Port dues
P.E.T.	Potentially exempt transfer
P.F.P.	Pension fund plans
P.G.	Plate glass
P.H.I.	Permanent health insurance
P.I.	Personal injury. Professional indemnity. Premium income.
P.I.A.	Peril insured against
P.I.A.S.	Personal Insurance Arbitration Service
P.I.I.	Professional indemnity insurance
P.I.L.	Payment in lieu
P.L.	Public liability. Partial loss
P-L	Property-liability (insurance) (U.S.)
P.L.A.	Purchased life annuity
PLC	Public limited company
P.L.E.	Primary loss expectancy
P.L.L.	Passenger legal liability (aviation)
P.L.R.	Primary loss retention
pm.	Premium
P.M.I.	Pensions Management Institute
P.M.L.	Probable maximum loss. Possible maximum loss
P.O.D.	Pay on delivery
P.O.R.	Port of refuge
p.p.	Per procurationem (On behalf of)
P.P.I.	Policy proof of interest
P.P.W.	Perfect party wall
P.R.	Port risks
p.r.	Pro rata (In proportion)
P.R.A.G.	Pensions Research Accountants' Group
PRF	Personal reserve fund
P.R.P.	Pensioner's rights premium
P.R.X.L.	Per risk excess-of-loss
P.S.A.C.	Policy Signing and Accounting Centre
P.S.O.	Policy Signing Office
P.T.	Premium transfer. Perte totale (Total loss)
P.T.F.	Premiums Trust Fund
P.V.C.C.	Pressure Vessels Consultative Committee

P.V.Q.A.B.	Pressure Vessels Quality Assurance Board

Q

Q.C.	Queen's Counsel

R

r. & c.c.	Riot and civil commotion
R. & K.	Ransom and kidnap (insurance)
r.c.c. & s.	Riot and civil commotions and strikes
Rad. C.Ex.C.	Radioactive contamination exclusion clause
RATAS	Research and Technical Advisory Services (Lloyd's Register of Shipping)
R.D.C.	Running down clause
R.H.A.	Road Haulage Association
RI	Registro Italiano
R.I. or R/I	Reinsurance
R.I.B.A.	Royal Institute of British Architects
R.I.C.C.	Reinsurance of common account
R.N.I.	Return of premiums with no interest
R.N.R.	Renewal not required
R.O.A.	Reinsurance Offices Association
R.O.F.	Return of accumulated fund
R.O.J.A.	Reinsurance of joint account
ROLAC	Registry of Life Assurance Commissions (defunct)
RoSPA	Royal Society for the Prevention of Accidents
R.P.	Return premium
R.P.K.	Revenue passenger kilometres
R.P.M.	Revenue passenger miles
R.R. & I.	Respective rights and interests
R.T.B.A.	Rate to be agreed
R.V.I.	Residual value insurance
R.W.I.	Return of premiums with interest

S

S/A	Subject to acceptance. Salvage Association
s/a	Subject to approval
S/A L/U	Subject to acceptance by the insured, to be notified to the leading underwriter only
s.a.n.r.	Subject to approval no risk. Subject acceptance no risk
s.a.p.l.	Sailed as per list
SAR	Search and rescue
S. and A.	Signing and accounting

S. and L.	Sue and labour
S &/or N.D.	Shortage and/or non-delivery
s.b.s.	Surveyed before shipment
S/C	Salvage charges
S.C.A.	Settlement of claims abroad
S.D.	Sea damaged
S/D	Short delivery
S.D.H.F.	Standard Dutch Hull Form
S.D.P.	Social, domestic and pleasure
S.D.R.	Special drawing rights
S.E.P.C.	Self employed pension certificate
S.E.R.A.	Self-employed retirement annuity
S/F	Survey fee
S.F.O.	Superannuation Funds Office
S.G.	Ship and goods. (Letters, now meaningless, at head of traditional marine policy form)
S.I.	Sum insured. Short interest. Statutory Instrument
S.I.B.	Securities and Investments Board
S.L.	Salvage loss
S/L	Sue and labour charges
S/L C.	Sue and labour clause
S/O	Shipowner
S.O.L.	Shipowner's liability
S.O.L.A.S.	Safety of life at sea
SOPA	Schedule of percentage adjustments
S.P.	Single premium. Short period
S.P.C.	Society of Pension Consultants
S.R. & C.C.	Strikes, riots and civil commotions
S.R.C.C. & M.D.	Strikes, riots, civil commotions and malicious damage
S.R.L.	Ship repairer's liability
SR&O	Statutory Regulations and Instruments
SRO	Self-regulatory organisation
S.S.	Steamship
S.S.A.(P.)S.	Small self-administered (pension) schemes
S.S.O.	Struck submerged object
S.S. or B.	Stranded, sunk or burnt
S. to A.	Subject to average
S. to S.	Station to station
Std.	Standard
Strd	Stranded
S.T.S.	Space transportation system
S.V.	Stop valve

s.v.	Sailing vessel
S.W.D.	Sea water damage
S.W.S.	Special wording scheme
Syn.	Syndicate
Synd.	Syndicate

T

T. & C.C.	Technical and Clauses Committee
T. &/or C.T.L.	Total and/or constructive total loss
t. & s.	Touch and stay
T.B.A.	To be advised. To be agreed
T.B.E.	To be entered
T.B.I.	To be identified
T.C.A.T.L.V.O.	Total or constructive or arranged total loss of vessel only
T.C.M.	Convention on the International Combined Transport of Goods
T.D.W.	Tonnage deadweight
T.I.V.	Total insured value
T.L.	Total loss
T.L.O.	Total loss only
T.L.O.excs.	Total loss only and excess liabilities
T.L.O.exs	Total loss only and excess liabilities
T.L.R.	Times Law Reports
T.L.V.O.	Total loss of vessel only
T.M.	Town's main
T.O.R.	Time on risk
TOVALOP	Tanker Owners' Voluntary Agreement Concerning Liability for Oil Pollution
T.P.	Third party
T.P.B.I.	Third party bodily injury
T.P.L.L.	Third party legal liability (aviation)
T.P.N.D.	Theft, pilferage and non-delivery
T.S.I.	Total sum insured
T.T.F.Clauses	Timber Trade Federation Clauses

U

U/A	Underwriting account
U. & O.	Use and occupancy
U.C.B.	Unless caused by
UKCIBC	United Kingdom Credit Insurance Brokers' Committee
UKIBEC	United Kingdom Insurance Brokers' European Committee

20

ul.	Unlimited
U.L.	Underwriters Laboratories (U.S.)
UNCITRAL	United Nations Commission on International Trade Law
UNCTAD	United Nations Commission on Trade and Development
U.N.L.	Ultimate net loss
U.O.R.	Under one roof
U.P.tax	Underwriters pay tax
U/R	Under repair. Underwriting
U/W	Underwriter

V

VAT	Value added tax
V.C.	Valuation clause. Vice-Chancellor
V.D.	Vehicle damage
Vd	Valued
V.L.S.	Valuation linked scheme
V.O.P.	Valued as in the original policies
V/s	Various

W

W.A.	With average (marine)
W.A. Clauses	Institute Cargo Clauses, with average
W.B.S.	Without benefit of salvage to the insurer
W/d	Warranted
W.O.C.M.	Warranted original class maintained
W.O.L.	Wharf-owner's liability
W.P.	Without prejudice
W.P.A.	With particular average
W.R.O.	War risk only
Wtd.	Warranted
W/W	Warehouse to warehouse

X

XL	Excess of loss
XS Loss	Excess of loss reinsurance

Y

Y	There. Hence Yat for thereat, Yafter for thereafter, Yin for therein, etc.
Y.A.R.	York-Antwerp Rules
Y.O.A.	Year of account

Definitions

A

Ab initio
From the beginning.

Abandonment
The cession by the insured to the insurer of the remains of his property, and rights relating to it, when a total loss is claimed.

Abandonment policy
A policy covering the insured against loss resulting from the abandonment of an event as, for example, when a cricket match is washed out by rain.

Abnormal risk
An insurance having some unfavourable feature in comparison with the average.

Abstainers insurance
The insurance of total abstainers from alcoholic liquor on terms, in life, health and motor insurance, more favourable than those available to the public generally.

Acceptance
Notification by a party to a proposed contract that he accepts the offer of the other party of the terms proposed, as where an underwriter initials a slip or the proposer of a life assurance, on receiving an offer to insure from assurers, signifies his acceptance by paying the premium.

Acceptance letter
Life assurers, on receiving a proposal, issue a letter indicating that they are prepared to accept it on payment of the premium. This constitutes an offer which the proposer can accept by paying.

Accepted value
A value on property insured that is accepted by the insurer as its true value and is not therefore disputable in the absence of proof of fraud on the part of the insured.

Accepting office
An insurance company that accepts a reinsurance.

Accident
An unlooked-for mishap or an untoward event that is neither expected nor designed.

Accident frequency
A measurement of the number of accidents occurring in a given period.

Accident insurance
1. Insurances of persons, property or liability against injury, loss or damage other than that covered by life, fire or marine insurances.
2. Personal accident insurance (U.S.).

Accident severity
A measurement of the seriousness of accidents occurring within a given period, judged either by their cost or by the nature of the damage or injury to which they give rise.

Accidental bodily injury
The phrase commonly used in liability policies in relation to claims for injury to the person as distinct from damage to property.

Accidental means
Words used in relation to an event giving rise to a claim under a policy to indicate that an event must arise fortuitously so far as the insured is concerned.

Accommodation business
Business accepted by an insurer not because he thinks it desirable in itself but to oblige an agent or policyholder whose other business he values.

Accord and satisfaction
The ending of a contract by an agreement whereby one party gives consideration to the other to be freed of his obligation under the contract.

Account agent
Same as *Credit agent*.

Account sales
A marine claims document giving details of goods sold, gross proceeds and sales charges, and net proceeds.

Accountants clause
A clause in a business interruption policy entitling the insured to employ his own accountants to prepare a claim.

Accrued interest
Interest earned but not yet paid.

Accrued rights premium

A payment to the State by a private pension scheme which has ceased to be contracted out of the State pension scheme to provide for assumption by the State of liability for the accrued rights of its members to eventual guaranteed minimum pensions.

Accumulating society

A friendly society providing sickness benefits at a rate of contribution according to age at entry calculated to provide enough revenue for the accumulating of a fund to meet the higher cost of claims in the later years of a member's membership.

Accumulation

Concentration of risk, as where an insurer may find that he has many policies on properties or liabilities that could result in losses occurring at one and the same time.

Accumulation factor

In life assurance the amount payable in the event of survival secured by a single premium of 1, taking into account interest and the probability of survival.

Accumulation (or accumulator) unit

A unit in a linked life assurance where the dividends or interest are not paid out but are added to the capital value.

Acquisition expenses

The insurer's expenses in obtaining a new insurance.

Active underwriter

The person who conducts underwriting on behalf of a Lloyd's underwriting syndicate.

Act liability only

Term used to describe a third party motor insurance which covers only the liability for bodily injury required to be insured by the Road Traffic Act 1972.

Act of God

An event that is the result of natural forces, arising without human intervention, which no human foresight could have provided against and of which human prudence was not bound to recognise the possibility.

Actual deaths

Deaths that have occurred, as opposed to expected deaths.

Actual total loss

There is an actual total loss (a) where the subject matter of insurance is completely destroyed; (b) where it ceases to be a thing of the kind insured; or (c) where the insured is irretrievably deprived of it.

25

Actuary
> A person concerned with the application of probability and, statistical theory to problems of insurance, investment, financial management and demography.

Ad hoc
> For this purpose.

Ad valorem
> According to the value.

Adaptable funding
> A system of costing for pension schemes based on *controlled funding* (q.v.).

Added years
> A number of years added to the service of a member of a pension scheme where each year gives entitlement to a fraction of pension and the member has either been credited with service with a previous employer or has paid additional voluntary contributions.

Addendum
> A document setting out agreed alterations to a reinsurance treaty or other contract.

Addition to age
> Where a proposer is an under-average life the assurers in calculating the premium may apply a higher rate applicable to someone x years older.

Additional benefit
> A benefit added to a policy beyond its standard cover.

Additional insurance
> In some forms of insurance the insurers may require to be notified of additional insurances effected or may require the insured to warrant that he will not effect them.

Additional perils
> Perils added to a fire policy, such as damage by storm, tempest or flood.

Additional premium
> Extra premium charged either because the insurance is more hazardous than normal or because additional benefits are added to the policy.

Additional voluntary contribution
> An additional contribution made voluntarily by a member of a pension scheme to augment the contributor's ultimate pension.

Adjustable premium
> A premium that is variable to correspond with the extent of the subject-matter of insurance, for example, according to

variations in the number of persons insured or the value of goods covered.

Adjuster
See *Average adjuster, Claims adjuster, Loss adjuster.*

Adjusters' note
Explanatory remarks appended to a report by an *average adjuster* (q.v.).

Adjustment
1. The calculation of a variable premium.
2. The calculation of a loss.

Administration bond
A bond given against defaults by a person administering the estate of another.

Administrator
1. A person appointed by the court to administer an estate, other than an executor named in a will.
2. A person who deals with the day-to-day running of a pension scheme, who may or may not be a trustee.

Admitted assets
The assets of an insurance company that are recognised by a supervisory authority for the purpose of determining the company's financial condition (U.S.)

Admitted insurer
An insurer authorised to do business in a state (U.S.)

Admitted liability
A form of aviation liability insurance under which insurers agree to pay claims up to a low limit without discussing the question of liability, subject to a complete release of liability from the claimant.

Advance payments bond
A guarantee to one who makes an advance payment under a contract.

Advance premium
U.S. description of *Deposit premium* (q.v.).

Advance profits insurance
Business interruption insurance of the expected profits of a business newly starting.

Advanced call
See *Call.*

Adventure
A business venture. The sending to sea of ship or goods.

Adverse selection
Same as *Selection against the insurer.*

27

Affidavit
> A written declaration on oath.

Affiliated society
> A friendly society with branches.

Affirm
> 1. Assert positively.
> 2. Ratify the judgment of an inferior court.
> 3. Declare solemnly, without taking an oath, that one will give true evidence.

Affreightment
> Hiring a ship to carry a cargo. The contract is expressed in a bill of lading.

Age
> In life assurance the age next birthday is commonly used for calculation of the premium. For annuities the age attained is used.

Age admitted
> Phrase marked on a life assurance (or annuity) policy to indicate that the assurers agree the age of the life assured.

Age attained
> The age last birthday of a life proposed for assurance.

Agency
> 1. A legal concept where one party acts for another (the principal) in affecting relations with another party.
> 2. Used to describe the business of a person acting as an agent, e.g. for obtaining insurances.

Agency agreement
> An agreement setting out the terms under which an agent may act for a principal.

Agency inspector
> An insurance company employee who acts as liaison officer between the company and its agents.

Agency system
> The organisation of an insurer's intermediaries.

Agent
> 1. Anyone who acts on behalf of another.
> 2. A person who introduces purchasers of insurance to an insurer.

Agent's authority
> The power, express or implied, of an agent to bind his principal.

Aggravated risk
> A risk that presents some unfavourable feature from the point of view of insurance.

28

Aggregate excess of loss reinsurance
1. A limited form of marine stop loss reinsurance, providing cover on an excess of loss basis for losses arising from any one event (or any one vessel) in excess of the reinsured's retention up to an agreed limit, but only when the aggregate of claims otherwise recoverable under the excess of loss treaty exceeds a stated amount.
2. A supplementary marine reinsurance treaty that permits the insured to reinstate cover when his right to reinstate cover under his original excess of loss treaty has been exhausted.

Aggregate limit of indemnity
The maximum amount that a liability insurer will pay under a liability policy in respect of all claims arising within specified period of insurance.

Aggregate mortality table
A mortality table combining the experience of selected lives during a *select period* (q.v.) and thereafter.

Aggregate stop loss reinsurance
A reinsurance that pays any amount in excess of a stipulated sum in respect of claims arising from the insurer's whole portfolio in a given branch of insurance.

Aggregation
A provision in an excess of loss reinsurance contract whereby the cost of successive claims may be added together for the purpose of establishing the sum recoverable.

Agreed returns
Returns of premium payable to the insured in accordance with the express terms of the policy.

Agreed value policy
Same as *Valued policy*.

Aircraft hull insurance
The insurance of aircraft hulls as distinct from liability.

Aircraft or aerial devices
Damage caused to property on the ground by aircraft or aerial devices or articles dropped therefrom (excluding damage by sonic booms) is an additional peril that can be covered by a fire policy.

Aircraft passenger insurance
Insurance in respect of liability to aircraft passengers; also personal accident insurance to provide specified benefits regardless of such liability.

Airliner
A passenger aircraft normally engaged in operating regular scheduled services over fixed routes.

Airport owners' and operators' insurance
Liability insurance for the owners and operators of airports.

Aleatory contract
A contract depending on an uncertain event or contingency.

Alien company
An insurance company established outside the U.S.A.
(U.S.). Not to be confused with *Foreign company* (q.v.).

Alien enemy
The term comprises (a) subjects of a hostile state, and (b)
persons of any nationality carrying on business in a hostile
state. Persons in category (a), when carrying on business in
the U.K. or in a country that is not hostile, are not, for the
purpose of a contract of insurance, deemed to be alien
enemies.

All Risks
Term used to describe a policy covering fortuities generally
though not inevitabilities such as wear and tear or depreciation. Sometimes loosely used to describe a policy that
covers a number of specified risks, though not all.

Allied company
A company linked with another whether one has acquired the
other or is a subsidiary or the linkage is by way of amalgama-
tion or merger.

Allocation amount
The proportion of the premium on a linked life assurance
which is invested by the insurance company in units of a trust
or an internal fund, the units being then notionally allocated
to the policy for the purpose of calculating its benefits.

Allocation of surplus
Division of a life company's surplus, e.g., to shareholders and
policyholders.

Allotment of bonus
The process of dividing up a life company's surplus among
policies.

Alphabet brokers
The leading U.S. insurance brokers, known by their initials,
e.g., J. & H. (Johnson & Higgins).

Always Open
Term used in placing *open covers* (q.v.) to denote that
the insurance remains continuous until ended by cancellation.

Amortisation
1. Writing off part of the value of an asset in a company's
books at intervals until the value of an asset is extinguished.

30

2. Meeting the cost of a potential liability to pay a pension, by periodical payments.

Amount
Actuarial term for the total sum produced by the accumulation of a single sum or periodical payments at compound interest over a period.

Amount at risk
Actuarial term for the difference between the sum insured and the mathematical reserve.

Anchor Policy
Any Lloyd's policy form bearing the anchor symbol of Lloyd's.

Animals Act 1971
An Act governing liability for the actions of animals.

Annual Audit
Verification by accountants of the affairs of an insurance company or Lloyd's syndicate.

Annual premium method
A method of calculating premiums under a pension scheme. The insurance company calculates at the outset the cost of providing benefits and expresses it as a level annual premium, subject to additional premium if benefit entitlement increases.

Annual subscriber to Lloyd's
A person, not being a member of Lloyd's, who is admitted to Lloyd's on payment of an annual subscription without being entitled to underwrite.

Annuitant
One to whom an annuity is payable.

Annuity
1. A series of regular payments.
2. A contract that provides an income for a specified period, e.g., during life.
3. The sum paid each year under 1 or 2.

Annuity bond
A deed evidencing the grant of an annuity.

Annuity certain
A series of regular payments made for a specified number of years.

Annuity-due
An *annuity-certain* (q.v.) where the first payment is made immediately the annuity is entered upon.

Annuity option
The right to buy a pension when a lump sum becomes payable under a pension scheme.

31

Antedating
    Where a policy is expressed as operating from a date before
    final agreement was reached on its terms it is said to be
    antedated.
Anti-selection
    Same as *Selection against the insurer.*
Anticipated freight
    Freight which a shipowner expects to earn but is likely to lose
    if his ship is lost.
Anticipatory credit cover
    Credit insurance to protect a buyer who has made payments
    in advance of delivery.
Anton Piller Order
    A court order enabling a party to an action to enter the
    property of another party and to remove documents.
Any one bottom (or Any one policy)
    Term applied by a reinsurer to a limit in a marine reinsurance
    treaty to avoid a potential accumulation of liability.
Apportionable annuity
    An annuity under which a proportionate payment is made in
    respect of the period between the last regular payment and
    the date of the annuitant's death.
Apportionment
    The division of an amount in some recognised proportion,
    e.g., in cargo insurance where several packages are insured
    for their global value, or in property insurance where two or
    more insurers must contribute to a loss.
Apprehensive period
    A period during which normal rates for riot and civil
    commotion insurances are suspended because disturbances
    are occurring or are thought imminent.
Approved scheme
    To qualify for tax relief an occupational pension scheme must
    be approved by the Superannuation Funds Office of the
    Inland Revenue. Full tax relief is available only to schemes
    which are set up under a trust and meet various conditions;
    these are cabled exempt approved schemes.
Aquacultural insurance
    Insurance of fish farmers against the mortality of their
    fish.
Arbitration
    Settlement of a difference by a person or persons agreed on
    by the parties in dispute. The arbitrator's decision is called an
    award.

Arbitration clause
A clause in a policy providing that certain differences which may arise between the parties shall be determined by arbitrators chosen in some specified way.

Architects', surveyors' and consulting engineers' fees
An item for such fees that may be incurred in the event of a loss under a property insurance may be included in the insurance.

Arranged total loss
A compromise settlement where a total loss has not in fact occurred.

Arrears
Overdue premiums.

Arrests, restraints and detainments
A marine insurance policy refers to the peril of "arrests, restraints and detainments of all kings, princes and people...". This means political or executive acts but not war losses, arrests for local infringements of regulation, or arrests by ordinary judicial process.

Arrived damaged value
The value of cargo which has been damaged in transit, at the time of its arrival at the place where the adventure terminates.

Arrived sound value
What the value of cargo would have been if it had arrived undamaged at the place where the adventure terminates.

Articles of Association
The by-laws of a company, complementing its Memorandum of Association.

As expiry
Expression used where it is proposed that an insurance should be renewed on its previous terms.

As original
Term used in reinsurance to denote that the reinsurance is on the same conditions as the original insurance.

Assault risk
The risk that persons concerned with money will be assaulted in the course of their duties is insurable under a money policy.

Assessment insurance
A system of insurance whereby premiums are not fixed in advance but are calculated each year on the basis of the sum needed to maintain the insurers' solvency in the light of the claims payable and the insurers' expenses.

Assessmentism
In life assurance, charging a premium estimated as sufficient

to meet claims (and expenses) arising during the year without taking into account the increasing death risk in future years as age advances.

Assessor

A person appointed to assess and agree on the settlement of a claim under an insurance policy. In modern fire insurance the term refers to such a person appointed by the insured, the insurers' appointee being designated an adjuster.

Assigned risk

Term used to designate an insurance that insurers generally are unwilling to accept of their own free choice but are compelled to accept by law or agreement (U.S.)

Assignee

One to whom a right of property is transferred.

Assignment

1. Transfer of a right.
2. The document making the transfer of a right. The right transferred may be an interest in the subject-matter of insurance, in the contract of insurance, or in policy moneys due to the insured.

Assignor

One who transfers a right to another.

Associate

An individual elected as an Associate at Lloyd's for the purpose of entering the Room to provide services for underwriters as, e.g., a solicitor, a loss adjuster or an accountant.

Associated company

A company linked with another.

Association scheme

A programme for the insurance on specially designed terms of the members of an association.

Assume

Accept all or part of a risk.

Assuming company

A company accepting a reinsurance (U.S.).

Assumption certificate

A statement by a reinsurer that he guarantees that a party other than the ceding company will be paid.

Assurance

Same as *Insurance*.

Used commonly for the life business and in the traditional form of marine policy. Charles Babbage in 1826 suggested that assurance was a contract on the duration of life which must either happen or fail and insurance a contract relating to any other uncertain event which may partly happen or partly fail, but the distinction has never been universally accepted.

Assured

Same as *Insured*.

Used commonly in life and marine insurance, in Lloyd's practice, and in the courts.

Assurer

Same as *Insurer*.

Used in life assurance and in the traditional form of marine policy.

Atomic risks

The British insurance industry has formed pools for insuring the public liability and material damage risks of atomic installations, viz.,

(a) atomic reactors and atomic power stations and plant (not part of or in any waterborne vessel or aircraft);

(b) any other premises or facilities related to the production of atomic energy or its incidental processes.

Minor radioactive hazards from isotopes, X-ray machines and particle accelerators are insured by individual insurers.

Attachment

1. The coming into force of an insurance.

2. The seizure of property.

Attachment date

The date on which insurance cover comes into force.

Attachment of risk

The coming into force of an insurance.

Attachment slip

A supplementary slip, attached to the original slip, used when it is necessary to obtain an insurer's agreement, by signature, to an amendment or addition.

Attestation clause

A clause in a policy evidencing its signature or sealing.

Attorney

1. One appointed to act for another.

2. A lawyer (U.S.)

Audit

Examination by accountants of the records of an insurer to check that they are properly prepared and that the financial position is as stated. In the case of Lloyd's underwriters the auditors must also satisfy themselves that Lloyd's regulations have been complied with.

Augmentation
The award of discretionary extra benefits from a pension scheme.

Authorisation
The power granted to someone to act, e.g., to transact insurance in a country.

Authority
The power given by a principal to an agent to act on the principal's behalf.

Automatic cover
A provision whereby an insurance applies despite a change of circumstances such as a change of interest or an increase in values, without prior action by the insured being required.

Automatic cover clause
A clause in an engineering policy extending cover to newly acquired plant without prior notification by the insured. (Subsequent notice may be required.)

Automatic personal accident insurance
1. In aviation insurance a form of personal accident cover arranged by the aircraft operator for named or unnamed passengers. Benefits are payable without the insurers having a right to a release of liability from the passenger.
2. Incorrectly, an "admitted liability" (q.v.) insurance.

Automatic reinstatement
A provision in a policy that in the event of a loss the sum insured shall not be reduced by the amount of the loss.

Automatic reinsurance treaty
A treaty under which direct insurances are automatically reinsured by the treaty.

Average
1. The arithmetic mean.
2. In marine insurance, loss or damage.
3. In non-marine property insurance, where average is said to apply and there has been under-insurance, the insured's claim is reducible in proportion to the under-insurance.

Average adjuster
One who assesses and apportions losses in marine insurance, notably general average losses.

Average agent
An agent engaged in the assessment of cargo claims and the surveying and treatment of damaged goods.

Average bond
1. See *General average agreement*.
2. U.S. description of *Average guarantee* (q.v.).

Average clause
  1. A clause in a marine cargo policy dealing with the application of the *franchise* (q.v.).
  2. In non-marine property insurance, same as *Average condition*.
Average condition
  A condition in a non-marine property insurance policy that if the property value has been understated the insured's claim for a loss is reduced proportionately to the undervaluation.
Average disbursements
  See *General Average disbursements*.
Average guarantee
  See *General Average guarantee*.
Average irrespective of percentage
  "Partial loss is payable without reference to the franchise on the policy" (marine).
Average rate
  A rate used in fire insurance when several properties are insured for one sum. A weighted average is used, taking into account the rate and the sum insured in respect of each property.
Average salary scheme
  A pension scheme in which benefits are based on the average of annual earnings during employment.
Average statement
  The statement prepared by an average adjuster to show the contributory values, losses and expenses applicable to a *General Average* (q.v.).
Average unless General
  "The insurance will pay for particular average but not *general average*" (q.v.).
Average warranty
  An express warranty in a marine insurance policy stipulating the franchise or excess applicable to partial losses.
Aviation hull insurance
  In aviation insurance practice hull insurance is distinguished from cargo, passenger and liability insurance.
Award
  The decision of an arbitrator.

B

Back-to-back
  Term used to describe complementary transactions in the

nature of hedging, as where a life policy and an annuity are effected simultaneously on the life of one person.

Backdating

Same as *Antedating*.

Back-service

A period of employment that may be credited to the member of a pension scheme in respect of years of work before the member entered the scheme.

Baguio

A violent cyclonic wind in the Philippines; a hurricane.

Bail bond

A bond given to obtain the release of an imprisoned person. It may guarantee that he will subsequently appear in court on pain of forfeiture of a specified sum (U.S.) or, as in some countries, that damages will be paid for a road accident for which he was responsible.

Bailee

One in temporary possession of the property of another.

Bailee clause

A clause in a marine insurance cargo policy requiring the insured to take all measures to avert or eliminate a loss and to ensure that all rights against carriers, bailees or other third parties are preserved and exercised.

Bailment

The entrustment of property to another.

Bailor

One who entrusts his property to another.

Balance settlement

An arrangement whereby by an account is kept of premiums and claims payable and the balance is paid over at the end of a specified period.

Balance table

A statement prepared in respect of a pension scheme showing the balance of pension for each employee that has to be purchased by the employer.

Balanced portfolio

The total business of an insurer that has been so arranged by selection and reinsurance as to safeguard the financial equilibrium of the company.

Balancing charges

Term used to describe the tax which a shipowner may have to pay if he receives an insurance claim payment in excess of the book value of his ship and is therefore deemed to have made a profit accordingly.

Bank guarantee
An undertaking by a bank that liability under a document will be honoured or a contractual obligation met.

Bank Urgent
Lloyd's expression for a policy requiring to be signed urgently for deposit in a bank as part of the security for credit granted.

Barratry
An act by the master or crew of a ship committed without the privity of the owner and detrimental to his interests.

Base premium
A ceding company's premiums to which the rate of premium for reinsurance is applied.

Base value
In a valuation-linked property insurance the value at the outset of a period of insurance is termed the base value.

Basic specification
The specification in a standard fire policy with columns for buildings, machinery, plant and other contents, stock and materials in trade, and miscellaneous.

Basis of valuation
To protect the insurer under an open cover where shipments may be declared and added to the insurance even after a loss a clause in the policy defines the basis to be adopted for their valuation.

Basis rate
The rate of premium for a business interruption insurance, based initially on the material damage rate and adjusted in some cases by a consequential loss loading, is termed the basis rate, the ultimate rate depending on the period of indemnity chosen.

Batch clause
A clause in a products liability insurance providing that all claims for injuries arising out of one prepared or acquired lot of the product resulting from a common cause, shall be considered as resulting from one accident and shall therefore be governed by the limit per accident.

Bearer policy
A policy the proceeds of which are expressed as payable to whomsoever holds it.

Beneficiary
One receiving a benefit or advantage from, e.g., a will or an insurance.

Benefit
A right to money or services under an insurance.

Benefit of insurance
    Term used, e.g., in a contract of carriage, where some person
    such as a bailee stipulates that he shall receive the benefit of
    insurance effected by the owner.

Benefit of salvage
    An insurer under a contract of indemnity who pays the value
    of property lost or destroyed becomes entitled to the salvage.
    See *Without benefit of salvage.*

Benefit policy
    An insurance policy that prescribes the sum payable on the
    happening of the event insured against, as distinct from an
    indemnity policy where the sum payable depends on calcula-
    tion of the insured's loss; for example, a personal accident
    policy.

Betterment
    Term used to describe an improvement in property insured
    under a contract of indemnity resulting from its reinstatement
    or repair. The insurer may seek to reduce his liability on the
    ground of betterment.

Bid bond
    A bond required of a contractor tendering for a contract to
    ensure that the bid is being made in good faith.

Bill of lading
    A shipping document containing a description of the goods to
    be shipped.

Binder
    1. U.S. term for temporary cover issued by an insurer, or a
       reinsurer.
    2. An authority by an underwriter to an agent to grant cover
       on the underwriter's behalf.

Binding authority
    An authority given by an insurer (or a reinsurer) to an agent
    to accept risks on the insurer's behalf.

Binding clause
    1. A clause in a reinsurance treaty setting out the parties and
       the extent of the liabilities of each.
    2. A clause in the S.G. form of marine policy in which the
       underwriters bind themselves and specify their respective
       liabilities.

Blanket policy
    A policy in which a single sum insured covers a number of
    separate items such as buildings in a fire policy or employees
    in a fidelity guarantee policy, without being divided up among
    them.

Blanket rate
An insurance rate applied uniformly over a number of items insured to which different rates might ordinarily apply.

Blind treaty
A reinsurance treaty under which the reinsurer dispenses with the provision of regular information about individual premium and loss items.

Block limit
The maximum value that an insurer will cover in respect of a given city block.

Block policy
1. A policy used primarily for inland transit risks on cargo issued for a fixed premium without the need for sendings to be declared.
2. An "all risks" policy issued to certain trades, e.g., jewellers (U.S.).

Block system
A common system in industrial life assurance whereby an agent is allotted a block of territory to which he confines his canvassing and collecting.

Blood relative clause
A clause in an industrial life assurance policy which provides that the assurer's liability shall be discharged by payment of the policy moneys to the husband or wife of the proposer or a relation by blood or connection by marriage.

Blue Cross
U.S. schemes of hospital and medical expenses insurance.

Blue List
Lloyd's Shipping Index.

Blue Shield
U.S. surgical and medical expenses insurance supplementary to Blue Cross schemes.

Boiler insurance
Insurance of boilers against damage by explosion or collapse and sudden and specified unforeseen events such as overheating.

Bond
1. A written obligation to pay a sum or to perform a contract.
2. An undertaking by a surety to pay compensation or a penalty if the person guaranteed by the bond fails to fulfil some legal obligation.
3. A single-premium life assurance policy.

Bonded warehouse
A warehouse for goods on which duty has not been paid and

whose keeper is the subject of a bond to ensure that any duty which may become payable will be paid.

Bonding company

A company approved by the U.S. courts for the issue of bonds such as those necessary to effect the release of a ship from arrest (U.S.)

Bonus

1. A part of the surplus of an insurance company distributed to policyholders.
2. A free distribution of shares or money.

Bonus allocation

The apportionment of the available surplus of a life assurance company to its policyholders.

Bonus declaration

An announcement of the rate at which bonuses are to be credited to life assurance policies.

Bonus loading

A sum added to the pure premium to allow the margin necessary to pay bonuses to holders of with-profits policies.

Bonus reinforcement policy

A life assurance policy used to facilitate the purchase of a house on mortgage by means of with-profit rather than non-profit assurance. The assurance is for such a sum as will, with the addition of bonuses to be expected, enable the mortgage to be redeemed at the end of the term. To protect the mortgagee the with-profits assurance is reinforced by a decreasing term assurance so that in the event of the mortgagee's death before the bonuses have built up, the total proceeds will suffice to pay off the mortgage.

Bonus reserve

A provision retained by a life assurance company for the payment of future bonuses to its policyholders.

Bonus reserve system

A system whereby a life assurance fund is valued to show what future rates of bonus the fund will be sufficient to provide, upon suitable assumptions as to future mortality, interest rates and expenses.

Book debts insurance

Insurance against loss through inability to collect debts due because accounting records have been destroyed.

Book interest

The interest that an industrial assurance agent has in his right to collect premiums from the policyholders named in his collecting book. This goodwill was at one time commonly bought or sold and the practice survives in the case of some assurers.

Book value

The value of an asset as shown in the owner's accounting records.

Bordereau

A schedule or list. Commonly used in reinsurance practice for periodical statements of insurances, premiums and losses.

Both to Blame Collision Clause

Under a contract of affreightment cargo is normally carried at the risk of the cargo-owner who insures it. Where a collision between two ships damages the cargo, and both ships are to blame, the cargo owner will sue the third party shipowners who, by the law of some countries, can then recover part of the cargo claim from the carrier in whose ship it was carried. The Both to Blame Collision Clause in the contract of affreightment allows the shipowner in these circumstances to obtain reimbursement from the cargo owner. The Both to Blame Collision Clause in a marine cargo policy indemnifies the cargo owner for such a payment.

Bottomry

A loan to the master of a ship for the purpose of completing the voyage, repayable only if the voyage is completed (Obs.).

Bouquet (of treaties)

Reinsurances of different classes of insurance transacted by an insurer offered as a package deal to a reinsurer.

Bourse

A continental exchange at which insurance is transacted, e.g., at Amsterdam.

Box

An underwriter's seat and desk at Lloyd's.

Bracketed provisions

Same as *Exceptional circumstances clause.*

Branch

1. A class of insurance, e.g., life, marine.

2. A local office of an insurance company.

Breach of contract cover

A form of credit insurance effected by a company to protect another against loss through failure of the company to complete contractual obligations of a financial nature.

Breach of statutory duty

In the case of many statutes a breach of a duty imposed by the statute gives a right of action in tort to a person injured by the breach.

43

Breach of Warranty endorsement
> An endorsement to extend cover under an aircraft hull insurance to protect the interest of the mortgagee or lessor of the hull even if the insured has been guilty of an act or omission that would invalidate his own cover.

Breach of warranty of authority
> A person who purports to act on behalf of a principal impliedly warrants that he has the principal's authority so to act. A third party who relies on the warranty and who sustains loss as a consequence may sue the "agent" for breach of warranty.

Breakdown
> Engineering insurance in traditional form covers the breakdown of mechanical and electrical plant defined as (a) actual breaking or burning out of any part of the plant whilst in use from either mechanical or electrical defect causing sudden stoppage and necessitating immediate repair or replacement and (b) fracturing of any part of the plant by frost which renders the plant inoperative.

Breakdown insurance
> A form of motor insurance covering the expenses incidental to the breakdown of a car, such as towage, hire, getting the car home, and hotel expenses.

Breaking the warranty
> 1. Same as *Opening the warranty*.
> 2. A breach by the insured of a warranty in an insurance policy which requires him to do, or not to do, something.

Broker
> An independent person whose business it is, for remuneration, usually in the form of commission, to bring together the buyers and sellers of goods or services.
> See *Insurance broker*.

Brokerage
> The commission payable to a broker. In insurance this is normally paid by the insurer.

Broker's cover
> See *Master cover*.

Broker's daily statement
> In Lloyd's practice a statement issued to brokers by Lloyd's Policy Signing Office, not necessarily daily, of insurances that have been notified to underwriting syndicates.

Broker's lien
> The legal right of an insurance broker to hold a policy pending receipt of the premium from the insured.

Broker's pseudonym
An abbreviation identifying a Lloyd's broker in dealings with Lloyd's Policy Signing Office and Lloyd's Data Processing Service.

Broker's slip
See *Slip*.

Brokers' wording
A policy wording drafted by an insurance broker, often to suit the particular needs of a trade in whose insurances he specialises.

Broking deposit
A deposit payable by an insurance broker on admission to Lloyd's and held by Lloyd's in trust under a security deed.

Builder's risk
1. Marine insurance applicable to a ship under construction.
2. U.S. term for *Contractors' all risks* (q.v.).

Building rate
The rate of premium applicable to buildings in fire insurance, which may differ from the contents rate.

Building-Society linked assurance
Life assurance in which the premiums (less a charge for the death risk) are invested on the policyholder's behalf in a building society.

Bumbershoot
A type of marine insurance providing liability cover in excess of normal limits for protection and indemnity risks.

Bumbershoot
A liability insurance covering risks over and above a pre-existing insurance (U.S.).

Bureau
A policy signing office

Burglary
The crime of entering a building as a trespasser and (a) stealing or attempting to steal anything in the building or inflicting or attempting to inflict bodily harm on any person in the building, or (b) intending to commit any of the acts listed in (a). (Cf. *Theft Act 1968*.)

Burglary insurance
See *Theft insurance*.

Burning cost
The cost of claims under a group of insurances or a reinsurance treaty, used to obtain certain ratios. In U.K. fire insurance the ratio may be of claims cost to premiums or sums

insured. In reinsurance the ratio is of reinsurance losses incurred to the ceding company's premium. Use of the term is not confined to fire insurance.

Burning ratio

The cost of claims expressed as a percentage of premiums.

Business interruption insurance

Same as *Interruption insurance.*

Business risk

A risk inherent in a business such as a change in supply or demand whereby, if things turn out badly, a trading loss will be suffered or profit reduced.

Buyer's interest

The insurable interest of a buyer of goods.

Buy-out bond

An insurance contract which invests the *transfer value* (q.v.) from an occupational pensions fund to provide eventual retirement benefits. The contract is usually written under section 32, Finance Act 1981.

C

Call

The sum payable by a member of a *Protection and Indemnity Club* (q.v.) for his right to indemnity by the club. A call payable at the outset of each period is termed an advanced call. Additional payments (supplementary calls) in respect of a period may be made subsequently if required to meet claims arising.

Cancellation

The termination of a policy by notice or mutual consent.

Cancellation clause

A clause in a policy setting out the conditions under which the policy may be cancelled by notice.

Cancelling returns only

A provision found chiefly in hull reinsurance that no return of premium will be allowed except where the policy is cancelled.

Capacity

The maximum amount of insurance that an insurer or the insurance market will be prepared to accept.

Capital additions clause

A provision in a fire policy to cover new buildings or machinery added by the insured during the period of insurance.

Capital annuity
> Same as *Split annuity*.

Capital benefits
> Lump sum benefits under a personal accident policy, e.g., for death or loss of limb or sight.

Capital bond
> A contract, whether in the form of a deferred annuity with cash option, or a life assurance, which, in consideration of a premium, promises payment of a larger sum at the end of a term of years.

Capital redemption policy
> An insurance to provide a capital sum at the end of a term in order to replace one's capital (because e.g., a lease will expire or debentures will become repayable).

Capital sum
> The sum payable under a life policy (other than income benefits) when a claim falls due for payment.

Captains' Room
> The restaurant at Lloyd's, so called from the room at Lloyd's Coffee House which was originally used as a meeting-place for seafaring men and a venue for the sale of ships and goods by auction.

Captive insurance company
> An insurance company formed by a trading company, a trade association or the like, primarily for the insurance of the founder's own risks.

Capture and seizure
> In marine insurance capture includes every act of seizing or taking by an enemy or belligerent. Seizure goes beyond this to embrace every act of forcible possession either by a lawful authority or by overpowering force.

Cargo insurance
> The insurance of goods transported by sea or air.

Cargo interest
> Insurable interest relating to cargo, other than the interest of the cargo owner.

Carnet
> An official document permitting motorists to cross frontiers without payment of customs duty on their car.

Carpenter plan
> Same as *Spread loss reinsurance*.

Carriage of Goods by Sea Act 1971
> An Act laying down the respective responsibilities, liabilities, rights and immunities of carriers and cargo owners in respect

of the carriage of goods by sea. The Act incorporated the internationally agreed Hague-Visby Rules and came into effect on 23 June 1977.

Carrier
1. A person who carries passengers or goods by land, sea or air.
2. An insurer or reinsurer (U.S.).

Cash agent
An agent introducing insurance who is not allowed any period of credit for payments to the insurer of the premium.

Cash benefit scheme
A scheme for the payment of a cash benefit on retirement.

Cash bonus
A bonus on a life policy that is paid in cash, as distinct from a reversionary bonus.

Cash insurance
Same as *Money insurance*.

Cash loss
An arrangement in a reinsurance treaty or under a direct insurance whereby if a large claim arises it is settled immediately without waiting for a periodic adjustment of accounts.

Cash-in value
Same as *Surrender value*.

Cash option
An option to take cash in lieu of a benefit in some other form, such as an annuity.

Castle Reserve Scheme
A state scheme to provide graduated pensions from which employers may contract out. Introduced by the Social Security Pensions Act 1975 when Mrs Barbara Castle was Secretary of State for Social Services.

Casualty insurance
U.S. term for non-life insurance other than fire, marine or surety business.

Catastrophe
A sudden and severe disaster causing very large loss.

Catastrophe hazard
The hazard of very large loss arising out of a single cause.

Catastrophe reinsurance
Reinsurance to protect an insurer against an accumulation of losses arising from a single catastrophic event such as an earthquake.

Causa causans
Same as *Proximate cause*.

Caveat emptor
Let the buyer beware.

Cavity barrier
A construction to close or divide a cavity against penetration by flame or smoke.

Ceasing age
The age at which benefit under a permanent health policy ceases.

Cede
To buy reinsurance.

Cedant
Same as *Cedent*.

Cedent
An insurer who transfers risks by means of reinsurance.

Ceding company
An insurance company that transfers risks by means of reinsurance.

Centralised society
A friendly society without branches.

Certificate of entry
A policy issued by a Protection and Indemnity Association in respect of a vessel entered in the Association.

Certificate of existence
Same as *Survival certificate*.

Certificate of insurance
See *Insurance certificate*.

Cessation of payment of premiums
Some long-term policies provide that the annual premium shall cease to be payable at some date before the termination of the policy, e.g., when the insured attains a given age, the cover remaining in force.

Cession
Insurance that is reinsured.

Cestui que trust
One for whose benefit property is held in trust.

Change in temperature clause
An exclusion in a fire policy on goods in a cold store of damage to perishable goods caused by a change in temperature.

Change of voyage clause
A clause in a marine insurance cargo policy providing that if the voyage is changed or there is any omission or error in the description of the interest, vessel or voyage the insurance will be held covered at a premium to be arranged.

Charge note
>Same as *Debit note.*

Charges of insurance
>The premium (marine).

Charter aircraft
>Aircraft available for hire under a special contract.

Chartered freight
>The hire paid or payable to a shipowner for the use of the entire ship for a voyage or for a period.

Chartered Life Underwriter
>A U.S. designation, based on examination and experience, for a person concerned with the sale of life assurance.

Chartered loss adjuster
>A *loss adjuster* (q.v.) who is a member of the Chartered Institute of Loss Adjusters.

Chartered Property and Casualty Underwriter
>A U.S. designation, based on examination and experience, for a person concerned with the sale of property and casualty insurance.

Charterparty
>A contract for the hire of a ship.

Chattels
>Personal property.

Chattels personal
>Movable things.

Chattels real
>Leasehold interests in land.

Checked baggage
>Such personal property accompanying a passenger on an aircraft as is defined by the air carrier, as distinct from cargo.

Child's deferred assurance
>Assurance on a young child under which the sum assured becomes payable only on death after attainment of a specified age.

Chomage insurance
>Same as *Percentage of fire loss insurance.*

Chose in action
>A thing of which one has not the present enjoyment but which one has a right to recover by legal action, e.g. the proceeds of an insurance policy.

Civil commotion
>A disturbance of the peace involving numbers of persons but falling short of a rebellion or revolution. A stage between a riot and a civil war.

Civil law
1. A legal system derived from Roman law, in which most of the law is expressed in codes of law, as in France or Germany.
2. The national or municipal law of a state, in contrast with public international law.
3. The laws of a country excluding some field of fields of law such as criminal or military law or in some countries, administrative law, ecclesiastical law or commercial law (which governs merchants and trade).

Civil Liability Convention for Pollution Damage from Persistent Oils 1969
An international convention, effective from 1975, which places liability on shipowners for pollution damage caused by oil spillages.

Claim agent
The agent appointed by a marine insurance company to settle a claim (U.S.).

Claim settlement rate
The speed at which claims are brought to finality.

Claiming cash
A right which insurers may have to ask reinsurers for immediate settlement of a substantial claim rather than wait for the regular periodical settlement.

Claimright insurance
Insurance to the consignor of goods in respect of money withheld by the consignee in accordance with the contract of sale, pending arrival of the goods.

Claims adjuster
One who negotiates settlement of a claim on behalf of an insurer.

Claims Advisory Committee
A committee at Lloyd's which advises underwriters defending legal actions whether they should proceed to trial, having regard to Lloyd's good name.

Claims broker
The employee of an insurance broker who handles claims on behalf of clients.

Claims Bureau
1. Any office set up by insurers to handle claims.
2. Lloyd's Underwriters' Claims Office, used by most marine underwriters at Lloyd's to handle claims, including reinsurance matters.

Claims condition
> A condition in many types of insurance policy setting out the insured's duties in the event of a claim.

Claims cooperation clause
> A clause in a reinsurance treaty providing for early notice of possible claims and cooperation in the defence of claims that may affect the reinsurer and stipulating that the insurers shall not admit liability for such a claim without the reinsurer's consent.

Claims equalisation reserve
> A reserve by an insurance company to smooth the cost of claims which occur at irregular intervals, e.g., through natural phenomena such as exceptionally adverse weather, so as to prevent undue fluctuations in the revenue account.

Claims expenses
> The expenses of investigating and settling claims, e.g., adjusters' fees as distinct from the claims themselves.

Claims made basis
> The basis of a policy which confines the liability of an insurer to claims made during the currency of a policy, as opposed to a policy on an *occurrence basis* (q.v.).

Claims payable abroad
> A provision that may be inserted in a policy to permit the collection of claims payments from some specified person overseas.

Claims reserves
> The provisions made by an insurer for (a) claims notified but not paid and (b) claims that may have arisen but that have not yet been reported.

Claims-settling agent
> One instructed on behalf of an insurer both to assess a loss and to pay it on the insurer's behalf.

Claims sharing agreement
> An agreement between two property and liability insurers that in the event of claims arising in which both are interested on behalf of different parties, such claims shall be shared between them on some specified basis without regard to the degree of legal responsibility of the respective policyholders.

Classification
> 1. The selection of factors on which to base premium rates, e.g., location, activities.
> 2. A class.

Classification clause
> A clause in a marine cargo policy specifying the minimum

standard of the vessels to be used in the carriage if additional premium is to be avoided. Vessels must be fully classed by a recognised classification society but additional premium may be required if a vessel is over a specified age.

Classification society
A society formed to inspect ships and to describe and grade them for the information of insurers, e.g., Lloyd's Register of Shipping. An approved ship is said to be fully classed.

Clause
A section of a policy or other legal document such as a will or parliamentary bill.

Clause 19 (2)(a)
A clause in the Royal Institute of British Architects model conditions of contract for building which requires a contractor to maintain certain liability insurance in the joint names of the employer and the contractor.

Claused Bill
A bill of lading which records some defect in goods shipped or in their packaging.

Clawback
Claim back by Inland Revenue of tax relief allowed on life assurances in certain circumstances, e.g., where the policy is made paid up in its early years.

Clean cut basis
A method of accounting in treaty reinsurance whereby the right of a reinsurer to receive premiums or his liability to pay claims is treated as ceasing upon cancellation of the treaty.

Closed fund
An insurance company's long-term fund on which new business is no longer written.

Closed line
A broker is said to close a line when he decides how much of an insurance shall be attributed to an underwriter who has written a line. The total lines written may have exceeded 100% of the insurance required or the value provisionally stated may have proved an over-estimate.

Closed scheme
A pension scheme closed to new entrants. Existing members will either continue in full membership or will cease to receive increases in benefit.

Closed year
A year of account for which the financial outcome has been determined; usually, at Lloyd's, after three years, when remaining liabilities are reinsured.

Closing
> Completion of an insurance.

Closing slip
> A form of advice to an insurer from a broker detailing an insurance so that a policy can be prepared.

Cloth cap scheme
> A *Provident fund* (q.v.).

Club
> See *Protection and Indemnity Club.*

Club calls
> The contributions that shipowner members of a Protection and Indemnity Club are called on periodically to make to meet the claims paid and expenses incurred by the club.

Co-assurance
> Same as *Co-insurance* (1).

Co-assurer
> Same as *Co-insurer.*

Code Civil
> A code of law governing the rights and duties of parties in civil matters, such as has existed in France from the time of Napoleon, spreading to many other countries.

Coded excesses method
> A system of rating reinsurances to adjust automatically premiums payable for excess-of-loss covers arranged on an individual basis, in line with changes in the reinsurer's exposure as revealed by changes in the ceding company's portfolio and its distribution by sums insured.

Codification
> Assembling and stating the law relating to some topic in a single logically arranged form, as for marine insurance, in the Marine Insurance Act 1906.

Coefficient of variation
> The *standard deviation* (q.v.) divided by the mean of a number of standard deviations.

Co-insurance
> 1. Where a number of insurers each cover part of a risk or where a policy requires the insured to bear a part of each loss there is said to be co-insurance.
> 2. In the U.S. the term is used to describe the application of an *average condition* (q.v.) whereby if the sum insured is inadequate the insured has to bear a proportionate part of a claim.
> 3. Reinsurance on the same terms as the original insurance (U.S.).

Co-insurer
1. Each of a number of insurers participating in an insurance.
2. An insured whose policy requires him to bear part of a loss.

Collapse
A peril covered by a boiler policy and commonly defined as "the sudden and dangerous distortion (whether or not attended by rupture) of any part of the plant caused by crushing stresses by force of steam or any other fluid pressure (other than pressure of ignited flue gases)".

Collecting book
A book in which an industrial life assurance agent records the premiums he collects.

Collecting commission
Commission paid to a broker by the insured where the broker has collected a marine insurance claim on his behalf.

Collecting note
A document empowering a broker to collect a marine insurance claim on the insured's behalf.

Collecting society
A friendly society that transacts industrial life assurance.

Collection commission
Commission paid by an insurer to an agent for the collection of premiums.

Collective policy
1. A policy issued on behalf of a number of insurers.
2. A policy in respect of a number of persons, with insurance in respect of each separately.

Collector
An agent employed by an industrial life assurance company with the duty of collecting premiums.

Collision
The violent encounter of two objects. In marine hull liability insurance a distinction is drawn between "collision" with vessels and "contact with fixed objects" such as piers, wharves and fastened buoys, the latter not being covered by collision clauses.

Collision clause
A clause in a marine hull policy covering the shipowner in respect of his liability (or frequently three-quarters of his liability) for claims by third parties arising out of collisions.

Collusion
Secret agreement or understanding for a deceitful purpose. A

theft insurance sometimes excludes losses arising out of collusion with an insider such as an employee.

Combination company
An assurance company that transacts both ordinary and industrial life assurance (U.S.).

Combination plan reinsurance
A combination of excess of loss and quota share reinsurance in one contract.

Combination policy
A policy issued by two or more insurers embodying two or more kinds of insurance each insured with a separate insurer (U.S.).

Combined claim
A claim under an environmental impairment liability insurance which relates partly to insured and partly to excluded losses.

Combined company policy
A policy issued on behalf of a number of insurance companies, each insuring a portion of the risk.

Combined liability policy
A policy combining employers' liability and public liability cover.

Combined policy
A policy issued on behalf of two or more Lloyd's underwriters or two or more insurance companies.

Commission
Remuneration to an agent for services such as arranging an insurance.

Committee of Lloyd's
Until Lloyd's Act 1982, the governing body of Lloyd's. Now a committee which, under the Council of Lloyd's (q.v.), conducts the day-to-day administration of Lloyd's.

Common account
When an original insurer who already has reinsurance effects further reinsurance with another reinsurer it may be either wholly for his own protection or also for the protection for the first reinsurer. In the latter case it is said to be reinsurance for the common account.

Common carrier
One who carries goods for hire, his services being offered to the public generally without discrimination.

Common hazard
Same as *General hazard*.

Common law
1. A legal system based on precedent rather than on a legal code.
2. The law, other than that contained in the principles and rules of *equity* (3., q.v.).
3. Legal rights, remedies, crimes and the like which exist without being expressed in statutes.
4. In countries with a civil law system, the law common to the whole country as distinct from peculiarities of law in one area.

Communication
Connection between buildings whereby fire could spread from one to another, i.e., where the buildings are not separated by a party wall.

Commutation
Payment to discharge an actual or potential liability to make payments in the future.

Commutation clause
A clause often found in Lloyd's reinsurance treaties which provides for the estimation and discharge of all liabilities by payment of a lump sum.

Company limited by guarantee
A company without share capital the liability of members for its debts being limited to a sum specified in its constitution.

Compensation
A payment to make good a loss.

Complete annuity
Same as *Apportionable annuity*.

Completion
Taking the final formal step in the conclusion of a contract so that it comes into force forthwith.

Completion bond
A bond guaranteeing one who advances money in respect of a building that the building work will be completed.

Component parts clause
A clause under an aviation hull policy which restricts the insurer's liability in respect of a given component part to a stated proportion of the sum insured.

Composite company
An insurance company that transacts a number of classes of insurance, including both life and non-life.

Compound reversionary bonus
A sum added to the sum assured under a with profits life assurance to be payable when the policy becomes a claim and

meanwhile to be aggregated with the sum assured as the basis for calculation of subsequent bonuses.

Comprehensive policy
A policy covering a number of perils.

Compulsory excess
A provision in a policy, imposed by the insurer, that the insured shall bear the first £x or the first y% of a claim.

Compulsory insurance
Insurance that a person is obliged to effect. For example, a motorist is required by the Road Traffic Act 1972 to have in force an insurance in respect of liability for bodily injury to third parties arising out of the use of a motor vehicle on a road.

Concealment
Deliberate suppression by a proposer for insurance of a material fact relating to the risk.

Concurrent insurances
Insurances are said to be concurrent when they cover only the same property or classes of property in the same situation(s), when none extends to any risk not covered by the other(s), and when none contains a specific provision that would prevent the policies from ranking uniformly in their application.

Condition of average
Same *Average condition*.

Condition precedent of the policy
A condition of an insurance a breach of which by the insured entitles the insurers to avoid the policy.

Condition subsequent of the policy
A condition of an insurance a breach of which by the insured entitles the insurers to sue for damages though not to escape liability for a claim.

Condition precedent to liability
A condition of an insurance a breach of which by the insured entitles the insurers to deny liability for a claim under the insurance.

Conditional probability
The probability of an event given the occurrence of some other event or combination of events.

Conditional receipt
A receipt for the intial premium on an insurance proposal, subject to a condition, e.g., that the insurance will not be effective until the insurers have considered and notified acceptance of the proposal.

Confiscation insurance
The confiscation risk for overseas plant and equipment may be covered by insurance. For marine insurances distinction is drawn between confiscation resulting from war, which is part of war risks insurance, and any other confiscation, e.g., in respect of cargo. Both types of confiscation risk may be covered under a marine insurance.

Conflagration
A destructive fire spreading over many properties.

Conflagration area
An area over which a destructive fire is thought to be capable of spreading, or has already spread.

Conloss
Abbreviation of consequential loss.

Consensus ad idem
Perfect agreement between the parties to a contract. An essential to the making of the contract.

Consequential loss insurance
Insurance against pecuniary loss, other than material damage, resulting from an insurable peril.

Consideration
For a contract to be valid in English law each party must give something of value, whether in the form of money, goods, services or a promise of them.

Consolidated option
An option in a business interruption insurance, effected on the Dual Wages basis, for the insured to elect to receive full protection against loss in respect of wages for a longer period than the initial period specified in the policy.

Consolidated period
The initial period specified in a business interruption insurance on the Dual Wages basis *plus* the extension of the period provided for under the *Consolidated option* (q.v.).

Consortium
A number of businesses working jointly on a project, e.g., contractors, consulting engineers, architects and surveyors in a construction project.

Constant premium
A premium that does not vary from time to time.

Construction cost index
An index showing variations in the cost of construction work, which may be used for determining automatic changes to sums insured.

Constructive total loss

In marine insurance a constructive total loss occurs where the subject-matter insured is reasonably abandoned on account of its actual total loss appearing unavoidable or because it could not be preserved from actual total loss without an expenditure which would exceed its total value after the expenditure had been incurred. In non-marine insurance the insured has no right of abandonment but the term is used when repair of the subject matter would be uneconomic.

Consultation condition

A clause in a credit insurance policy that requires the insured to consult with the insurers when they have cause for concern over the creditworthiness of insured buyers or when an insured debt becomes overdue.

Contact damage

In marine insurance, damage to a ship or conveyance by contact with some external substance other than water or another ship. (Damage through contact with another ship is termed collision damage.)

Contents rate

The rate of premium for fire insurance applicable to the contents of a building as distinct from that applicable to the building itself.

Contingency fund

A fund held as a reserve against some event that may happen but is not certain to happen.

Contingency insurance

1. Insurance against relatively remote possibilities e.g., loss arising through the reappearance of a missing beneficiary, or secondary liability arising because a person primarily liable is not indemnified by an insurer.
2. Marine insurance and reinsurance under which the insurer or reinsurer undertakes to pay a fixed amount in the event of a contingency occurring.

Contingency reserve

A fund set aside to meet unforeseen occurrences of a specific type.

Contingent annuity

An annuity that becomes payable only if some event or series of events occurs, e.g., if A and B predecease C.

Contingent assurance (life)

A life assurance that becomes payable only if some event or series of events occurs, e.g., if A and B predecease C.

Contingent bonus
A bonus granted conditionally, e.g., if the life assured survives for X years.

Contingent commission
A commission payable to an agent that is dependent on some feature of the business to which it relates, e.g., its profitability.

Contingent debt
A reduction applied to the sum assured under a life policy if death occurs within a specified period.

Contingent fee
A fee, the payment of which is contingent on some event, e.g., as where, in the U.S.A., a lawyer acts for a client in a lawsuit without payment unless the suit succeeds.

Contingent liability
A liability arising in some secondary way.

Contingent liability (motor) insurance
Third party insurance indemnifying an employer or one who hires out vehicles against any liability that may rest on the insured if the insurance effected by the user of the vehicle proves non-existent or ineffective.

Contingent life assurance
Life assurance under which the sum assured becomes payable only if a certain state of affairs exists at the time of the death of the life assured, e.g., if another person has died meanwhile.

Contingent survivorship assurance
An assurance on two or more lives that becomes payable only in a certain contingency, e.g., if the deaths occur in a particular order.

Continuation Clause
A clause in a marine insurance hull policy providing that if at expiration of the policy the ship is at sea or in distress or at a port of refuge or of call it may on previous notice be held covered to its port of destination at a pro rata premium.

Continuation option
An option in a group life or permanent health insurance for an individual leaving the group to maintain insurance in respect of himself.

Contra entry
An accounting entry set against another entry.

Contra preferentem rule
A rule of construction whereby if one party to a contract has drawn it up, any ambiguity in the contract will be construed by the courts against that party rather than in his favour.

Contract
An agreement based on the meeting of minds and requiring a consideration in the form of an act or a promise to be given by each party.

Contract guarantee
A bond whereby A, a guarantor, promises to pay B a sum of money if C does not perform a contract entered into between B and C.

Contract for services
A contract whereby one party undertakes to perform services for the other party as an independent contractor and not as a servant of that other party. Cf. *Contract of service.*

Contract of adhesion
A contract in a standard form prepared by one party without options as to its terms on the part of the other party.

Contract of indemnity
A contract the intention of which is to make good financial loss as nearly as possible.

Contract of service
A contract whereby one party agrees to work as the servant of the other party who can stipulate the way in which the work shall be done. Cf. *Contract for services.*

Contract price clause
A clause in a fire policy whereby in respect of goods that have been sold but are still the responsibility of the insured the insurers agree that the price named in the contract shall be the basis of indemnity in the event of a claim.

Contract signing scheme
A system at Lloyd's whereby underwriters may agree that certain policies shall be signed by Lloyd's Policy Signing Office without immediate notification to all underwriters concerned.

Contract works insurance
Same as *Contractors' all risks.*

Contracting out
Excepting oneself from an obligation that would otherwise rest on one in law. For example:
(a) the members of an approved occupational pension scheme may be contracted out of part of the social security retirement scheme;
(b) a haulage contractor may stipulate that goods he carries shall be at their owner's risk.

Contractors' all risks
Insurance in respect of contract works covering damage to

property on the site however caused (though with exceptions) and third party liability.

Contractual liability
Liability that arises by virtue of a contract, as distinct from liability at common law.

Contractual savings
Sums that a saver undertakes to save regularly over a period.

Contribution
1. The principle whereby if two or more insurers indemnify the insured in respect of the same subject matter against the same peril on behalf of the same interest, they share the loss or liability proportionately.
2. Money paid for a pension under a pension scheme.

Contribution clause
A clause in an insurance contract of indemnity providing that the insurer shall not be liable for more than a rateable proportion of a claim if there is in force another insurance covering the claim.

Contribution method
A method of allotting bonuses to different classes of life policyholders in proportion to the contribution that each is assumed to have made to the company's surplus.

Contributions equivalent premium
A payment made by a pension scheme to the State when a member leaves service, representing the additional contributions that would have been payable to the State if the member had not been contracted out.

Contributory negligence
Where a person sues for damages the damages may be reduced by a proportion by virtue of the fact that his own negligent conduct contributed to causing the event giving rise to the claim or enhanced the injury suffered.

Contributory pension scheme
A pension scheme in which employees make contributions towards the cost of the scheme.

Contributory reinsurance
Same as *Quota share reinsurance.*

Contributory value
The value if a ship, its cargo and freight, on which general average contributions are based.

Control law
The laws of a state that regulate the operations of insurers.

Controlled funding
A system of paying for a pension scheme whereby the

ultimate cost of pensions is estimated, and either (a) the scheme's money is spent on buying pensions for the oldest members first, or (b) pensions are not allocated to individual members until they reach retirement.

Controller
1. An official, such as one who supervises the application of insurance control laws.
2. A person who controls an insurance company, as defined by the Insurance Companies Act 1974, s.7., including a managing director, chief executive, a person controlling one-third or more of the voting power, or a person in accordance with whose directions the directors are accustomed to act.

Controlling authority
The government department or office that controls the operations of insurers in a country — in Britain the Insurance Division of the Department of Trade and Industry.

Conversion
1. The wrongful use or disposition of property that is in one's lawful possession.
2. Changing a contract from one form to another, e.g., converting a life assurance policy which provides for the payment of an annual premium, into a policy for a reduced sum assured with no further premiums being required.

Convertible
Capable of being converted by exchange into property of another kind.

Convertible currency
In Lloyd's practice a currency other than that of the U.K., the U.S.A., or Canada.

Convertible term assurance
A temporary life assurance that can be exchanged for a permanent life assurance at the assured's option.

Cooling-off period
A period during which one who has agreed to enter into a transaction such as a life assurance or a hire purchase agreement may withdraw without penalty.

Cooperative society
A society owned by the consumers (or the producers) of a product.

Coordinating agent
An underwriting member of Lloyd's who writes business under more than one underwriting agent is required to

nominate one of them to coordinate the allocation of his *premium limit* (q.v.).

Copyright
The ownership of a work, including industrial designs, plans and drawings, by its originator.

Corporation loan
A loan to a public authority.

Correspondent
An overseas broker whose business is placed at Lloyd's by a Lloyd's broker.

Cost escalation cover
A facility offered by the Export Credits Guarantee Department to protect traders and contractors against a part of the risk of large increases in cost.

Cost, insurance and freight
A term of sale for goods in transit whereby the price paid by the buyer includes the insurance premium and the shipping charges.

Cost-of-living index
An index, such as the Retail Prices Index, which measures changes in prices over a period.

Co-surety
One of a group of sureties participating directly in a bond.

Council of Lloyd's
The governing body of Lloyd's since 1982. Certain members of the Council are elected by Lloyd's Names (q.v.) and form the Committee of Lloyd's which, under the Council, conducts the day-to-day administration of Lloyd's.

Counter guarantee
Security given to a guarantor to indemnify him against any liability he may incur as a result of having given his guarantee.

Counter indemnity
Same as *Counter guarantee*.

Counter life
The life involved in a contingent survivorship assurance whose death brings the insurance to an end without payment of the sum assured.

Counter selection
Same as *Selection against the insurer*.

Country damage
Damage to baled or bagged goods prior to loading on a vessel, caused by the absorption of excessive moisture or deterioration from grit, dust or sand due to inclement weather.

Coupon insurance
>Insurance effected by completing a coupon and sending it to the insurer.

Coupon policy
>A life assurance policy with coupons attached, each of which entitles the holder to payment of a guaranteed cash bonus on a stated date (U.S.).

Court bond
>A bond given to a court of law to guarantee the due performance of certain duties by a principal.

Court of Protection bond
>A bond given to the Court of Protection in respect of a person responsible for the affairs of a mentally incapacitated person.

Cover note
>An interim document evidencing the grant of insurance cover.

Coverage
>Insurance protection (U.S.)

Coverholder
>An agent authorised by an underwriter to grant cover on the underwriter's behalf.

Craft risks
>Risks arising when cargo is being landed or transhipped in a small vessel.

Credit accident insurance
>Insurance to relieve a debtor of his obligations to pay during periods of inability to earn as a result of accidental injury.

Credit agent
>An agent introducing insurance who collects the premium for which he is allowed a period of credit before he must pay it to the insurer.

Credit card insurance
>Insurance of the liability of a credit card holder for the misuse by a third party of his card.

Credit control
>The measures taken by a business to safeguard itself against loss through slow payment, or failure to pay, by debtors.

Credit guarantee
>A guarantee to a seller that a purchaser will pay.

Credit insurance
>1. Insurance for creditors against their inability to collect debts due to them.
>2. Insurance whereby debtors are relieved of their obligations if they die (see *Credit life assurance*) or while they are

prevented from earning by, e.g., accidental injury or sickness or unemployment (cf. *Credit accident insurance*).

Credit life assurance

Assurance to provide for the repayment of a loan in the event of the borrower's death.

Credit note

A document notifying the placing of a credit to an account.

Creditable service

A period of service that counts in the determination of eligibility for membership of a pension scheme or in the calculation of pension.

Cremation expenses insurance

Insurance effected by an individual to provide for the expenses of his ultimate cremation.

CRISTAL

Contract Regarding an Interim Supplement to Tanker Liability for Oil Pollution. A cargo owners' scheme to provide compensation for oil pollution additional to that provided by *TOVALOP* (q.v.), with a top inclusive limit of $30m, met from contributions by oil company members of the scheme.

Crop hail insurance

Insurance against damage to crops by hail.

Crop insurance

Insurance for farmers against failure or diminution of a crop resulting from either one specified peril (hailstorm) or more general perils such as flood and adverse weather.

Cross liabilities

1. Where two vessels, A and B, are in collision in circumstances where both were partly to blame, so that A is liable to B for part of B's damage and B is liable to A for part of A's damage, the Admiralty Court makes a single award to the party who has a net balance in his favour. Marine hull policies provide that claims shall be settled under the policy on the basis of cross-liabilities, viz., as if each party had been compelled to pay his proportion of the other's damage.

2. Where a liability policy indemnifies two or more persons it is possible that one of the insured may incur a liability to another of the insured. A cross-liabilities clause makes it clear that each insured is separately indemnified so that such a liability is covered.

Cross-risks

Marine insurances on voyages between ports outside the United Kingdom.

Cumulative preference share
A *preference share* (q.v.) which entitles the holder, if his dividend is unpaid in any year, to receive it out of the profits of a subsequent year.

Current annuity
An annuity in course of payment.

Current cost method
Same as *Single premium method.*

Current risks
Insurances in effect at any given time.

Current service pension
The pension earned by an employee in a pension scheme during his service after his entry into the scheme.

Curtate annuity
Same as *Non-apportionable annuity.*

Custody and control
Public liability policies often exclude liability for damage to property in the insured's custody and control but the exclusion may require modification or deletion, e.g., in the case of insured who provide car parks or cloakrooms.

Custom and usage
Custom and usage of a particular trade or market may be a defence to an otherwise valid claim if the parties can be taken to have accepted it, provided the custom or usage is not unlawful.

Custom of Lloyd's
Practice peculiar to the Lloyd's market which binds those taking part but not if it is unreasonable (unless they have assented to be bound) or unlawful.

Customary deductions
Deductions, by a custom of Lloyd's, from claims for particular average to ship, usually one-third where new work replaces old in repairs to hull or machinery. In practice waived by the insurer.

Customary groundings
See *Customary strandings.*

Customary strandings
In marine hull insurance underwriters agree to pay the cost of inspecting the bottom of the vessel after a stranding or grounding, even if no damage is found, except if the stranding or grounding takes place in certain specified areas known as areas of customary strandings or groundings.

Customers' extension
An extension of a property insurance policy to cover cus-

tomers' goods in the insured's custody often subject to the proviso that the insured is responsible for them.

Customs and Excise bonds
Bonds given to the Commissioners of Customs and Excise to secure the eventual payments of duty that has become or may become due.

Cut-off
1. The date after which a reinsurer is not liable under a reinsurance contract.
2. Separation between buildings so that each is assumed to be a separate fire risk.

Cut-through clause
A clause in a reinsurance contract providing that in the event of the ceding insurer's insolvency the reinsurer will be liable for his share of a loss to the insured and not to the ceding insurer's liquidator.

Cycle insurance
Insurance of cycles against one or more perils, viz., accidental damage, fire, theft and third party liability.

Cyclone
A system of winds blowing spirally inwards towards a centre of low pressure, especially a violent cyclonic wind in the Bay of Bengal, the South West Indian Ocean and Australia; loosely, a hurricane.

D

Da Costa clause
Same as *Blood relative clause.*

Damaged value
The actual value on arrival at destination of a vessel or goods which have been damaged. For hulls it is taken as the value without any repairs being taken into account. For cargo the gross damaged value is the value of the damaged cargo after landing charges and duty have been paid. Net value is that before payment of landing charges and duty.

Damages
The sum awarded by a court as compensation for loss, damage or injury.

Damnum fatale
(Literally, fatal damage.) Damage caused by a chance event or an inevitable accident for which, since there is no negligence, there may be no liability on the part of a person such as a *bailee* (q.v.).

69

Dangerous Wild Animals Act 1976
An Act requiring persons, other than zoos and circuses, who keep dangerous wild animals, to be licensed. One requirement for a licence is the holding of an insurance in respect of third party liability.

Datum level
In credit insurance, a *franchise* (q.v.).

Datum line cover
Credit insurance which allows the insured to propose a specific debtor for inclusion in the cover only after his indebtedness has attained a certain level, called the datum line.

Days of grace
A period after the renewal date of a policy during which cover continues provided the premium is paid before the end of the period and the insured has not evinced an intention not to renew.

De die in diem
From day to day.

De facto
As a matter of fact.

De jure
As a matter of law.

Death benefit
1. The sum stated in a policy as payable on the death of the insured.
2. A national insurance benefit for fatal industrial injuries.

Death-in-service benefits
Benefits payable in a pension scheme in respect of an employee who dies while still in service, in the form of either a lump sum or a pension to dependants.

Death strain
The amount paid on death claims less the reserve held on the policies concerned.

Debenture
A written acknowledgement of a debt, usually one owed by a company and often secured by a charge over all or part of its property.

Debit
1. The collection of industrial life assurance premiums.
2. The total premiums due to be collected by an industrial life assurance agent.

Debit note
An advice that an account is to be debited with a sum of money.

Debris removal clause
A clause in a fire insurance policy providing for payment of the cost of removing debris after a loss.

Debt
A life policy issued in respect of a substandard life may provide that in the event of early death the sum assured shall be reduced by a specific amount, referred to as a debt.

Décennale liability insurance
Liability insurance for contractors, architects and consulting engineers covering both liability for accidents on the site during a construction period and subsequent liability for collapse or defects for up to 10 years.

Declaration
1. A statement on a proposal form signed by a proposer affirming certain things, e.g., the truth of the proposer's answers.
2. A periodical statement under a policy with an adjustable premium, giving details of items on which the premium depends, e.g., wages under an employers' liability policy or sendings under a cargo open policy.

Declaration of bonus
Same as *Bonus declaration*.

Declinature
The refusal by an insurer of a proposed insurance.

Decline list
A list of risks that an insurer will not accept.

Decreasing term assurance
Temporary life assurance under which the sum assured is reduced from time to time.

Deductible
1. Same as *Excess*.
2. Allowable as an expense for tax relief.

Deductive item
A pension scheme may relate pensions to pay in excess of a fixed figure, known as the deductive item.

Deed
A written document signed, sealed and delivered.

Deed poll
A deed to which there is only one party.

Defalcation
Same as *Embezzlement*.

71

Defamation insurance
Insurance against liability for libel or slander. Cover is commonly effected by publishers of books and newspapers, local authorities and professional persons. Criminal and intentional libels are likely to be excluded and the insured may be required to bear a proportion of any claim by way of co-insurance.

Defective Premises Act 1972
An Act imposing liability for defects in premises on landlords, developers, buyers and sellers of buildings, and builders and architects.

Deferred account
An agreement whereby an insured or reinsured is allowed to pay premiums by instalments.

Deferred annuity
An annuity that does not become payable until some time after its purchase.

Deferred pension
1. A pension, which will become payable at retirement age, to which a right has accrued. (See *Frozen pension*.)
2. A pension not yet payable to a member of a pension fund because he or she has continued working beyond normal retirement age.

Deferred period
A period specified in a permanent health policy that must elapse after disablement occurs before benefit starts to run.

Deferred share
A category of share whose right to dividend arises only after the entitlement of the holders of other classes of share has been met to a defined extent.

Deficit clause
A clause in a reinsurance contract under which profit commission is payable, whereby if the reinsurer makes a loss in any year his deficit is carried forward for the purpose of calculating the profit commission in a subsequent year or years.

Definite advice
A firm statement, following a provisional one, as where, in cargo reinsurance the insurer who has taken a line gives provisional notice to the reinsurer and sends confirmation after a shipment has been made.

Definitive trust deed
A trust deed setting out the full details of a trust.

Del Credere
>A guarantee to a seller by an agent selling on credit that the buyer is solvent.

Delegatus non potest delegare
>"An agent cannot delegate his authority". A general rule, subject to exceptions, in the law of agency.

Delivery
>An act done in relation to a deed which has been signed and sealed to evince an intention to be bound by the deed. (Delivery of a deed does not necessarily mean handing it over to the other party.)

Delivery guarantee cover
>A form of credit insurance providing compensation if a supplier fails to meet his obligation to deliver.

Demolition value
>The value of property sold as only fit for demolition.

Demurrage
>1. Money paid to a shipowner as compensation for the delay of a vessel beyond the period allowed in a charterparty for loading or discharging.
>2. Any loss of hire period suffered by a shipowner.

Demutualisation
>Turning a mutual insurance company into a proprietary company.

Denial of access
>Business interruption insurance may be extended to cover loss through denial of access to the insured's premises arising out of a peril insured against.

Department of Trade bonds
>Bonds in respect of receivers and liquidators appointed by the Department of Trade.

Dependant's option
>An option in a pension scheme which may allow a member to give up some of his pension in exchange for a pension to a dependant after the member's death.

Dependant's pension
>A pension payable to a dependant of a pension scheme member after the member's death.

Deposit
>1. A sum paid on account, e.g., of a premium to be determined later.
>2. A sum deposited by an insurer with the authorities in a country to entitle the insurer to transact business in that country.

3. A sum left by a reinsurer in the hands of a direct insurer as security for payment of claims for which the reinsurer may ultimately become liable.

Deposit administration
A system whereby money is held by an insurance company for the ultimate purchase of pensions at retirement age and is increased by interest.

Deposit of Poisonous Waste Act 1972
The Act regulates the deposit of poisonous waste and imposes a liability on the depositor for damage caused.

Deposit premium
A payment in advance as a deposit pending determination of the actual premium.

Deposit society
A friendly society providing sickness and sometimes other benefits, which allocates part of the member's contribution to a deposit account in his name from whch withdrawals may be made in accordance with the society's rules.

Depreciation
Loss in value through time.

Determination
Winding up a pension scheme when a trust ceases to exist.

Development risks
Risks attaching to products which could not have been anticipated when the products were launched in the light of scientific or technical knowledge at that time.

Development statistics
A statement by an original insurer showing details of every claim falling within a proposed reinsurance with figures for the amounts paid and outstanding at the end of each year from the date of occurrence until final settlement.

Deviation
The departure of a vessel from the course laid down for it or, if no course has been laid down, from the customary course.

Deviation clause
1. A clause in a marine hull policy providing that the insured shall not be prejudiced by a deviation that is beyond his control.
2. A clause in a charterparty or bill of lading allowing the vessel to deviate without resultant liability of the carrier to the cargo owner.

Difference in conditions policy
Where a company operating internationally has a number of policies covering similar risks and effected in various coun-

tries it may also effect a master policy providing indemnity for claims excluded by a condition found exceptionally in any local policy.

Difference insurance
A fire insurance covering the difference between the value of property at the time of a fire and its reconstruction or replacement value.

Direct action
In English law a third party does not as a rule have a right of direct action against a liability insurer, but in some legal systems he has.
But see *Third Parties (Rights against Insurers) Act 1930*.

Direct business
Insurance placed with an insurer direct and not through an intermediary.

Direct costs
Costs that vary directly with the amount of business transacted.

Direct insurance
Insurance as opposed to reinsurance.

Direct reinsurer
A reinsurer who accepts business directly from an original insurer.

Direct writing
Transacting insurance in direct contact with the public.

Directive
A formal instruction issued by the E.E.C. to its member-states requiring each state to align its law in the matters indicated in the directive.

Directors' and Officers' liability insurance
Insurance against the liability of directors and officers of a company in respect of wrongful acts such as negligence, breach of trust or wrongful advice.

Dirty Bill
Same as *Claused Bill*.

Disability benefit
A right under a life policy, such as entitlement to waiver of premiums, if the policyholder becomes totally disabled.

Disability percentage table
A table showing various disabilities (e.g. loss of an eye or a finger) and the percentage of total disability that each is deemed to represent.

Disablement benefit
Benefit payable under a personal accident, sickness or perma-

nent health insurance in respect of a period during which the insured is unable to follow his occupation in whole or, in some cases, in part.

Disbursements
Payments for expenses: notably, in marine insurance, expenses in running a vessel.

Disbursements Clause
A clause in a marine insurance hull policy defining and restricting the extent to which additional insurances in respect of disbursements, freight etc, may be effected in relation to the ship.

Discharge
1. A document acknowledging that one whose claim has been settled renounces all rights in that respect.
2. The unloading of cargo from a vessel.

Disclosure
1. See *Duty of Disclosure*.
2. A stage in legal proceedings at which the parties to a suit must disclose to each other documents in their respective possession.

Discount
A reduction.

Discounted bonus
The present value of a reversionary bonus.

Discounted bonus policy
A with-profits life assurance policy for which the premium is reduced by part of the expected value of future bonuses.

Discovery cover
A reinsurance treaty which covers losses discovered during the term of the treaty, regardless of when they were sustained.

Discovery period
The period within which a defalcation covered by a fidelity guarantee insurance has to be discovered and notified to the insurers. The period may be longer or shorter than the term of the policy.

Discretionary (endowment) scheme
A scheme for the provision of benefits on retirement of employees in cases where the employer retains a discretion as to who shall join or what benefits shall be provided, the benefits usually being provided by endowment assurance.

Disregard
Same as *Deductive item*.

Distribution unit
A unit in a unit trust in respect of which the net income from the securities in the trust fund is paid to investors periodically.

Dividend
1. A payment to a shareholder of his proportion of the profits of a company.
2. A payment to the holder of a life assurance policy of his share of the company's surplus (U.S.).

Dividing society
A friendly society which annually distributes in cash among its members the whole or the bulk of the excess of its income over its expenditure.

Dol
An intentional act which is wrongful or unlawful.

Domestic company
An insurance company established in the country where it is doing business. In the U.S.A. the term is used in each state to describe a company established in that state, a company established elsewhere in the U.S. being described as a foreign company, while a company established outside the U.S. is an alien company.

Donor policy
A life assurance policy effected by one person on the life of and for the benefit of another.

Double endowment assurance
A form of endowment assurance under which the sum payable on maturity is twice that payable on earlier death.

Double indemnity
A provision in a life or personal accident policy that the benefits will be doubled if a claim arises from a particular cause.

Double insurance
More than one insurance on the same risk.

Drencher
A fire prevention appliance which covers a building externally with a curtain of water to prevent fire from spreading from one building to another.

Drive-in claims service
A service offered by some motor insurers whereby motorists can bring damaged cars to the insurers' premises for inspection.

Dual valuation clause
A clause in a marine hull policy providing one value for a total loss and another for all other purposes.

Dual (Wages) basis
A basis for the insurance of wages in a business interruption policy giving the insured full cover against having to pay unproductive wages for one period and more limited cover for a further period.

Due date
The date on which a premium is due for payment.

Duration certificate
A certificate sought by an insurance company from a private medical adviser during the currency of a life or permanent health insurance.

Duty of disclosure
A common law duty on the part of a proposer for insurance to disclose to the insurer all material facts, viz., all facts that would influence a prudent insurer in deciding whether to grant the insurance and, if so, on what terms.

Dynamic (or dynamised) pension
A pension the rate of which is automatically increased from time to time on some specified basis, e.g., by 5% per annum.

E

Each or Line
Term marked against the single reinsured amount in respect of a fleet of vessels to indicate that each vessel is reinsured for that sum or the original insurer's line on the vessel, whichever is the less.

Early signing
Where a broker has difficulty in getting money out of a country, the underwriter may agree to the signing of a policy before the actual premium can be noted.

Earned-incurred basis
A basis for calculating an insurer's loss ratio by comparing the premiums earned in a period with the estimated cost of claims arising during the period.

Earned premium
Premium is said to be earned by a particular date to the extent that the insurance has by then run its course.

Earthquake
Damage occasioned by or happening through earthquake is excluded from the standard fire policy but may be insured as an additional peril. Earthquake damage is the subject of separate insurance in some countries.

Earthquake fire damage
Damage by fire occasioned by or happening through an earthquake.

Earthquake shock damage
Damage by earthquake shock as opposed to earthquake fire damage.

Earthquake zone
1. An area particularly subject to earthquakes.
2. A division of a country that is particularly subject to earthquakes, made by insurers for the purposes of rating and of controlling the extent of their exposure to risk from a catastrophe.

Economy wording
Where, in fire insurance, co-insurers issue separate policies the full specification may be included only in the policy of the leading insurer, other policies containing an outline only, as a measure of economy.

ECU
The European Currency Unit, a unit of value, based on a number of European currencies and used by the European Community to express sums of money.

Effective date
The date on and from which an insurance comes into force.

Effects
Goods and chattels.

Eighty-five per cent reinstatement average scheme
A scheme for the insurance of buildings under the reinstatement clause of a policy whereby average is applied only if the sum insured is less than 85% of the reinstatement value.

Ejusdem generis rule
A legal rule of construction. Where a specification of things of the same nature, or *genus*, is followed by a general word or phrase (e.g., "etc." or "and all other perils") it will be interpreted as being confined to things of the same *genus*.

Elective benefits
Benefits as to which the beneficiary has an option either whether to insure or, if he insures, as to the form in which to take the benefit.

Electrical clause
A clause in a fire insurance policy to exclude damage to electrical plant and apparatus caused by abnormal currents or self-heating.

Embezzlement
Fraudulent diversion to one's own use of the money or property of another that is in one's care.

Emergency medical treatment
Under the Road Traffic Act 1972, s. 155, a motor insurer must pay a fee to a medical practitioner who renders emergency treatment to a person injured in an accident arising out of the use of the insured vehicle on a road.

Employer's form
The proposal form in fidelity guarantee insurance.

Employers' Liability (Compulsory Insurance) Act 1969
An Act that made it obligatory for businesses to insure in respect of their liability to employees for bodily injury or disease arising out of and in the course of their employment.

Employer's Liability (Defective Equipment) Act 1969
An Act rendering an employer liable for personal injury to employees caused by defects in equipment provided by the employer, even if the defect is attributable to the fault of a third party such as a manufacturer or repairer.

Employers' liability insurance
Insurance by employers in respect of their liability to employees for injury or disease arising out of and in the course of their employment.

Endorsement
1. Any writing on a policy in addition to its normal wording which supplements or modifies its terms. It may be added when the policy is prepared, or subsequently.
2. Writing on the back of a document, e.g., the payee's signature on the back of a cheque.

Endowment assurance
Life assurance providing for the payment of a sum of money at the end of a specified period or on death if death occurs meanwhile.

Engineer-surveyor
An engineer employed by an insurance company to inspect plant and machinery.

Engineering insurance
The insurance of various perils arising out of plant and machinery, such as explosion or collapse of boilers, breakdown of electrical or mechanical plant and lifts and cranes, and resultant damage to the insured's surrounding property and liability to third parties.

Engineering interruption insurance
Insurance covering the insured's pecuniary loss resulting from

interruption to or interference with the insured's business caused by an accident to machinery or a failure in public supply (e.g., of water or electricity).

Enhanced ordinary charges
Increases in the charges for handling insured cargo resulting from the fact that the cargo has been damaged.

Environmental impairment liability insurance
Insurance against liability for accidents or loss arising out of impairments of the environment by the insured, such as the escape of pollutants or smells, noises, vibration or heat.

Equal access
Statutory provision whereby pension schemes for male and female members must treat the sexes alike in various respects.

Equalisation fund
A fund that may be set up by insurers to smooth out the incidence of claims over a number of years, as where the incidence of insured perils, such as damage by hail, is irregular.

Equity
1. Fairness, natural justice.
2. The application of a standard of what seems just in particular circumstances, as opposed to the strict enforcement of legal rules when that would result in unfairness.
3. A body of principles and rules developed by chancery courts in England to mitigate the rigours of other courts. Since 1875 these principles and rules have been applied in all courts.
4. The value of property in excess of any charges upon it.

Equity-linked policy
A life insurance policy the benefits of which are calculated according to the value from time to time of certain specified categories of ordinary shares.

Equity of redemption
The right of a mortgagor, on paying off his debt, to recover the mortgaged property notwithstanding any agreement to the contrary.

Erection all risks
See *Contractors' all risks*.

Errors and omissions insurance
Insurance against losses due to errors or unintentional omissions.

Escalation
Provision for automatic increases on some defined basis in premiums and sums insured.

Escalator clause
A clause in a builders' risk marine policy providing for a possible increase in the insured value of the object under construction on account of inflation or rising costs.

Escalator pension
Same as *Dynamised pension.*

Escape clause
A clause in a reinsurance treaty enabling the reinsurer to terminate the contract upon notice.

Escrow
A document which has been sealed and delivered to a person who is not a party to it on the understanding that it is not to take effect until some event happens or some condition is fulfilled.

Estimated maximum loss
Same as *Probable maximum loss.*

Estimated premium
A provisional premium subject to eventual adjustment.

Estoppel
A rule of evidence which prevents a person from being heard to say that a particular state of affairs does or does not exist, because either (a) a judgment has established to the contrary, (b) he has made a contrary statement in a deed, or (c) he has previously made a contrary statement or has acquiesced in a contrary statement, so allowing another person to act on the strength of that statement.

European accident statement
A form issued by motor insurers in many European countries to their policyholders for use if an accident occurs. It is for completion and signature by the parties concerned on the spot so that the basic facts about the accident can be established at the outset.

Evidence of age
In life and health insurance and before paying annuities insurers require evidence of the insured's age as the premium rate or even eligibility for insurance is affected.

Evidence of health
Evidence of good health is required by insurers at the outset of a life or health insurance and when a lapsed policy is to be revived. In group schemes it is sometimes waived. It is not required on renewal of a permanent life or health insurance. Policies with options to effect additional insurances may grant the option without further evidence of health being required.

Ex gratia payment
A sum paid by an insurer who maintains that he is not liable to make the payment.

Ex parte
A step in a legal action taken by one party in the absence of the other is said to be ex parte.

Ex turpi causa non oritur actio
No (right of) action arises out of an immoral cause.

Exception
A peril or contingency specifically excluded from the insurance cover.

Exceptional circumstances clause
A clause in a business interruption policy providing that adjustments shall be made in calculating the amount of a claim by allowing for the trend of the business and other circumstances which would have affected the business if the material damage had not occurred.

Excess
1. An amount being the first part of the cost of a claim, which the insured has to bear in accordance with the terms of the insurance.
2. The balance of a risk that cannot be placed in an insurance market, so that additional cover is needed.

Excess floating policy
A collective fidelity guarantee policy which provides that in addition to the specified sum insured in respect of each employee there is a further floating amount which can be used to indemnify the insured against unexpectedly large losses.

Excess insurance
An insurance that takes effect only in respect of losses exceeding a stated amount or the amount covered by a previous (or primary) insurance to which it does not make contribution.

Excess line broker
An insurance broker who places a *surplus line (2)* (U.S.)

Excess of average loss reinsurance
Excess of loss ratio reinsurance where the excess point is recalculated annually as a moving average of the loss ratio experienced over an agreed number of preceding years and the ceding company is required to bear an agreed share of any loss in excess of that average.

Excess of line reinsurance
The marine insurance equivalent of *Surplus reinsurance* (q.v.).

Excess of loss policy

A policy that covers claims only to the extent that they exceed a stated amount.

Excess of loss ratio reinsurance

Reinsurance under which the reinsurer agrees that if the loss ratio on the original insurances exceeds a given percentage he will pay a proportion (say, 90%) of the loss in excess thereof, subject to some maximum.

Excess of loss reinsurance

Reinsurance covering claims only the extent that they exceed a stated amount.

Excess point

Term used in excess of loss reinsurance for the point at which the reinsurance comes into effect.

Excess reinsurance

Reinsurance whereby the ceding company retains the whole amount up to a specified limit and the reinsurer covers the excess beyond that amount though subject as a rule to some specified maximum.

Excess value policy

A policy effected by an insured to protect himself where the value of a vessel stated on a marine hull policy is less than its true value and the insured may therefore incur liabilities, e.g., for salvage payments or general average contributions, in proportion to the under-valuation.

Exclusion

A part of the insurance contract that limits its scope.

Execution of policy

The formal act of completing a policy whether by signing or by sealing.

Executor

A person appointed by a will to give effect to it after the testator's death.

Executrix

A female *executor* (q.v.).

Exemplary damages

Exceptionally heavy damages awarded by a court to deter persons from behaving as the defendant has done. Cf. *Punitive damages*.

Exempt approved scheme

See *Approved scheme*.

Exit

The removal of a life from mortality statistics on account of death or the maturity of a policy.

Expectation of life
The number of years which an individual aged exactly X would expect to live if he (or she) were subject to the same probabilities of death as the rest of his age group. Complete expectation of life includes fractions of a year; curtate expectation excludes them.

Expected value
The results obtained by multiplying the value of each possible event by its respective probability and totalling.

Expense loading
The addition made to the pure premium for an insurance to allow for the insurer's expenses.

Expense ratio
The proportion that the expenses of the insurer bear to his income from premiums.

Experience
The comparison of claims, or claims and premiums, over a period, in respect of a particular insured or a group of insurances.

Experience rating
Rating of an insurance based on the record of a particular insured.

Experience refund
In life reinsurance, a refund by the reinsurer of part of the premium in proportion to the profitability of the business.

Expiry
The ending of the period of insurance.

Explosion
A standard fire policy covers damage by fire, whether resulting from explosion or otherwise, and explosion of domestic-type and heating or lighting boilers only. It excludes other damage by explosion, whether the explosion is caused by a fire or not. Other explosion damage may be covered as an additional peril. Boiler explosion is also the subject of engineering insurance.

Expona clauses
Clauses in reinsurance treaties that define the extent if any to which exposure to liability in North America is included.

Export credit insurance
Insurance for exporters against the risk of non-payment for political and/or commercial reasons.

Exposure
1. The state of being subject to the possibility of loss.
2. The measurable extent of risk.

3. The possibility of loss to insured property caused by its surroundings.

Exposure hazard
The extent to which property is subject to the possibility of a fire spreading from a nearby building.

Express warranty
A promise by the insured, set out in a policy, that a given thing shall or shall not be done or that a state of affairs will or will not exist.

Expression of wish form
A form on which a member of a pension scheme may indicate his wishes as to the disposal of benefits accruing on his death, for the guidance of those administering the scheme in the exercise of any discretion they may have.

Expropriation
The act of taking over property or rights in property by a sovereign body or an authority vested with powers thereby.

Extended protest
A declaration by the master of a vessel more detailed than a *protest* (q.v.) made in view of litigation.

Extended terms insurance
A form of export credit insurance where credit is being granted in excess of 180 days.

Extension
A clause in a policy which gives extra cover, e.g., in a business interruption policy, cover in respect of loss through fire at a supplier's premises, or in a cash policy, cover in respect of personal accident benefits to injured employees.

External member (or External Name)
An underwriting member of Lloyd's who is not (or was not, just before retirement) occupied principally with business at Lloyd's by a broker or underwriting agent. (Cf. *Working member*).

Extra-contractual obligations
A term used in reinsurance contracts to cover or exclude damages awarded in courts against an insurer that go beyond the insurer's contractual liability because, for example, the insurer has been negligent in negotiations or has failed to pay a claim promptly.

Extra premium
An amount added to the premium for some increase in hazard.

Extraneous perils
Perils covered by an "all risks" policy on marine cargo other

than navigation perils, e.g., negligence, short delivery, leakage.

F

Facility
An agreement by an insurer allowing a broker to accept insurances of a defined category on the insurer's behalf.

Factor
An agent whose ordinary course of business is to sell goods with the possession of which he is entrusted by his principal. A debt factor is one who collects debts on behalf of a principal.

Factory Mutuals
A group of U.S. mutual insurance companies specialising in the insurance of factories highly protected against fire.

Facultative obligatory treaty
A reinsurance treaty under which an insurer may elect whether to offer a risk of a specified type for reinsurance, the reinsurer being obliged to accept it if offered.

Facultative reinsurance
The reinsurance of risks that the original insurer may elect whether or not to offer for reinsurance, the reinsurer being free to accept or reject the offer.

Facultative treaty
A contract setting out how *facultative reinsurance* (q.v.) shall be handled by an insurer and a reinsurer.

Failure of consideration
When a risk for which the insurer has accepted a premium fails to attach there is said to be a failure of consideration and the insured, if he acted in good faith, may recover the premium.

Family income benefits
Benefits under an endowment assurance, in addition to the principal sum assured, which provide an income for dependants for the period between the death of the assured and the maturity date of the policy.

Faute lourde
Gross negligence though without wrongful intention. (Cf. *dol.*)

Fidelity guarantee
An insurance guarantee to A against the dishonesty of B or B's failure to perform an obligation.

Field staff
1. The sales force of an insurance company.
2. The employees of an insurance company who are in contact with the public, as opposed to those at head office.

Final pensionable salary
A definition in a pension scheme of what constitutes the final salary with reference to which the pension will be calculated. It may provide for averaging over a period. (See *Pensionable salary*.)

Final salary scheme
A pension scheme under which the rate of pension is based on the *final pensionable salary* (q.v.) before retirement.

Fine arts insurance
The insurance of works of art, traditionally undertaken in the U.S.A. by inland marine underwriters.

Fire
In fire insurance "fire" means actual ignition of something that should not be on fire, the cause being accidental or fortuitous in origin.

Fire extinguisher
An appliance, mechanical or otherwise, used for the extinguishment of fires.

Fire insurance
Term used to cover not only insurance against fire but the insurance of additional perils such as explosion and weather.

Fire interruption insurance
Insurance against pecuniary loss consequent upon a fire or other perils commonly covered by a fire insurance policy.

Fire loss
A claim under a fire insurance policy.

Fire mark
A plaque affixed to the wall of a building bearing the name or device of an insurance company and often its policy number, to denote that the building or its contents was insured by that company. Fire marks of the 17th and 18th century were nearly always of lead. Cf *Fire plate*.

Fire plate
Term used to describe the successors to the *fire mark* (q.v.), in the later 19th and earlier 20th century. They are mostly of copper or tin and do not bear a policy number.

Fire prevention
Measures taken to prevent the outbreak of a fire.

Fire protection
Measures taken to protect property from loss by fire and to minimise such loss.

Fire resistance
A measure of the extent to which a building by its construction will resist fire and so reduce its spread.

Fire stop
A seal to close an imperfection of fit between components of a construction in order to restrict the penetration of flame or smoke.

Fire surveyor
One who inspects property to determine the degree of hazard to which it is subject from fire and to assess the premium payable for fire insurance.

Fire wall
A wall that divides a property into separate fire areas.

Fireproof construction
Formerly used in fire insurance practice to distinguish buildings that conform to a high standard of construction, although no building is in fact completely fireproof.

Fires Prevention (Metropolis) Act 1774
An Act, not confined in its operation to London, that empowers persons with an interest in a building insured against fire to require an insurance company to apply policy moneys to reinstatement of the building after a fire.

First line reinsurance
Same as *Flat line reinsurance*.

First loss
In credit insurance, an *excess* (q.v.).

First loss insurance
Property insurance where the sum insured is accepted to be less than the value of the property but the insurer undertakes to pay claims up to the sum insured.

First party insurance
Insurance to provide benefits for a person as distinct from third party insurance which provides for one's liability to another.

First surplus treaty
A reinsurance treaty whereby a reinsurer agrees to reinsure a stated proportion of any insurance in a given range of amounts over and above an agreed proportion retained by the original insurer, the losses being shared proportionately between the insurer and the reinsurers who are party to the

treaty. For higher amounts there may be second, third, fourth, etc., surplus treaties with other reinsurers.

First Three
The first three *leading* underwriters on a broker's slip, not necessarily the first three underwriters to have signed.

Fixed objects
In marine hull liability insurance a distinction is drawn between "collision" with vessels and contact with "fixed objects" such as piers, wharves and fastened buoys, the latter not being covered by collision clauses.

Fixed premium
A premium fixed at the outset and not subject to adjustment during the year or other period of insurance.

Fixed rate treaty
A reinsurance treaty under which the rate of premium is fixed at the outset as a percentage of the ceding insurer's premium income less premiums paid for reinsurance effected in priority to reinsurance under the treaty.

Fixed sum excess
A provision under a policy that the insured shall bear the first £x of any loss.

Fixed term assurance
An assurance under which the sum assured is payable at the end of a fixed term irrespective of the insured's survival. Premiums cease on his death.

Fixed treaty
A reinsurance treaty under which the original insurer binds himself to cede, and the reinsurer binds himself to accept, the risks specified.

Fixtures
Chattels annexed to land or buildings which as a general rule become part of the realty so that ownership vests in the landowner, with certain exceptions for tenant's fixtures and trade fixtures.

Flat line reinsurance
Reinsurance of a fixed amount, whether the whole or part of the insurer's line.

Fleet
Originally a group of ships but applied to groups of other vehicles and in the U.S. to a group of insurance companies in one ownership.

Fleet policy
A single policy covering a number of motor vehicles or hulls in one ownership.

Fleet rating
A rating applied to a number of motor vehicles or hulls in one ownership, having regard to claims experience.

Flexible endowment assurance
An endowment assurance which expressly allows the assured the option to surrender the policy in part or in whole at a date convenient to him after the policy has been in force for a period, usually ten years.

Flexible funding
A system of costing for pension schemes based on *controlled funding* (q.v.).

Flight risks
The risks attaching to an aircraft whilst in the air as opposed to ground risks.

Floater
Same as *Floating policy*.

Floating policy
A policy where the sum insured covers different situations or persons with no division of the sum insured among them.

Flood insurance
Insurance against damage by flood which is easily obtainable where the risk is comparatively remote but not, as in parts of the U.S.A., where it is endemic and where a federal insurance scheme has proved necessary.

Foam installation
Fixed pipework connected to an apparatus producing foam which it discharges to suppress a fire.

Follow the fortunes
A clause in a reinsurance treaty whereby the reinsurer undertakes to follow the fortunes of the insurer. Thus, if the insurer settles a claim ex gratia, the reinsurer may be expected not to deny liability for his share in the settlement.

Follow the lead
The custom in an insurance market, e.g., Lloyd's, whereby once a leading underwriter (q.v.) has accepted part of an insurance, other underwriters will tend to follow him.

For declaration only
A policy which does not specify the insurance or state the premium pending subsequent declarations of specific insurances.

Force majeure
Some physical or natural restraint which prevents an intention being carried out and which is outside the control of the person who had the intention. The term thus includes *Acts of*

God (q.v.), strikes, war and legislative or administrative intervention.

Force of morality

The proportion of persons of exact age *x* who would die within one year if the observed mortality were to remain constant.

Forcible and violent means

Term used in theft insurance when cover is given only for theft following on entry by forcible and violent means, thus excluding losses following entry gained by a trick, by the use of a key, or by entering through an unlocked door or window.

Foreign company

Term used in the U.S.A. to describe an insurance company established in one U.S. state when it is operating in another.

Foreign jurisdiction clause

A clause in a policy providing that claims shall be settled in a jurisdiction other than that of the country where the insurers are based.

Forfeiture

Loss of a right in consequence of a crime or breach of engagement. Thus, rights under a life assurance policy may be forfeited if the insured fails to pay the premium. Where an insurance has been obtained by fraud on the part of the insured he forfeits both his rights under the policy and any premium paid.

Forgoing

Giving up part of one's salary on the understanding that one's employers will use the money forgone to buy pension or life assurance benefits.

Form of subrogation

An authority signed by the insured which enables the insurer to pursue his subrogation rights without having to prove them in some other way.

Fortuitous

Happening by chance.

Fortuitous event

A chance happening.

Forward contract

An agreement for insurance to come into force at some future date.

Forward exchange rate cover

Credit insurance against the exporter's risk of loss from an unfavourable movement in the rate of exchange.

Forwarding charges
Expenses of carriage of cargo to destination from a place of refuge or port of forced discharge.

Foundations clause
A clause in a fire policy excluding damage to foundations where the sum insured does not include their value.

Franchise
1. A minimum percentage or amount of loss which must be attained before insurers are liable to meet a claim. Once it is attained the insurers must pay the full amount of the loss.
2. The amount of salary disregarded under an occupational pension scheme because it is taken care of by a state scheme.

Franked income
Investment income in the form of dividends or other taxable distributions from which income tax has been deducted by the payer.

Franking
Reducing liability to pay a pension by deduction of benefits payable under some other pension scheme.

Fraud
A deliberate act done with intent to deceive.

Fraud or dishonesty
Terms used in a fidelity guarantee policy to describe the employee's conduct insured against. The words are not statutorily defined.

Frauds, Statute of, 1677
S.4 of this Act, still in force, provides that no action may be brought on a promise to answer for the debt, default or miscarriage of another, unless it is evidenced in writing and signed by or on behalf of the promisor.

Fraudulent misrepresentation
Misrepresentation made knowingly with intent to deceive, or recklessly without care whether it be true or false.

Free asset
An asset of an insurance company that is not earmarked for the fulfilment of a limited class of obligations such as satisfying claims in one section of its business only.

Free cover
The extent to which death-in-service benefits will be made available under a group life assurance without investigation of an individual's health.

Free limits
1. The geographical area within which the holder of a life or health policy is covered without payment of additional premium.
2. Limits of amount up to which an insurance will be granted automatically.

Free of capture and seizure clause
A clause in a marine policy to exclude war risks.

Free of particular average
A marine insurance expression. Where it is used insurers are not liable for partial damage other than a general average loss. Limited cover for partial damage is however given by the so-called Institute Cargo Clauses (F.P.A.).

Free of particular average absolutely
A marine insurance expression. Where it is used insurers are not liable for partial damage other than a general average loss, and limited cover for partial damage such as is provided by the Institute Cargo Clauses (F.P.A.) is not given.

Free of particular average unless
A marine insurance expression. Where it is used insurers are not liable for partial damage unless (a) the vessel in which the cargo is carried is stranded, sunk or burnt, or (b) an insured package is totally lost in the loading, transhipment or discharge, or the loss or damage is attributable to fire, explosion or collision or impact of the vessel with an external substance other than water.

Free of particular average unless caused by
A marine insurance expression. Where it is used insurers are not liable for partial damage unless (a) such damage is caused by the vessel being stranded, sunk or burnt, or (b) an insured package is totally lost in loading, transhipment or discharge, or the loss or damage is attributable to fire, explosion or collision or impact of the vessel with an external substance other than water.

Free of premium
No further premium is payable.

Free policy
In industrial life assurance a policyholder who has discontinued his policy has in some circumstances a statutory right to a paid-up policy for a reduced sum insured, called a free policy.

Free reserves
The reserves of an insurance company for any purpose, over

and above technical reserves, e.g., for outstanding claims or unexpired risk.

Freedom of establishment
The right to set up an office or establishment in a country other than that in which one has one's principal place of business.

Freedom of services
The right to provide services in a country without necessarily having an office or establishment in that country.

Freezer insurance
Insurance of the contents of deep freezers against damage caused by an undesigned change of temperature.

Freight
By the Marine Insurance Act, 1906, s.90, "freight" includes the profit derivable by a shipowner from the employment of his ship to carry his own goods or moveables, as well as freight payable to a third party, but does not include passage money.

Freight insurance
Insurance of the money earned for carrying goods.

Friendly society
A mutual society established for the relief or maintenance of its members or their relatives during sickness or other infirmity or in old age or widowhood, or for life assurance and certain other purposes.

Fringe company
A company, other than a major British company, by whom or on whose behalf insurance is written in one of the underwriting rooms near Lloyd's.

From the ground up
A statement of an original insurer's experience of a class of business offered for reinsurance is said to be from the ground up (F.G.U.) when it shows the number and distribution by amount of all claims however small even though reinsurance is required for large claims only.

Front-end loading
A system under which the expenses of a life assurance company are charged more heavily against premiums payable in the earlier years of a policy than in later years.

Fronting company
A company whose services are used by a reinsurer, the company accepting direct insurance in its own name and forthwith reinsuring it with the reinsurer.

Frost
In marine insurance frost is not considered a peril of the sea.

Frozen pension
> A pension payable at a fixed rate from a future date to which a right has accrued because either a scheme member has left a pension scheme before retirement age or the pension scheme has been discontinued.

Frustration
> The premature determination of a contract owing to the occurrence of an intervening event or a fundamental change in circumstances not contemplated by the parties at the outset.

Frustration clause
> A clause in a marine insurance policy covering war risks that excludes any claim based upon frustration of the insured voyage or adventure.

Full reinsurance clause
> A clause in a facultative reinsurance contract, where all or nearly all a risk is reinsured, to give the reinsurer control over claims settlements.

Full value insurance
> An insurance where the insured is required to warrant that the sum insured represents the full value of the insured property.

Fund
> A provision or reserve.

Fund Convention 1971
> An international convention which requires cargo owners to contribute to the cost of oil spills if the shipowner's liability limit does not suffice to meet claims.

Funding
> Setting aside assets to meet an eventual obligation.

Future service pension
> 1. A pension that will be earned during employment in the future.
> 2. Pension earned after a new pension scheme starts or after improvement of benefits in an existing scheme.

G

Gambling
> Staking money on a chance.

Gambling Policies Act
> Same as *Marine Insurance (Gambling Policies) Act* 1909.

Gaming
> Playing a game of chance for money.

Gaming Act 1845
An Act providing that all contracts or agreements by way of gaming or wagering are void.

Gearing
1. The ratio of non-profit assurances to with-profits assurances in the portfolio of a life assurance company.
2. The ratio of fixed interest capital, including prior charges, to the ordinary share capital of a company.

General agency system
The system of obtaining insurance business through general agents rather than through branch offices.

General agent
1. An agent with wide powers.
2. An agent, often with an exclusive territory, employed by an insurance company to obtain business for it.

General average
The principle in maritime law that when a sacrifice is made or an expense voluntarily incurred to preserve the rest of a venture the loss or expense should be shared among all the interests involved in proportion to their value.

General average act
A sacrifice made or an expense incurred voluntarily to preserve a marine venture, e.g., jettisoning a part of the cargo.

General average adjustment
A statement of losses, values and proportionate contributions prepared by an average adjuster nominated by the shipowner for the purpose of adjusting a general average loss.

General average agreement
When a *general average act* (q.v.) occurs the carrier has a lien on the cargo to secure the consignee's contribution. To remove this the consignee must deposit money or provide an insurer's guarantee. Collaterally the consignee must execute a general average agreement (or average bond) undertaking to abide by the decision of the average adjuster and to accept liability for the general average contribution.

General average bond
See *Average bond.*

General average contribution
The payment due from a party in a marine venture to pay for a general average loss. It is in proportion to the value of his interest as compared with the total values of all interests in the venture.

General average deposit
A deposit which a shipowner requires of a cargo owner as a condition of releasing his lien on cargo that is subject to a general average contribution.

General average expenditure
Expenditure incurred by a shipowner in connection with a *general average act* (q.v.), e.g., the hire of a tug to pull a vessel off a strand.

General average fund
A fund collected jointly by a shipowner and his average adjuster consisting of *general average deposits* (q.v.) and available for the payment of general average expenditure and, eventually, of contributions.

General average guarantee
An insurer's guarantee that may be accepted by a shipowner in lieu of a *general average deposit* (q.v.).

General average sacrifice
The sacrifice of one of the interests in a marine venture made to preserve the other interests from a total loss.

General bond
A customs and excise bond covering all transactions during a specified period.

General business
By the Insurance Companies Act 1974, s. 1, "general business" is defined as insurance not being *long term business* (q.v.).

General damages
Compensation at law, e.g., for pain and suffering, which cannot be quantified and proved specifically as can *special damages* (q.v.).

General expenses
The overhead expenses of an insurance company that have not been allocated to the account of any one class of the company's business.

General hazard
A feature tending to the inception or spread of fire found in most classes of risk, as opposed to a special hazard in a particular class.

Gentleman's agreement
An understanding, binding in honour only, that is not expressed in a formal document intended to have legal effect.

Geographical limits
Same as *Territorial limits*.

Gilt-edged security
    A British Government security.
Glass insurance
    The insurance of glass used commercially or domestically against breakage.
Global policy
    Same as *Blanket policy.*
Gold Clause Agreement
    An agreement between insurers, shipowners and merchants' associations which relaxes certain limitations of carrier's liability for damage to goods contained in the Hague Rules, prescribing, inter alia, a higher limit per package than that provided in the gold clause (Article IV) of the Hague Rules and a longer period than that there allowed for the bringing of an action.
Gold franc
    A unit of value found in international conventions, consisting of 65.5 milligrammes of pure gold.
Golfer's insurance
    Insurance of golf clubs with, often, the addition of personal accident benefits, third party liability, and a cash benefit to cover hospitality costs if the insured holes in one.
Good faith
    See *Utmost good faith.*
Goods
    By the Marine Insurance Act, 1906, First Schedule, Rule 17, "goods" means goods in the nature of merchandise, and does not include personal effects or provisions and stores for use on board.
Goods-in-transit insurance
    The insurance of goods in transit domestically or internationally other than purely by sea. The insurance may cover either the goods or the carrier's liability for them.
Government bond
    A guarantee given by a surety such as an insurance company to a government department in respect of the actions of a third party, referred to as the principal.
Graded schedule scheme
    An insured pension scheme under which benefits are calculated according to earnings in each year of membership.
Grades of construction
    A scheme of grading buildings for appraisal for fire insurance, issued by the Fire Offices' Committee and replacing the F.O.C.'s former *standards of construction* (q.v.).

Graduation
The adjustment of crude data in a statistical table to produce smooth functions.

Grantee
One on whom legal rights are conferred.

Green card
A document evidencing the existence of third party motor insurance, issued to a motorist for use internationally.

Gross arrived damaged value
See *Damaged value.*

Gross earned premiums
Premiums received by or due to an insurer, without deduction of the cost of any reinsurance, but adjusted to take account of the difference between the unexpired risk reserves at the beginning and end respectively of the period concerned.

Gross fund
A fund not liable to tax on income or capital gains.

Gross line
The share of an insurance accepted by an underwriter before a deduction is made for any reinsurance by him.

Gross net premium
The gross premium for a marine insurance, before deduction of brokerage and discounts but less gross returns of premium.

Gross premium
The total premium before deduction of brokerage or discounts.

Gross proceeds
By the Marine Insurance Act, 1906, s.73, gross proceeds of the sale of goods or merchandise means the actual price obtained at a sale where all charges on sale are paid by the seller.

Gross system
A system of preparing accounts without offsettable items, specifically without allowing for the effects of reinsurance.

Gross value
By the Marine Insurance Act 1906, s.71, gross value means the wholesale price of goods or merchandise or, if there be no such price, the estimated value with, in either case, freight, landing charges, and duty paid beforehand.

Gross written premiums
Premiums received by or due to an insurer without deduction of the cost of any reinsurance or any adjustment for the fact that some of the income has to be reserved for unexpired risks.

Gross yield
The interest or dividend on an investment without deduction of tax payable on it.

Ground risks
The risk of damage to an aircraft while stationary on the ground.

Grounding
1. The running aground of a ship.
2. The withdrawal of an aircraft from service.

Grounding risk
The risk under an aviation products liability insurance that the manufacturer will incur liability if aircraft are grounded pending investigation and rectification of an alleged defect.

Group
1. A number of insurance companies acting under a single control.
2. A body of persons, such as the employees of a company or the members of an association. They may be insured either under a single master policy or under separate contracts. In some cases all members are insured. In others, members of the group have an option whether to insure or not.

Group insurance
The insurance of groups of persons, as distinct from individual insurance. See *Group* (2).

Group life assurance
Life assurance on groups of persons as distinct from individual life assurance. See *Group* (2).

Group underwriting
The centralisation of underwriting within a group of insurance companies, thus maximising the group's underwriting capacity.

Growth bond
Same as *Capital bond*.

Guarantee
1. A written undertaking given by one party to another to answer for the fulfilment of the obligations of a third party.
2. A facultative reinsurance.

Guarantee deposit
A deposit by way of security as a guarantee against obligations.

Guarantee fund
One-third of the margin of solvency prescribed for general insurance companies by the E.E.C., subject to a minimum that varies according to the classes of business transacted. A

company that does not maintain its guarantee fund is required to submit a short-term financial scheme to redress its affairs.

Guaranteed annuity
A life annuity of any kind which has a proviso that it shall be paid for at least a stated number of years in any event.

Guaranteed annuity option
In respect of a life assurance or a pension scheme producing a benefit in the form of a lump sum the assurance company may offer the option to take an annuity of a guaranteed minimum amount.

Guaranteed bonus
Where a life assurer guarantees that a given rate of bonus will be added to the sum assured each year the assurance becomes in effect a without-profits assurance for an automatically increasing sum assured.

Guaranteed minimum pension
The minimum amount of pension that a vocational pension scheme must provide for periods during which a member is contracted out of the state scheme.

Guaranteeing office
In life reassurance, the reassurer.

Guarantor
One who gives a guarantee.

H

Hague-Visby Rules
A set of internationally agreed rules governing the rights and immunities of carriers of goods by sea. They are incorporated in the Carriage of Goods by Sea Act 1971 which came into effect on 23 June 1977.

Hailstorm insurance
Insurance against damage to crops or glass breakage caused by hailstorm.

Halving agreement
An agreement between two insurers to share equally the cost of claims made against one or both of them arising out of an occurrence, regardless of the liability of their respective insured.

Hamburg Rules
Proposed rules for the carriage of goods by sea which substantially eliminate shipowners' exemptions from liability for damage to cargo arising from, e.g., fault in management, fault in navigation, or fire.

Hancock annuity
An annuity purchased by an employer for the benefit of an ex-employee in respect of which, subject to the fulfilment of certain conditions, tax relief on the purchase price may be obtained by the employer.

Hangarkeeper's liability insurance
Insurance of the liability of a provider of accommodation for aircraft on the ground.

Harmonisation
A process that the E.E.C. seeks to apply to the laws of its member-states in some fields so that their respective laws, while not made uniform, have a broadly similar effect.

Hazard
A physical or moral feature that introduces or increases the possibility of a loss arising from a peril or that may influence the extent of a loss.

Health and Safety at Work, etc, Act 1974
An Act to enforce provisions for the health, safety and welfare of persons at work and for protecting members of the public against health and safety risks.

Health Insurance
See *Permanent health insurance* and *Private health insurance*.

Heave
Horizontal displacement upwards, as distinct from subsidence.

Hedging
Protecting oneself against a risk of loss in respect of a transaction by entering into a countervailing transaction, e.g., when buying an annuity effecting a life assurance to recoup all or part of the annuity purchase money on death.

Held covered
1. A risk is said to be held covered when an insurer agrees to insure it temporarily pending completion of insurance arrangements.
2. A marine insurance policy may provide that some contingency which may or may not arise shall be held covered if it does arise, subject to notice and payment of an additional premium.

Hidden reserve
Under English law insurance companies are allowed to hold reserves that do not appear in their published accounts which may, for example, show their investments at less than their true value.

Hold-harmless agreement
An agreement by one party to indemnify another against claims of a defined nature.

Hold-up cover
Cover for theft accompanied by violence or the threat of it.

Holloway society
A *deposit society* (q.v.) whose members' contributions increase progressively after age 30.

Home business
Insurance transacted with policyholders in the British Isles.

Home Foreign
Insurance from overseas effected in the U.K. market.

Home office
Head office (U.S.).

Home service insurance
Same as *Industrial life assurance*.

Home Trade insurance
Marine insurance within the U.K., and including trade with European ports between the Elbe and Brest.

Honeycomb slip
A slip with a honeycomb of boxes in which the syndicate numbers of insurers on the risk are inserted in the same order as they appear on the original slip. The slip is used when special agreements are added to the initial slip to ensure that none of the original underwriters has been omitted.

Honour policy
A policy that has no legal effect and is binding in honour only.

Honourable undertaking
Reinsurance treaties commonly contain a clause saying that the agreement is an honourable undertaking, the purpose of which is not to be defeated by a strict or narrow interpretation of the language used in the treaty.

Hospital and medical expenses insurance
Insurance against hospital and medical expenses. Used by persons not wishing to rely wholly on the national health service.

Hospital cash insurance
Insurance providing for payment of a cash sum during a period of treatment as a hospital in-patient, regardless of whether the patient is incurring expenses for treatment.

Hospital charges
The Road Traffic Act 1972 entitles a hospital to recover its charges (up to a specified amount) for treatment of a person injured in a road accident when a third party motor insurer

has made a payment under its policy in respect of the injury. The maxima were increased in 1980.

Hotel Proprietors Act 1956
An Act setting out the strict liability of hotel proprietors for the property of guests up to £50 any one article or £100 in the aggregate.

Hours clause
A clause in an excess of loss property catastrophe reinsurance which specifies the number of hours after an accident or catastrophe during which losses must occur in order to be aggregated for the purpose of calculating a claim against the reinsurers.

House purchase assurance
Endowment assurance issued for the purpose of repaying a mortgage at the end of its term or on the death of the assured if this occurs meanwhile.

Household goods and personal effects
Furniture, clothing and the other customary contents of a private dwelling.

Householders' insurance
A package of insurances for private householders, including the insurance of contents against fire, theft and other perils and the liability of the householder as occupier.

Housekeeping
The care, cleanliness and maintenance of premises, including the systematic collection and disposal of waste.

Houseowners' insurance
A package of insurances for the owners of private dwellings, including the insurance of buildings against fire and other perils and the liability of the owner to third parties.

Housing Cost Index
An index of building costs prepared by the Royal Institution of Chartered Surveyors, used as a guide in determining replacement values of buildings for insurance purposes.

Hovercraft insurance
The insurance of air cushion vehicles in respect of damage to hull or liabilities. The insurance, though placed mainly in the aviation insurance market, is governed by the Marine Insurance Act 1906. Liability to passengers in the United Kingdom is governed by the Hovercraft (Civil Liability) Order 1971, made under the Hovercraft Act 1968.

Hull
A ship, boat, hovercraft or aircraft.

Hull insurance
>Insurance on a ship, boat, hovercraft or aircraft, including its machinery and equipment. Marine hull insurance commonly includes indemnity for ¾ of collision liability.

Hull interest
>An insurable interest connected with a ship exposed to maritime perils, e.g., the interest of shipowner, charterer or mortgagee.

Hull Paramount clauses
>Clauses in a marine hull policy which override anything in the policy with which they are inconsistent. Notably, war risk exclusion.

Hull returns
>Returns of premium allowed under a hull policy, notably when the vessel insured is laid up.

Hull syndicate
>A marine insurance syndicate engaged primarily in hull insurance.

Hundred per cent treaty basis
>A basis of rendering accounts to a number of treaty reinsurers by showing only the full amounts of premiums and claims etc, and not the proportion applicable to each reinsurer, the proportion being given solely for the net balance due to or from each reinsurer.

Hurricane
>A wind of over 74 mph, especially a cyclonic wind in the Caribbean.

Hybrid policy
>A policy which contains two different types of cover.

Hybrid scheme
>A company pension scheme partly self-administered and partly managed by an insurance company.

I

Ice deviation clause
>A clause in a marine cargo policy permitting a vessel to deviate to discharge cargo at the nearest accessible port if the destination port is inaccessible on account of ice.

Ice deviation risk
>Insurance to pay £x per ton of cargo discharged short of destination because of icing at the destination port or its closure due to icing.

Ice exclusion clause
A clause in a marine hull policy excluding damage caused by contact with ice during winter months.

Immediate annuity
An annuity coming into operation from the date of completion of the contract.

Immediate participation guarantee contract
A contract providing that the insured shall participate from the outset in the actual experience of a pension scheme as to mortality, expenses, interest income and profit or loss on the sale of investments.

Immunisation
The investment of assets in such a way that the insurer's existing business is immune to a general change of interest rates in the future.

Impact damage
Damage to fixed property by a moving object.

Impact damage agreements
Agreements whereby liability insurers agree to pay and the owners or insurers of fixed property agree to accept, a stated proportion of damage to the property caused by an insured vehicle, without regard to legal liability.

Impaired lives
Persons who suffer from some condition that may shorten their life.

Implied authority
The power of an agent to bind his principal that has not been expressly stated but that can be deduced from the principal's conduct.

Implied condition
A condition to which a policy is subject that is not expressed in the policy, the fulfilment of the condition resting with either the insured or the insurer.

Implied obligation
An obligation not expressed in a contract, to which the contract is subject.

Implied warranty
A condition to which a policy is subject that is not expressed in the policy, the fulfilment of the condition resting on the insured.

Importation of average
A condition in a policy whereby if a claim is covered by two policies one of which is expressed as subject to average and one not, the latter is made subject to average in like manner.

In and out policy
> A policy covering stockbrokers against losses due to the infidelity of staff, dealings in forged or stolen documents, and the misappropriation of documents or money.

In camera
> In private.

In force
> A contract is said to be in force so long as it remains operative until it expires or is cancelled.

In transitu
> In transit.

Inception date
> The date on which an insurance begins to operate.

Inchmaree Clause
> See *Negligence Clause.*

Incidental non-marine
> Insurances written by a marine underwriter as an adjunct to his marine insurance account.

Income benefit
> A benefit by way of regular payments to the dependants of a deceased person under a life assurance, or to the insured during a period of disablement under a health insurance.

Income bond
> A contract combining life assurance and an annuity under which an income is payable for a term certain.

Income tax relief
> See *Life Assurance Premium Relief.*

Incontestability clause
> Same as *Indisputability clause.*

Increase in cost of working
> Under a business interruption policy the occurrence of the event insured against may cause the insured to incur increases in his costs in endeavouring to maintain production. The insurance provides some cover in this respect.

Increased risk
> An insurance that presents some unfavourable feature.

Increased value and excess liabilities policy
> Same as *Excess value policy.*

Increasing bonus
> A bonus under a with-profits life assurance at a rate increasing with the length of time the policy has run.

Increasing claim payments
> A permanent health insurance may provide for the benefits when they become payable to increase annually by a stated

percentage as a measure of compensation for inflation.

Incurred but not reported (I.B.N.R.)
At the end of a period of account a reserve in respect of property, liability and pecuniary insurances to cover the expected cost of losses that have occurred but have not yet been reported to the insurer or reinsurer.

Incurred loss ratio
The percentage of losses incurred to premiums earned.

Incurred losses
Losses arising during a period of insurance whether settled or not.

Indemnification aliunde
The liability of insurers under a contract of indemnity is to make good the insured's loss. If the insured's loss is made good *aliunde* (from another source) the insurers are entitled to credit accordingly for any sum received.

Indemnity
1. The making good of a loss by means of a monetary payment.
2. An agreement by one party to make good a loss sustained by the other party.

Indemnity period
In business interruption insurance the period from the date of an occurrence giving rise to a claim in respect of which losses are payable by the insurer in accordance with the terms of the insurance.

Indenture
A deed to which there is more than one party.

Independent company
Same as *Non-tariff company*.

Independent liability method
A method of apportioning a claim covered by two or more insurances. The liability of each insurer is calculated independently and each insurer contributes in proportion to the amount of his liability thus ascertained.

Independent range
Insurance policies are said to be of independent range when one covers property of certain classes or at certain situations and the other covers classes of property or situations which are not identical. If there is some overlap in cover the respective insurers must contribute in the settlement of a loss.

Independent risk unit
Part of the subject-matter of an insurance which is separate from and independent of other parts.

Index clause
> A clause in a contract of insurance or reinsurance which links premiums and sums insured or limits of indemnity to an index of prices as a measure of combating the effects of inflation.

Indexed annuity
> An annuity under which the calculation of the annual payment due is made by reference to a cost-of-living index.

Indicate
> A broker who has obtained a quotation from a leading underwriter for a line of an insurance is said to indicate a rate when he informs his client of this.

Indirect business
> Insurance received by an insurer through a broker or agent entitled to commission, or through another insurer, as distinct from business transacted directly between the insurer and the insured.

Indisputability clause
> A clause in a policy providing that after a stated period the insurer may not dispute the validity of the policy in the absence of fraud on the part of the insured, thus relieving the insured of the consequences of any innocent non-disclosure or misrepresentation.

Individual life assurance
> Life assurance effected by individuals as distinct from group life assurance.

Indivisibility of premiums
> A principle whereby when a premium has been agreed for a period it is payable in full even though the insurer has covered the risk for only a part of the period.

Industrial all risks insurance
> Insurance of industrial property against loss or damage where the perils insured against are not specified but exceptions are.

Industrial fire insurance
> Fire insurance of business property as distinct from the insurance of the property of private individuals.

Industrial injuries insurance
> A form of social insurance providing benefits for employed persons for injuries arising out of and in the course of their employment.

Industrial life assurance
> Life assurance the premiums on which are paid to collectors at intervals of less than two months.

Industrial property rights insurance
> Insurance against the infringement or alleged infringement of

patent, design, trademark, trade name or copyright, or actions for passing off, in respect of goods sold or supplied.

Inevitable accident
Where a defendant seeks to escape liability for the consequences of an accident on the ground that it was inevitable, it must be shown that he did (or omitted to do) nothing that a person exercising ordinary care, caution and skill would not have done, (or would not have left undone, as the case may be).

Inflation factor
An adjustment of premium to allow for a rise in costs due to inflation.

Infra
Below

Infringement (of industrial property rights) insurance
Insurance against the financial consequences of inadvertently infringing rights such as patents, trademarks or copyright.

Ingestion damage
Damage caused by foreign bodies being drawn into the air intake of the turbine engine of an aircraft.

Inherent vice
A quality in goods that produces damage to them by its own action without the assistance of an outside agency.

Initial period
In business interruption insurance a period of so many weeks after the occurrence of material damage during which the insured is protected against loss in relation to wages to the full extent of his wage roll.

Initial premium
The premium charged at the outset of insurance subject in some cases to subsequent adjustment.

Initialling
The initialling of a slip by an underwriter binds him to accept his line of the insurance. Similarly he signifies his acceptance of subsequent amendments or agreements by initialling a document.

Injunction
An order of the court to do, or not to do, some specified act.

Inland marine insurance
A category of marine insurance relating to inland water and inland transit risks. In U.S. practice it includes the insurance of movables such as jewellery and personal effects and instrumentalities of transport such as bridges.

111

Innkeeper's liability
>In English law an innkeeper is liable for the safety of the property of his guests. The Hotel Proprietors Act 1956 describes and circumscribes the liability.

Inside staff
>The employees of an insurance company who work within its offices and who are not wholly or mainly engaged in making outside calls.

Insolvency clause
>A clause providing that the reinsurer shall be liable for his share of a loss even though the insurer has become insolvent.

Inspection clause
>A clause in a reinsurance treaty entitling the reinsurer to inspect the books of the ceding insurer.

Inspector
>An official of an insurance company concerned with the selling and servicing of insurances.

Instalment premium
>In life assurance a premium that is expressed as annual but is met by a series of payments at more frequent intervals, the total being payable even if death occurs while one or more instalments are outstanding.

Instant certificates
>Provisional certificates provided by Lloyd's for the use of the insured in connection with open covers and the like pending the availability of printed certificates.

Institute Agent
>An agent appointed by the Institute of London Underwriters and authorised to settle claims payable abroad.

Institute Clauses
>Clauses approved by a committee of company and Lloyd's underwriters as standard clauses for use in the marine insurance market, and published by the Institute of London Underwriters.

Institute Warranties
>A set of standard warranties issued by the Institute of London Underwriters for inclusion in marine hull policies. The warranties deal mainly with navigational matters.

Insurability
>Able to be insured against. In principle one may insure against the financial consequences of any event where it is a matter of fortuity whether the event will occur or when it will occur. One cannot insure against the consequences of one's deliberate acts or where insurance would be against public

policy. In practice a risk may be uninsurable where:
(a) the prospect of widespread loss is too great for the insurer to accept, e.g., war damage to property on land;
(b) the risk is entrepreneurial, e.g., the risk of a change of fashion rendering stock unsaleable;
(c) the risk is too great or unquantifiable.

Insurable interest

Insurance requires for its validity that the insured shall be so related to the subject-matter of the insurance that he will benefit from its survival or will suffer from loss or damage to it or may incur liability in respect of it. In the absence of such an interest, known as an insurable interest, the insurance will be invalid. Everyone has an insurable interest in his own life and spouses are deemed to have such an interest in the lives of each other.

Insurance

Insurance is a contract whereby one party, called the insurer, in return for a consideration, called the premium, undertakes to pay to the other party, called the insured, a sum of money or its equivalent in kind upon the happening of a specified event that is contrary to the interest of the insured.

Insurance agent

A representative of an insurer, whether an employee or an independent contractor, who negotiates, effects, and may service, contracts of insurance.

Insurance broker

One who advises persons on their insurance needs and negotiates insurances on their behalf with insurers, exercising professional care and skill in so doing. See *Insurance Brokers (Registration) Act 1977.*

Insurance Brokers (Registration) Act 1977

This Act provides for the setting up of an Insurance Brokers Registration Council to register persons and firms who use the description "insurance broker", "reinsurance broker" etc, and to set professional standards for them.

Insurance certificate

A document evidencing the fact of insurance where it is convenient to have such evidence separate from the policy, e.g.
1. for issue to a person covered under a group policy;
2. for shipments under a cargo open cover;
3. for users of motor vehicles to produce to show that they have the third party cover required by the Road Traffic Act 1972.

Insurance Ombudsman Bureau
> An independent bureau, financed by insurance companies who have agreed that its head shall investigate and, if required, adjudicate on, complaints by private policyholders against insurers who are members of the scheme.

Insurant
> Nineteenth century term for one who obtains an insurance.

Insure
> 1. To grant an insurance.
> 2. To obtain an insurance.

Insured
> The person covered by a policy of insurance.

Insured scheme
> A pension scheme where pensions are provided by an insurance company.

Insurer
> The party to a contract of insurance who is liable to pay claims arising under it.

Insurrection
> A rising of people against established authority with the object of supplanting it.

Integration
> The process of dovetailing a private pension scheme with the state scheme.

Intentional self-injury
> Intentional self-injury is commonly excluded from personal accident insurances.

Inter se
> Between themselves.

Inter vivos
> Between living persons.

Interest clause
> A clause in a liability reinsurance treaty providing that where interest is added to a claimant's damages it is payable by insurers and reinsurers in proportion to their respective shares of the claim.

Interest or no interest
> Phrase at one time used in a marine insurance policy where it was doubtful whether the insured had an *insurable interest* (q.v.). By the Márine Insurance Act 1906, s.4, a policy made with these words is deemed to be a gaming or wagering contract and is void.

Interest profit
> That part of the surplus of a life assurance company that is

attributable to the interest earned exceeding the rate of interest assumed at a previous valuation.

Interim bonus
A bonus on a life assurance policy at a rate applying until the next regular declaration of bonus.

Interim documents
Documents describing in broad outline a pension scheme for which formal documents are in course of preparation.

Interim trust deed
A trust deed empowering the trustees to act for a limited period pending execution of a *definitive trust deed* (q.v.).

Interinsurance exchange
U.S. term for *Reciprocal insurance* (q.v.).

Interlocking clause
A clause in a reinsurance treaty with a consortium of insurers, such as a pool, whereby each reinsurer undertakes that claims will be settled even though one or more of the reinsurers becomes insolvent.

Interlocutory
Incidental, partial or interim in the course of legal proceedings.

Intermediaries clause
A clause under a reinsurance treaty whereby a reinsurer accepts responsibility for losses arising out of the insolvency of the broker who negotiated the treaty.

Intermediary
An agent or broker through whom a transaction is arranged between parties.

Internal fund
A fund set up and managed by a life assurance company as part of its life fund for the benefit of the holders of linked life assurances.

Internal risks policy
A policy for a motor trader with special reference to his liability for loss or damage occurring on his premises.

International Oil Insurers
A voluntary association of insurers who have pooled their resources to write for common account a specialised class of insurance related to the oil, gas and petrochemical industries.

Interpleader
A legal procedure whereby if more than one person lays claim to property the party, such as the insurer, who is liable to one or the other, may ask the court to decide which.

Interruption hazard
The various features, whether inherent or extraneous, that contribute to the possibility of interference with the trading of a business in the period after damage has been caused by an insured peril.

Interruption insurance
The insurance of loss consequential on the interruption of business by an unforeseen event such as a fire or a breakdown of machinery.

Intruder alarm
An alarm that gives warning of entry to premises or some part of them.

Invalidity
Social security term for physical or mental disability.

Invalidity benefit
Same as *Disability benefit*.

Inventory
A list of items of property.

Investment insurance
Insurance for an investor against loss of value of his investment through expropriation or the like.

Inwards reinsurance
Reinsurance business received from other insurers or reinsurers.

Irrespective of percentage
A term in a marine policy providing that the insurers will pay claims however small the percentage of loss so that the *franchise* (q.v.) in the *Memorandum* (q.v.) will not apply.

Issue risk indemnity
An indemnity against the birth of a child where the effect of the birth is to defeat or prejudice a reversionary interest.

Issued capital
The nominal value of the shares issued by a company, whether or not all the shares have been paid up.

J

Janson clause
A clause applying an *excess* (q.v.) to a marine insurance policy.

Jeweller's block policy
A policy covering a jeweller's stock and goods entrusted to him against all risks, with certain exceptions.

Joint and several
If an obligation on several persons is joint and several each of the persons is liable for the whole and one or all may be sued.

Joint Cargo Committee
A committee of Lloyd's and insurance company underwriters which discusses problems relating to marine cargo insurance and makes recommendations to the market.

Joint Hull Committee
A committee of Lloyd's and insurance company underwriters which discusses problems relating to marine hull insurance and makes recommendations on rating or conditions to the market.

Joint Hull Returns Bureau
A bureau which approves applications by shipowners for returns of premiums as when a ship is laid up.

Joint hull survey
A survey of a ship carried out jointly by a surveyor on behalf of the insurer and a surveyor on behalf of the insured.

Joint Hull Understandings
A set of understandings formulated by the *Joint Hull Committee* (q.v.) and recommended to underwriters for adoption in the interest of having some uniformity in market practice, e.g., when considering the adjustment of renewal premium rates.

Joint insured clause
A clause in a policy which makes it clear that two or more persons are insured by the policy.

Joint life and survivor annuity
An annuity payable during the joint lifetime of two or more persons and during the life of the survivor(s). Sometimes the rate is subject to reduction after the death of one of the annuitants.

Joint life annuity
An annuity on the lives of two or more persons but ceasing on the death of one of them.

Joint life assurance
Assurance on two or more lives that becomes payable when the first of the lives concerned dies.

Jouissance security
A security issued by a joint stock company that does not give the holder the status of a shareholder but entitles him to a share in the profits of the company or in the proceeds of a winding up, etc.

117

Judgment rating
Rating an insurance on a discretionary basis without dependance on a tariff or schedule of rates.

Jumbo risk
An exceptionally large risk or insurance.

Jurisdiction
The power of a court to hear and determine law suits.

Jurisdiction clause
A clause in a policy that specifies what country's courts shall have jurisdiction in the event of a dispute under the policy or, in liability insurances, that excludes liability for third party claims brought in other than domestic courts.

K

Keyman insurance
Insurance of a business against financial loss caused by the death or disablement of a person whose work has a material effect on the profitability of the concern.

Keys clause
Clause in a theft insurance policy stipulating that keys of safes, etc, shall not be left on premises when closed for business.

Kidnap and ransom insurance
Insurance to provide ransom for a kidnapped person.

Knock-for-knock agreement
An agreement between insurers that in the event of an accident involving their respective policyholders neither party shall seek to recover the insured cost of repairing the damage caused to the vehicle it insures from the other insurer.

L

Label clause
A clause in a marine policy on cargo limiting liability for a claim to an amount sufficient to pay the cost of reconditioning and the cost of new labels and of relabelling.

Laches
Legal term for unreasonable delay in enforcing an equitable right.

Land risks
Insurances relating to land-based property. In respect of these commercial insurers do not grant war risk cover.

Landslip
The sliding down of a mass of land.
Lapsation profit
The addition of surplus to a life fund that accrues when insurances lapse and the reserve held in respect of them can be released.
Lapse
An insurance is said to lapse when it ceases to operate either because the insured does not pay the renewal premium or because the insurer does not invite its continuance.
Lapse ratio
The proportion of policies lapsed or surrendered during a year to those in force at the beginning of the year.
Larceny
The unlawful taking of the property of another with intent to deprive the owner of is use.
Last survivor annuity
Same as *Joint life and survivor annuity*.
Last survivor assurance
An insurance on two or more lives that becomes payable only on the death of the last life to survive.
Latent defect
A defect not apparent or discoverable by the exercise of reasonable care.
Launching state
A state from which a space object is launched into space, or one which performs or procures the launch.
Law of large numbers
A natural law of probability which states that the larger the number of exposures to risk of independent, homogeneous units the closer will be the actual number of casualties to the probable number in an infinite series.
Layer
Term used to denote a stratum of cover, e.g., for claims between £10,000 and £50,000, or between £50,000 and £250,000.
Layering
Effecting reinsurance divided between two or more reinsurers who charge different rates for identical cover.
Lay-up return
A return of premium made by marine insurers in respect of a period during which the insured vessel is laid up.
Lead
See *Leading underwriter*.

Leading underwriter
The underwriter who first accepts a share or line of an insurance.

Leading Underwriters' Agreement
An agreement in the London marine insurance market whereby when there are alterations to a risk that do not materially affect it, they may be accepted by certain underwriters only whose acceptance will bind the others.

Legal (costs and expenses) insurance
Insurance of the legal costs and expenses incurred by the insured in (a) pursuing a civil claim against a third party, (b) defending a civil action brought by a third party and (c) defending criminal proceedings where the offence alleged was not a deliberate wrongful act.

Legal costs extension
The extension of a liability insurance to provide for the payment of the insured's legal costs in litigation other than the defence of the insured against claims arising under the liability insurance (which costs are commonly covered by the insurance in any event).

Legal personal representative
The executor or administrator of an estate.

Legal protection insurance
Same as *Legal (costs and expenses) insurance.*

Legal reserve life insurance company
U.S. term for a life insurance company that operates under laws that specify a basis for the minimum reserves it must maintain.

Lessee
A person to whom a lease is granted. A tenant under a lease.

Lessor
A person who grants a lease. A landlord.

Letter of credit
A document authorising payment of an agreed sum to a named person at the risk of the issuer. If expressed as irrevocable the authority cannot be withdrawn.

Letter of indemnity
A written undertaking to indemnify the person to whom it is addressed against the consequences of some action or liability on his part.

Lettered Rules
Those of the York-Antwerp Rules (q.v.) that are prefixed by a letter as distinct from a number. The lettered rules are

applicable only in circumstances to which it is impossible to apply the numbered rules.

Letters of administration

An official document evidencing the title of personal representatives of a deceased person to administer his estate in a case where the deceased named no executors or those named are unable or unwilling to act.

Letters of mart and countermart

An obsolete expression describing licences formerly granted by the Crown to subjects entitling them to fit out armed ships to recoup themselves for losses inflicted on them by the subjects of other states by way of reprisal.

Level annual premium method

Same as *Annual premium method.*

Level premiums

In long-term life assurance, as the probability of death rises with age it would be logical to charge a higher premium year by year, with steep increases in the later years of life. Instead, it is customary for the assurer, having calculated the death risk and allowed for the effect of interest on premiums, to express the sum required from the assured as a premium payable at the same rate annually throughout the years during which premiums are payable.

Levy

A charge on insurers for some specific purpose, e.g., to meet the outgo of the Policyholders Protection Board which makes payments to safeguard those liable to loss through the insolvency of insurance companies in the terms of the Policyholders Protection Act 1975.

Liability insurance

Insurance in respect of liability to third parties, most commonly for accidents resulting in bodily injury and damage to property.

Liable or not liable

Term in a reinsurance contract where the reinsurer is prepared to indemnify the ceding insurer not only for claims for which there is clearly liability under the original insurance but also where the ceding insurer denies liability but makes a compromise or ex gratia payment.

Libel and slander insurance

Same as *Defamation insurance.*

Libel bond

A bond to secure the release of a vessel arrested because of a complaint (called a libel) made to a U.S.A. court.

Licence insurance
> Insurance against the financial consequences of losing a licence, principally granted in respect of licences to sell alcoholic liquor or to conduct a place of entertainment.

Lien
> 1. A legal right to hold the property of another as security for the fulfilment of some obligation.
> 2. In life assurance another word for <u>debt</u> (q.v.).

Lienholder
> A person entitled to a *lien* (1q.v.).

Life annuity
> A contract providing an income during the life of a person.

Life annuity certain
> An annuity payable for a minimum specified period and thereafter throughout the lifetime of the annuitant.

Life assurance
> Assurance providing for the payment of a sum of money on the death of the person assured or, in the case of endowment assurance, at the end of a specified term even though the person assured is still living.

Life Assurance Companies (Payment into Court) Act 1896
> An Act entitling a life assurance company to pay into court policy money where no sufficient discharge can be obtained for it in any other way.

Life Assurance Premium Relief
> A resident in the United Kingdom who pays premiums under a *qualifying policy* (q.v.) made before 14 March 1984 on his life or that of his spouse is allowed to deduct 15 percent by way of income tax relief when paying the premium.

Life assured
> The person on whose life an assurance depends is termed the life assured. He may or may not be the owner or holder of the life assurance policy.

Life contingency
> The probability of death, of survival, or of the duration of human life.

Life expectancy
> The average number of years that persons of a given age may expect to survive according to a mortality table.

Life salvage
> An award to a salvor for the saving of life.

Life table
    A table showing the number of lives that would survive to
    successive ages on given assumptions as to the rate of
    mortality.
Life tenant
    A person having a life interest in an estate.
Life underwriter
    1. The employee of an assurer who is responsible for
    considering the terms on which life assurances can be
    accepted.
    2. A life assurance salesman (U.S.).
Lift insurance
    The insurance of lifts against breakdown and accidental
    damage, coupled with third party liability.
Lightning
    A peril covered by a fire insurance policy.
Limit
    The insurer's maximum liability under an insurance.
Limit of indemnity
    The maximum sum payable under a contract of indemnity. It
    may be expressed as "per accident", "per event", "per
    occurrence", or "per annum".
Limit of liability
    Same as *Limit of Indemnity*.
Limitation
    A bar to a lawsuit on the ground that it has not been brought,
    or pursued, within some specified time.
Limitation of liability
    A statutory limitation to the amount of the liability of the
    owner or operator of a vehicle for claims against him, e.g.,
    under the Carriage of Goods by Sea Act 1971.
Limited conditions
    See *Limited terms*.
Limited liability company
    A company the liability of whose members for its debts is
    limited to the value of each member's shares.
    See also *Company limited by guarantee*.
Limited market
    Term used to describe the situation where only a few insurers
    are willing to accept insurance of a particular type.
Limited payment life assurance
    A life assurance on which premiums are payable for a limited
    number of years that may be less than the duration of the

assurance, e.g., a whole-life assurance with premiums ceasing at age 80.

Limited revaluation premium
A payment by a pension scheme to the State in respect of a member leaving the scheme, where the scheme limits to 5% per annum its liability for the revaluation of preserved benefits.

Limited terms
Insurance that excludes partial losses.

Line
1. A share of an insurance or of reinsurance business. Thus, the proportion of an insurance accepted by a Lloyd's syndicate is termed a line. In reinsurance the original insurer's retention is termed a line. Thus a ten-line reinsurance treaty is one under which the insurer retains one line (one-eleventh of the insurance) and can place with the various reinsurers ten lines (ten-elevenths of the insurance).
2. A category of insurance, e.g., fire (U.S.).

Line sheet
A schedule for the guidance of company underwriting staff, showing the maximum amount of insurance that the company will accept for different classes of risk.

Line slip
A slip in respect of a defined type of insurance, which, if initialled by a leading underwriter and a second underwriter, will bind other underwriters who have agreed in advance to the procedure. The broker presenting the slip may or may not have *binding authority* (q.v.).

Line stamp
A stamp impressed by a Lloyd's underwriter on a slip and bearing his syndicate's pseudonym and number.

Liner
A ship working to a regular time schedule.

Liquidation
The process of realising the assets and quantifying the liabilities of a company which it is proposed to dissolve. The court, on petition, may order the provisional liquidation of a company, in which case it may be resuscitated. Otherwise the court will issue an order for voluntary or compulsory liquidation.

Liquidator's bond
A bond in respect of the conduct of the liquidator of a company that is being wound up.

Litigation costs and expenses
A liability insurance provides indemnity in respect of litigation costs and expenses incurred in connection with a third
party claim against the insured.

Livestock insurance
Insurance against the death of livestock.

Living on top
Having a pension scheme which provides benefits in addition
to the full state pension.

Lloyd's (of London)
A corporation that organises the market of individual insurance underwriters in London and provides ancillary services
including a marine intelligence service.

Lloyd's Acts
Acts of 1871, 1911 and 1982 which regulate the constitution of
Lloyd's.

Lloyd's Agency System
An international network of persons appointed by Lloyd's to
provide intelligence and to perform certain services for
underwriters when so instructed by them.

Lloyd's Agent
A person appointed by Lloyd's to provide intelligence, e.g.,
as to shipping movements and, when so instructed by
underwriters, to carry out surveys and adjust claims.

Lloyd's arbitration
A procedure for settling by arbitration a dispute between
parties within the Lloyd's community.

Lloyd's Associates
Individuals, not being insurers, who are admitted to Lloyd's
Underwriting Room for business purposes, e.g., as accoun-
tants or solicitors.

Lloyd's Association
A group of individual underwriters who subscribe to insurances each one for his own proportion, on a basis similar to
that of Lloyd's of London (U.S.).

Lloyd's Broker
A firm or individual who is authorised to place insurance at
Lloyd's and who in doing so represents the insured. There are
over 250 Lloyd's brokers, large and small.

Lloyd's certificates
Insurance certificates issued by the Committee of Lloyd's.
They facilitate the payment of claims abroad.

Lloyd's Form
Lloyd's Standard Form of Salvage Agreement.

Lloyd's List
> A daily paper published by Lloyd's which records merchant shipping movements, news of chartering markets, law reports and other items relating to shipping, insurance, transportation and finance.

Lloyd's Name
> A U.K. resident who is an underwriting member of Lloyd's and works at Lloyd's having been for five years before election employed by a Lloyd's underwriting agent, or by a Lloyd's broker in the production, placing or servicing of insurances.

Lloyd's Open Form
> Lloyd's Standard Form of Salvage Agreement.

Lloyd's Shipping Index
> A daily publication listing over 20,000 merchant vessels on overseas voyages, with particulars of the vessels and their latest reported position.

Lloyd's Syndicate
> A group of underwriting members of Lloyd's who are bound by the signature of an active underwriter on their behalf. When an insurance is accepted on behalf of the syndicate each member is liable for his stated fraction only of the insurance but not for the fractions of other members. His personal liability is unlimited.

Lloyd's Underwriter
> 1. An underwriting member of Lloyd's.
> 2. The term is more often used to describe the active underwriter who accepts insurances on behalf of a syndicate of underwriting members and who may or may not be himself an underwriting member.

Lloyd's Underwriting Agent
> A person who acts as an agent for an underwriting member of Lloyd's
> (a) as a member's agent who acts in all respects for the member, other than in managing the underwriting syndicate, and/or
> (b) as a managing agent, who manages the affairs of the syndicate.

Loading
> 1. The placing of goods on a vessel for carriage.
> 2. Charging a higher rate of premium than normal, because of some adverse feature of an insurance.
> 3. An addition to the *pure premium* (q.v.) to allow for expenses, contingencies or profit desired.

Loading profit
The part of the surplus of a life assurance company that represents the amount by which the costs covered by the loading of the pure premium were less than the amount assumed for them in a previous valuation.

Loading the premium
Charging more than normal.

Loan value
The value of a long-term assurance policy up to which a loan will be granted on the security of the policy.

Loanback
A facility under a pension scheme for the policyholder to borrow money from the insurer, to be repaid out of the lump sum available on retirement.

Local government guarantee
A guarantee to a local or public authority required by the Local Government Act 1972, s.114, in respect of loss of money or other property happening as a result of fraud or dishonesty on the part of officials employed by the authority.

Local government indemnity
An indemnity to a local authority in respect of claims by third parties for loss sustained by reason of errors or omissions in registers of local land charges and the like, and notices issued in connection with them.

Location clause
A clause in an open cover limiting the insurer's liability on property in one location prior to shipment.

Location limit
A limit in an open policy on marine cargo restricting the liability of the insurers on cargo in any one location before shipment.

Long service death benefit
Death benefit under a pension scheme payable on death before retirement and increasing with length of service.

Long-tail claims
Claims notified or settled a long time after the expiry of a period of insurance.

Long-term agreement
An agreement in fire insurance whereby the insured undertakes, in consideration of a discount, to renew the insurance for a given number of years on the original terms if these are offered him by the insurers.

Long-term business
By the Insurance Companies Act 1974, s.1, defined as

ordinary long-term insurance business and industrial assurance business, including insurance business carried on as incidental only thereto.

Long-term insurance
1. Insurance forming part of *long-term business* (q.v.)
2. In fire insurance a contract that is expressed at the outset as being for a term of two or more years.

Loss
1. An event giving rise to a claim under an insurance.
2. A claim.
3. The disappearance of the subject-matter of insurance through theft or some other cause, as opposed to its survival in a damaged state.

Loss adjuster
One who, acting predominantly on the instructions of insurers, is habitually employed in a professional capacity in the negotiation and settlement of loss by fire or other contingencies.

Loss adjustment
The settling of an insurance claim.

Loss assumption clause
Same as *Cut-through clause*. (U.S.).

Loss development
An estimate correcting an initial estimate of the cost of a claim reported to an insurer or reinsurer.

Loss event
Term used in relation to the total claims payable by an insurer or reinsurer resulting from a single cause such as an earthquake.

Loss expectancy
An insurer's estimate of the cost of claims that could arise from the peril insured against.

Loss lag
Same as *Loss development*.

Loss loading
A factor applied to pure loss costs to produce a reinsurance rate of premium.

Loss of engagements
Where a shipowner is deprived of the use of a ship through an insured peril, e.g., collision, the loss consequential on loss of engagements is insurable.

Loss-of-licence insurance
Insurance to provide a benefit to the member of an aircrew

whose licence is withdrawn because of physical unfitness arising from accident or illness.

Loss of limb

In personal accident insurance the policy may grant a lump sum benefit for the loss of one or more limbs resulting from an accident.

Loss of profits insurance

Same as *Business interruption insurance.*

Loss of specie

There is said to be loss of specie when property the subject of insurance is so damaged that it ceases to be a thing of the kind insured, as where a motor cycle is crushed or clothes are burnt to ashes.

Loss of use insurance

Insurance of loss to an aircraft operator or a motorist consequential upon accidental damage to an insured vehicle, by way of indemnity or fixed benefit.

Loss portfolio

An amount payable by a reinsurer to a cedent in consideration of the release of the reinsurer from liability arising under a contract of reinsurance in respect of claims arising prior to a fixed date.

Loss prevention

Steps taken by insurers, by way of advice, research and the provision of information or the imposition of terms on an insurance, to prevent losses.

Loss ratio

The proportion of claims paid or payable to premiums earned.

Loss reserve

A fund set aside to pay claims outstanding at the end of a period of account.

Loss sustained cover

A reinsurance treaty which covers only losses sustained during the term of the treaty.

"Losses occurring" basis

A provision in a reinsurance treaty whereby the reinsurance applies to all losses occurring during the treaty period even if the risk attached before that period. The reinsurance does not apply to claims occurring after the reinsurance period even though the underlying insurance began to run during that period.

"Losses to extinction" basis

A basis whereby when profit commission is payable under a

reinsurance treaty and a loss is made in one year, it is carried forward so as to reduce the calculation of profit in the ensuing year. Any balance of loss remaining is similarly applied in subsequent years until it is extinguished.

Lost or not lost

Phrase in a marine policy meaning that the risk attaches even though, at the time of acceptance of the insurance, the insured property, unknown to the insured, had been lost.

Low start endowment assurance

An endowment assurance under which the premiums payable during the early years are lower than normal, while in the later years of the policy they are higher than normal.

Loyalty discount

A discount offered to the holder of an insurance which is renewable at his option to induce him to renew the policy with the same insurer.

Lutine Bell

The ship's bell of H.M.S. Lutine, wrecked 1799 while carrying a cargo of gold valued at £1,400,000. The bell hangs in the Room at Lloyd's and is struck when important announcements are to be made, once for good news and twice for bad. Its use nowadays is very rare.

M

Made good

The value of that part of a ship or cargo that is sacrificed in a *general average* (q.v.) is called the "made good". The owner is entitled to the cost of repairs to the ship or the net value of the cargo sacrificed.

Maintenance bond

A bond providing indemnity if work completed under contract is not of the required standard or does not function satisfactorily for a specified period.

Malicious damage

Deliberate damage by individuals in circumstances that do not constitute a riot.

Malingering

Pretending to be disabled from work when one is not.

Malus

A penalty addition to an insurance premium because one or more claims have been made.

Managed fund

A fund managed by an insurance company or other financial institution with a discretion in the choice of investments.

Managing agent
    See *Underwriting agent (2)*.
Manual
    A book containing a guide to its users on the practice of the insurer who publishes it. Thus an underwriting manual will set out premium rates, the classes of risk that are acceptable, and the conditions to be imposed in particular cases.
Mare and foal policy
    A livestock insurance covering a mare and her unborn foal against mortality risk.
Mareva injunction
    An injunction by a court restraining a party to an action from removing his assets out of the court's jurisdiction or disposing of them.
Margin of Solvency
    Same as *Solvency Margin*.
Marine and Aviation Insurance (War Risks) Act 1952
    An Act empowering the Department of Trade to reinsure war risks in respect of British ships and aircraft, and to reinsure cargo and foreign ships and aircraft when the United Kingdom is at war; also to insure directly British ships, aircraft and cargo against war risks if reasonable facilities are not otherwise available. Such insurance facilities may be extended to foreign ships and aircraft when the United Kingdom is at war.
Marine hull insurance
    Insurance on ships and their machinery and equipment.
Marine insurance
    The insurance of ships (including oil-rigs at sea) and their cargoes and freight.
Marine Insurance Act 1906
    An Act that codified the law relating to marine insurance.
Marine Insurance (Gambling Policies) Act 1909
    An Act prohibiting gambling on loss by maritime perils. The Act made anyone effecting a gambling policy, and brokers and insurers concerned, subject to fine or imprisonment. It has been rarely, if ever, invoked.
Marine insurance policy
    Marine insurance policies were till recently issued in traditional form. The so-called S.G. form is reproduced in the first schedule to the Marine Insurance Act 1906 though the Act did not make its use obligatory. S.G. stands for Ship and Goods but in practice separate policies were issued for hull and cargo, the traditional wording being largely overriden by sets of clauses endorsed on the policy.

Market capacity
> The amount of insurance that can be absorbed by all the insurers in the relevant market.

Market level indicator
> A factor statutorily applied in the calculation of premiums payable by a pensions fund to the Department of Health and Social Security when an employer ceases to be contracted out of the social security scheme and a payment for accrued and vested rights in respect of guaranteed minimum pensions becomes payable.

Market value
> The value of property, being what it will fetch in a transaction between a willing buyer and a willing seller.

Marketing
> The process of optimising the use of the resources of an enterprise by seeking to identify and satisfy the needs of consumers, actual or potential, in the best way for the enterprise.

MARPOL Convention
> The International Convention for the Prevention of Pollution from Ships, 1973.

MARPOL Protocol
> A draft instrument of 1978 giving effect to the *MARPOL Convention* (q.v.) subject to certain changes.

Marriage and issue risks
> Reversionary interests may be affected by the marriage of a person or if he or she should have issue. Where the contingency is remote by virtue of age or other circumstances insurance on behalf of persons who stand to lose financially if there is a marriage or issue may be effected to cover potential loss.

Married Women's Policies of Assurance (Scotland) Act 1870
> An Act applying to Scotland provisions about life assurance similar to those of the *Married Women's Property Act 1882* (q.v.) for England.

Married Women's Property Act 1882
> An Act enabling a person to effect an assurance on his or her life for the benefit of his spouse and/or children so as to create a trust for their benefit.

Master cover
> A form of open cover, usually operated by a broker or agent, under which a variety of insurances from a given source may be accepted.

Master policy
    A single policy in respect of a number of persons or insurances. In some circumstances certificates of insurance or even separate policies may be issued to persons concerned with a portion of the cover.

Matching
    Paying regard, in the selection of assets, to the dates on which liabilities will or may accrue, or the currencies in which they are payable, with the object of ensuring that the realisable value of the assets at any such dates will suffice to discharge the liabilities.

Material damage warranty
    A warranty in a business interruption insurance policy stipulating that before the interruption insurance becomes effective there must be a policy in force in respect of the material damage and a claim paid or admitted thereunder for such damage caused by an insured peril.

Material fact
    A fact that would influence the mind of a prudent insurer in deciding whether to accept a proposed insurance and, if so, on what terms.

Material property
    Tangible property as distinct from legal rights such as patents.

Mathematical reserve
    The amount required by an insurer to meet his potential liability under a life policy, taking into account interest and the discounted value of future premiums payable.

Maturity
    The time at which payment of the sum assured under a life assurance policy falls due at the end of its term.

Maturity bonus
    A bonus payable at the end of the term of a life assurance contract.

Maturity guarantee
    A guarantee by a life assurer that the value of a policy on maturity will be at least £x. Such a guarantee is common with unit-linked assurances.

Maximum possible loss
    The largest loss thought possible under a given insurance.

Maximum probable loss
    Same as *Probable maximum loss*.

Maximum value insurance
    A system used for fire insurance in some trades whereby the sum insured on stock represents the maximum amount at risk

at any time. A discount is allowed off the premium but no adjustment is made if the stock falls short of the maximum value.

Mean method of apportionment
A method of apportionment of loss between two or more property insurances that are non-concurrent and not subject to average.

Means test
An evaluation of the assets and/or income of a person for the purpose of determining his eligibility for social security benefits, or for underwriting membership of Lloyd's.

Measure of indemnity
The basis for calculation of the sum that an insured is entitled to recover in respect of a claim under an insurance that is a contract of indemnity.

Median
The value which divides a distribution into two halves, with as many below it as above it.

Member charge
A fixed sum per member added to the basic premium for a group insurance.

Member of Lloyd's
An individual elected to membership of the Corporation of Lloyd's either as an underwriting member or, very rarely, as a non-underwriting member.

Members' agent
See *Underwriting agent (2)*.

Memorandum, The
A clause at the end of the S. G. form of marine insurance policy which excludes claims for partial loss or damage to certain commodities and imposes a *franchise* (q.v.) on claims in respect of damage to other named commodities or to ship and freight.

Memorandum advice
An advance notification to an underwriter of a premium or claim.

Memorandum of Association
> The document that sets out the constitution of a company and states its objects. It is complemented by by-laws, referred to as Articles of Association.

Merger
> 1. The absorption of one company by another.
> 2. The principle that when a partial loss under an insurance policy is followed by a total loss the insurers are not required to pay for the partial loss in addition to the total loss.

Merit rating
> A system of calculating premium rates whereby some favourable (or unfavourable) feature is allowed for by deduction from (or addition to) the standard rate.

Metal workers' extension
> Extension of a fire insurance to cover property such as plant and machinery while in transit to or from or at the premises of machine makers, engineers, founders, metal workers, customers and sub-contractors.

Methylated spirits bond
> An excise bond guaranteeing that methylated spirits will be used only in permitted processes and that any duty becoming due on the spirits will be paid.

Minimising a loss
> It is the duty of a policyholder, when an insured loss occurs, to take all reasonable steps to minimise the loss, acting as he would in his own interest if the loss were uninsured.

Minimum premium
> Because of administration expenses insurers often prescribe a minimum premium for a particular class of insurance.

Minimum rate
> A rate of premium below which an insurer refuses to quote, as in fire insurance.

Misdescription
> An incorrect statement by a proposer in describing the risk proposed for insurance.

Misfeasance
> The improper performance of an act, as distinct from *nonfeasance* (q.v.).

Mismatching
> A situation where the term or nature of the assets of an insurance company is not adapted to the term or nature of its liabilities.

Misrepresentation
>An untrue statement.

Missing beneficiaries indemnity
>An indemnity given to executors, administrators or trustees who desire to distribute an estate when one of the beneficiaries is missing and they wish to divide his share among other beneficiaries.

Missing document indemnity
>Where it is desired to complete a transaction although a relevant document such as a share certificate or a life assurance policy is missing insurers may agree to indemnify against liability that coud arise if another person subsequently produces the document and substantiates a claim to payment or rights based on it.

Misstatement of age
>In life assurance the age of the life proposed for assurance is a material fact affecting the premium to be charged. A misstatement makes the assurance voidable but in practice ordinary life assurers on learnng the true age will treat the assurance as valid for a sum assured corresponding to the premium that should have been paid. For industrial life assurance this procedure is statutorily sanctioned by the Industrial Assurance Act 1923, s.20 (4).

Mixed policy
>A marine insurance policy covering both a voyage and a period of time.

Mixed schemes
>Pension schemes that are a combination of schemes approved under section 208 and 222 respectively of the Income and Corporation Taxes Act 1970.

Money purchase scheme
>A pension scheme under which the amount payable is governed by the value of the contributions rather than length of service or earnings in employment.

Moral hazard
>The hazard arising from the possible behaviour of the insured or his family or employees which may increase the possibility of loss by reason of carelessness or dishonesty.

Moratorium
>A legal authorisation to debtors to postpone payment.

Morbidity table
>A table showing the incidence of sickness in the population or in a selected group.

Mortality
Deaths.
Mortality function
Function depending on the duration of human life.
Mortality loss
A reduction in the surplus of a life assurance company that is attributable to the mortality experienced being less favourable than the rate of mortality assumed at a previous valuation.
Mortality profit
That part of the surplus of a life assurance company that is attributable to the mortality experienced being more favourable than the rate of mortality assumed at a previous valuation.
Mortality risk
The risk of death.
Mortality table
A table that includes the data in a *life table* (q.v.) as well as other mortality functions such as the rate of mortality and the expectation of life.
Mortgage
A conveyance of real or personal property as security for a debt, subject to the proviso that the property will be reconveyed when the debt is discharged.
Mortgage guarantee
A guarantee to a mortgagee that the sums owing to him will be paid.
Mortgage guarantee certificate
A certificate issued by the insurer of property to a mortgagee undertaking to inform the mortgagee if the insurance is changed to his detriment and not to settle a loss without the mortgagee's consent.
Mortgage protection policy
A life policy that provides by means of decreasing term assurance for a mortgage to be paid off in the event of the borrower's death.
Mortgage repayment plan
Any scheme whereby life assurance is used to ensure that a mortgage is eventually repaid. The money may be advanced either by a building society or by the life assurance company. In some cases the policy moneys serve to repay the mortgage. In others, where the building society lends, the role of life assurance is limited to paying off the mortgage in the event of premature death.

Mortgagee
A lender to whom property is conveyed as security for a debt on the condition that the property will be reconveyed when the debt is discharged.

Mortgagee clause
A clause in a property insurance policy giving beneficial rights to a lender.

Mortgagor
A borrower who conveys his property to another on condition that it will be reconveyed to him when the debt is discharged.

Mortuary bonus
An addition to the sum assured under a life assurance policy applicable to claims arising during some specified period.

Motor cycle insurance
A section of motor insurance embracing all two-wheeled power-driven vehicles.

Motor insurance
Insurance of motor vehicles, in British practice, provides a choice of three types of cover:
(a) comprehensive, including both accidental damage to the insured vehicle, loss by theft, and third party liability;
(b) third party liability for bodily injury or damage to property, with or without cover for loss or damage to the insured vehicle by fire and theft;
(c) third party liability for bodily injury only.

Mov(e)ables
Personal property as opposed to real property (interests in land). By the Marine Insurance Act 1906, s.90, means any moveable tangible property other than the ship, and includes money, valuable securities, and other documents.

Movement
Changes in the portfolio of a life assurance company (e.g., new business and exits) that affect its value.

Moving average
An average that is regularly recalculated on the basis of a time series. For example, a three-year moving average of claims paid will be based on the first place on years 1, 2 and 3. Next year it will be based on years 2, 3 and 4; and so forth.

Multiple birth insurance
Insurance to provide a stated sum of money in the event of a multiple live birth.

Multiple line insurer
An insurer who writes a number of classes of insurance (U.S.).

Multiplier
 1. A factor applied to pure loss costs to produce a rate of premium.
 2. In an action for damages for personal injury a factor applied to annual loss of earnings in calculating damages for death or permanent disablement.

Mutatis mutandis
 With the necessary changes.

Mutual insurance
 Insurance undertaken by a group of persons for their own benefit, without risk capital being provided from outside sources.

Mutual insurance company
 A company that conducts mutual insurance. In non-life insurance the company may confine its business to that of insurances of the risks of persons in the group that formed it, such as the members of a trade association, who may have subscribed capital. In life assurance it is common for the policyholders, especially the holders of with-profits policies, to become members (that is, nominally, part owners) on effecting a policy. A mutual life assurance company has no risk capital.

Mutualisation
 Turning an insurance company with risk capital into a mutual insurance company by buying out the shareholders.

N

Nail to nail
 Term used in transit insurance on paintings to denote that the cover operates from the time the object insured is removed from the wall-fastening for transit until it is fastened to the wall at its specified destination.

Name
 An underwriting member of Lloyd's in whose name a share of an insurance is accepted by an underwriter acting on behalf of a syndicate.

Name limit
 The maximum amount that a fire insurer is prepared to retain on insurances of a single insured in respect of goods at a particular location such as a warehouse or furniture depository, the balance being reinsurable under a surplus treaty.

Named policy
A marine cargo policy in which the vessel carrying the cargo is named.

Named steamer
Term used when the underwriters of a marine open cover stipulate that the cover will operate only provided they are advised of and approve the carrying vessel before each declaration attaches.

National insurance
The extensive scheme of social insurance that operates in the United Kingdom, providing benefits for retirement, sickness, unemployment, industrial injury, maternity and death.

Natural justice
Considerations to be observed by anyone adjudicating on the rights of others, such as acting fairly, in good faith and without bias, and giving each party the right to state his case.

Natural premium
In life assurance, the premium for the risk of death occurring within one year.

Natural premium method
Life assurance under which the premium for any year is governed by the risk of death occurring within that year.

Navigation clause
A clause in a marine hull policy excluding certain risks such as paid towage or salvage work or being towed except where customary or, to a limited extent, when in need of assistance.

Navigation risks
The risks incidental to a vessel navigating or at sea, as opposed to those arising while the vessel is in port or laid up.

Negligence
The omission to do something which a reasonable man, guided upon those considerations which ordinarily regulate the conduct of human affairs, would do, or doing something which a prudent and reasonable man would not do. It consists in a failure to exercise due care in a case in which a duty to take good care exists. It is a tort giving rise to civil liability.

Negligence Clause
A clause in a marine insurance hull policy which covers numerous perils, among them negligence of the master, officers or crew. It imposes an excess in some circumstances and makes a proviso that damage, to be covered, must not result from want of due diligence by the insured, the owners or the managers of the vessel.

Negotiable instrument
    A document of title to property that may be transferred from one person to another in the course of business.

Net absolute(ly)
    1. Term used in marine insurance to emphasise that all discounts, without exception, have been taken off a premium.
    2. Term used in facultative aviation reinsurance when no reinsurance commission is allowable.

Net earned premiums
    The premiums received or due to an insurer less the cost of reinsurance and after adjustment to allow for the cost of any unexpired risk.

Net line
    The amount of liability under a line of insurance that is retained by an insurer after cession by way of reinsurance.

Net premium
    1. The premium after discounts have been taken off.
    2. Term variously used to describe gross premiums (less return premiums) net of (a) reinsurance premiums payable, or (b) commission, or both (a) and (b).
    3. In life assurance valuation a hypothetical premium calculated as sufficient to secure the guaranteed benefits on the valuation bases of mortality and interest, but without allowance for commission, expenses or bonus.

Net retained brokerage
    Brokerage retained by a broker after deduction of allowances to third parties.

Net retained line
    Same as *Net line.*

Net value
    See *Damaged value.*

Net written premiums
    The premiums received or due to an insurer less the cost of reinsurance but without allowance being made for the cost of any unexpired risk.

Net yield
    The yield on an investment after deduction of tax payable on the interest or dividend, or of the expenses of management in the case of property.

New business
    New insurances as opposed to renewal of existing insurances.

New business inspector
    Same as *Inspector.*

New business strain
> In life assurance the reserve necessary for a new policy effected at an annual premium is likely to exceed the first premium after allowance for expenses, including commission, that are incurred at the outset. Writing new business, therefore, imposes a strain on the company's reserves.

New for old
> 1. A basis for property insurance on, e.g., household contents when the insurer agrees to pay the replacement cost of property lost or destroyed, without a deduction for depreciation.
> 2. By the Marine Insurance Act 1906, s.69 (1), insurers, in settling a claim for repairs to a ship, are entitled to make "the customary deductions" unless the policy expressly provides to the contrary. The customary deduction for new work in place of old is one-third the cost of repairs, with certain exceptions, e.g., for the ship's first voyage. In practice insurers waive their right but the waiver does not apply to allowances made in a general average adjustment.

No-claim bonus
> Same as *No-claim discount.*

No-claim discount
> A discount allowed from a renewal premium in consideration of there having been no claim paid or payable in the previous year of insurance. The use of no-claim discounts is widespread in U.K. motor insurance. Most are granted on a scale that rises with the number of consecutive claim-free years.

No claim for accident reported
> Where a marine insurance is accepted after the risk has attached and an accident to the vessel has already been reported the insurer may stipulate that there shall be no claim under the policy for it.

No claims return
> A return of premium on a marine insurance policy on which no claim has been made.

No cure no pay
> Where, in a marine venture, property is salved, the salvor becomes entitled to a salvage award based on the value saved. If nothing is saved there is no award.

No-fault liability
> Liability to pay compensation for bodily injury or, sometimes, damage to property, without regard to the question whether any party caused the loss by a wrongful act or omission.

Nominal value
1. The value stated on the face of a security.
2. A token value.

Nomination
A member of a friendly society may nominate a person to receive benefits payable on the member's death, up to certain limits of amount, and the society must pay the nominee. The nomination can be revoked and is automatically revoked by the member's marriage. (Friendly Societies Act 1974, ss. 66–69 and Administration of Estates (Small Payments) (Increse of Limit) Order 1975).

Non-admitted company
An insurance company not admitted to do business in a state (U.S.).

Non-admitted reinsurance
In the U.S.A., where an insurance company has placed reinsurance with a reinsurer who is not authorised to transact the business in the jurisdiction of a state, the reinsurance is termed non-admitted and the company cannot take credit for it in its statutory return.

Non-apportionable annuity
An annuity which ceases with the last periodical payment before death.

Non-assignability
A condition in a pension scheme that a member may not give or sell his right to benefit or pledge it as security for a loan.

Non-average policy
A policy free of any conditions of average.

Non-cancellable policy
An insurance contract that may not be cancelled by one or both parties. The term is usually applied to contracts which do not provide for cancellation by the insurer.

Non-cash advice
A preliminary advice to an underwriter about a premium or claim.

Non-concurrent insurances
Two or more insurances that cover some property in common though one or more covers (a) part only of the property covered by the other(s) or (b) property not covered by the other(s).

Non-contribution clause
A clause in a contract of indemnity which seeks to provide that in the event of another insurance covering a claim the

insurers with the non-contribution clause shall not be required to contribute to settlement of the claim.

Non-contributory pension scheme
A pension scheme in which the employees make no contributions towards the cost of the scheme.

Non-delivery
The failure of a whole cargo or a whole package to arrive at its destination, in contrast with *short delivery* (q.v.).

Non-disclosure
Innocent omission by a proposer for insurance to disclose a material fact relating to the risk proposed.

Nonfeasance
A failure to act, e.g., to repair a defective pathway.

Non-forfeiture condition
A condition in a life policy whereby some rights under the policy continue even though a premium due has not been paid.

Non-Institute company
A marine insurance company that is not a member of the Institute of London Underwriters.

Non-marine
General insurance other than marine insurance.

Non-medical business
Life or permanent health insurance where the proposer is not required to submit to a medical examination by a physician appointed by the insurance company.

Non-owned aircraft endorsement
An endorsement to an aviation policy indemnifying the insured against claims by passengers for which he is responsible when the passengers are being carried in an aircraft that is not the insured's property.

Non-participating employment
Employment between 1961 and 1975 in which members of a pension scheme earned some or all of their graduated pension from their employer's contracted-out scheme.

Non-payment risk
The risk that a debt will not be paid when due.

Non-profit
Same as *Without profits*.

Non-proportional reinsurance
Reinsurance such as excess of loss reinsurance where the reinsurer's liability is not calculated proportionately to the insurer's.

Non-selection limit
The amount of benefits under a group permanent health

insurance up to which persons will be accepted into membership of the group without evidence as to their health.

Non-standard

Same as *Substandard*.

Non-standard construction

Used in fire insurance to describe a building any part of which does not conform to the rules for the minimum grade of construction.

Non-tariff company

An insurance company that is not a member of a rate-fixing association and so is not bound to impose the rates and conditions prescribed by that body for its members.

Non-underwriting member

A member of Lloyd's who is not empowered to underwrite, e.g., a retired underwriter.

Normal pension date

See *Normal retirement date*.

Normal retirement date

A pension scheme commonly defines a normal retirement date for its members while making provision both for early and deferred retirement.

North American Warranty

A warranty in a marine insurance policy that the insured vessel will not proceed to certain places in the north at certain times.

Not taken up

Term used to describe an insurance that the proposed insured has not proceeded with.

Not to Inure clause

A clause in a marine cargo insurance policy providing that the insurance shall not inure to the benefit of the carrier or other bailee. In other words the clause reserves the insurer's potential right of recovery from the carrier or bailee.

Not under repair

The clause in a marine hull policy governing returns of premium when the vessel is laid up provides for a higher rate of return when the laid-up vessel is not under repair.

Notice of abandonment

Notice given by the insured to the insurer in marine insurance when he considers that he has a claim for a *constructive total loss* (q.v.) and is therefore prepared to abandon the insured vessel or cargo to the insurer.

Notification of claim

Non-life insurance policies normally contain a condition

requiring immediate notice of an occurrence that may give rise to a claim. In some cases a time limit is specified.

Notional reinstatement value cover

A form of property insurance cover whereby the insured declares the reinstatement value at the outset of the insurance period and estimates an amount to allow for inflation for which an additional premium is payable in arrear, based on an adjustment.

Novation

An agreement to substitute a new contract for an existing one, or to substitute a different person for one of the parties to a contract, with the agreement of all concerned.

Novus actus interveniens

A new and intervening act or omission, or a natural event, which breaks the causal connection between a previous act or omission and damage alleged to have resulted therefrom.

Nuclear contamination

Same as *Radioactive contamination.*

Nuclear Exclusion

Non-life insurance policies contain an exclusion of loss or damage or consequential loss or liability of any nature directly or indirectly caused by or contributed to by or arising from:

(a) ionising radiations or contamination by radioactivity from any nuclear fuel or from any nuclear waste from the combustion of nuclear fuel;

(b) the radioactive, toxic, explosive or other hazardous properties of any explosive nuclear assembly or nuclear component thereof.

Nuclear reactor

An installation for the purpose of generating heat from atomic fission for conversion into energy.

Nuclear risks

See *Atomic risks.*

Nuisance

The unlawful interference with a person's use or enjoyment of land, or of some right over or in connection with it, such as the right of free passage over a highway. A person committing a nuisance may be liable in tort for the consequences.

Numbered Rules

Those of the York-Antwerp Rules (q.v.) that are prefixed by a number. They are applied in priority to the lettered rules.

Numerical weighting system
A system of rating whereby the acceptability of a proposed insurance is judged and rated on a combination of factors to each of which a numericalweight is assigned.

O

'O' group
An informal meeting at Lloyd's of the Chairman, Deputy Chairmen and senior officials, to discuss current problems and events.

Obiter dictum
Any statement in a judgment that is not essential to the principle of law on which the court's judgment is based.

Objective risk
The measure of the degree of variation in the proportion of actual to expected events.

Obligatory reinsurance
Reinsurance that the insurer is bound to offer to a reinsurer by the terms of a reinsurance treaty or by law.

Oblige line
Same as *Accommodation line*.

Obligee
One to whom a surety such as an insurance company gives a bond in respect of a principal.

Occasional business use policy
A motor insurance policy indemnifying an employer and any employee who uses a vehicle on the employer's business when the specific insurance covering the vehicle is deficient, for example, because it does not cover business use.

Occupancy
The use to which a building is put by its occupiers.

Occupational accident
An accident arising out of and in the course of an occupation.

Occupational classification
A grouping of occupations for the purpose of rating, e.g., personal accident insurances.

Occupational disease
Impairment of health attributable to one's occupation.

Occupational extra
Additional premium imposed on an insured because his occupation is thought to render his insurance more hazardous.

Occupational hazard
A danger inherent in an occupation.

Occupational Pensions Board
A governmental body which supervises pension schemes in

relation to contracting out of the state scheme and their satisfaction of statutory requirements as to preservation of pension rights and equal access to pensions.

Occupier's Liability Act 1957
An Act that amended the law relating to the liability of occupiers of property for accidents at their premises.

Occurrence
When insurers insert in their policies a limit for "any one occurrence" they seek to avoid the ambiguity of a limit "for any one accident". Thus, if two passengers in a vehicle are injured in a crash it can be claimed that there were two accidents, one to each passenger, but that there was only one "occurrence".

Occurrence basis
A policy is said to be on an occurrence basis if it covers the consequences of events occurring during a period of insurance even though claims may not arise until later.

Ocean marine insurance
Insurance of seagoing ships, cargoes and freights, as distinct from *inland marine insurance* (q.v.) (U.S.).

Odd time
A period added to a calendar year for the purpose of making the renewal date of an insurance the date required by the insured.

Off risk
An insurer is said to be off risk when an insurance has been terminated.

Off slip
A *Signing slip*. (q.v.) copied from an original slip, used to sign risks off open covers, open slips and treaty reinsurance contracts.

Offer and acceptance
One of the essentials of a valid contract is that there must be full acceptance by one party of an offer made by the other. In matters of insurance the offer sometimes emanates from the insured and sometimes from the insurer.

Offer and acceptance note
A note requesting reinsurance with a space for reinsurers to signify their acceptance. They return it to the ceding insurer by way of confirmation.

Offer basis
The basis of a long-term agreement in fire insurance whereby the insured undertakes to offer his insurance to the insurer for a number of years at each renewal in consideration of a

discount off the premium, but the insurer does not bind himself to accept the offer.

Offer note
Same as *Request note.*

Office premium
The premium on a life policy as charged to the assured.

Off slip
A slip used for the noting of further items arising out of the original slip.

Omnibus clause
A clause in a liability insurance policy extending the indemnity to persons other than the insured, such as his servants.

Omnibus insurance
Insurance of the principal risks involved in a construction contract that is effected by the owner on behalf of himself and the various other parties concerned, thus avoiding subsequent disputes as to whose liability any given occurrence gives rise to.

On gross
Term used to describe the marine insurance premium to which a discount is to be applied — the gross premium before any deductions.

On net
Term used to describe the marine insurance premium to which a discount is to be applied — the gross premium less any previous deductions.

On risk
The insurer is said to be on risk once an insurance attaches.

Oncost
Overhead expenses.

One disaster or casualty clause
A clause in a reinsurance treaty to provide that all losses during a short period, usually 72 hours, shall be considered as caused by one disaster or casualty, e.g., a riot, a cyclone, or an earthquake, for the purpose of applying the limit of liability under the reinsurance.

One-man pension arrangement
A pension arrangement for an individual employee.

One outlet rule
A rule at Lloyd's that a broker must not be unduly dependent on one insurer in placing his business.

One source rule
A rule at Lloyd's that a broker must not be unduly dependent on one predominant source of business.

Open cover
1. Reinsurance where the reinsurer agrees to accept ob-

ligatorily a share of any business of a specified kind that is offered.

2. A contract for cargo insurance to cover all shipments from time to time as declared, a policy being issued in respect of each. The arrangement is subject to cancellation on notice by either party.

Open driving policy

A motor insurance policy with no restriction on who may drive provided the driver is not disqualified from holding a licence.

Open market option

An option open to the purchaser of a deferred annuity to use the proceeds of the contract, when the annuity becomes payable, to purchase an annuity from another insurer.

Open policy

1. A marine insurance policy which covers such risks as may be declared during the currency of the policy with no aggregate limit of cover.

2. A policy on which the sum insured has not yet been exhausted by declarations.

3. Formerly, an *unvalued policy* (q.v.).

Open slip

A form of slip used to cover a merchant contractor with a large contract to fulfil by several shipments, the total value of which is known in advance. Each shipment is declared and policies issued until the insured value is exhausted.

Open treaty

Same as *facultative obligatory treaty*.

Open year

A year of account or insurance in respect of which the financial outcome remains to be determined.

Opening the warranty

In marine insurance some exclusions begin with the words "Warranted free of...". Such a warranty is said to be opened when the insurers modify the extent of the exclusion.

Operating plan

The insurer's intended course of action in conducting his business.

Operative clause

That part of a policy that states what insurance is to be granted.

Option

A choice of alternative courses open to a party to a contract. In life assurance, for example, the assured may be entitled to effect further assurance without evidence of health, or to take the sum assured on maturity of his policy either in cash or in the form of an annuity.

Optional benefits
Benefits that may be added to an insurance policy at the insured's option, on payments of additional premium.

Optional treaty
Same as *Facultative obligatory treaty.*

Optionally renewable
Annual insurances are renewable only if both insurer and insured opt to renew them. In long-term life assurance and permanent health insurance the insurer is bound to renew during the stated term on tender of the premium by the insured.

Or as Original
Term used by a reinsurer to indicate that he accepts not only the risk as it is presented to him but also any variation that may exist in the original policy. The wording protects the ceding insurer in case an error has arisen in transmission of the facts about the risk.

Order
1. A request for insurance received by an insurer.
2. A friendly society with branches.

Ordinary bond
A Customs and Excise bond covering a single transaction, as opposed to a general bond.

Ordinary business
Ordinary life assurance (q.v.).

Ordinary freight
The reward paid to a shipowner for the carriage of goods in his ship to the port of delivery.

Ordinary life assurance
All life assurance other than *industrial life assurance* (q.v.).

Ordinary share
A share in the capital of a company which gives the holder a right to share in the distribution of its profits and in the residue of the company's assets after it has paid its creditors and preference shareholders whatever is due to them.

Original conditions
The conditions in an insurance policy which is the subject of a reinsurance.

Original cover
The original slip used for placing an open cover.

Original deductions/discounts
> The deductions or discounts allowed by a ceding insurer on a policy which is the subject of reinsurance.

Original gross premium
> The premium charged by a ceding insurer to the original insured without taking into account any discounts by way of commission or the like.

Original insured
> The insured under a policy which becomes the subject of reinsurance.

Original net premium income
> The net premium income of a ceding insurer.

Original net retained premium income
> That part of the net premium income of a ceding insurer that is retained by him after paying for reinsurance.

Original rate
> The rate of premium charged on an insurance which has become the subject of reinsurance.

Original slip
> The slip used for placing an insurance on which underwriters' acceptances are indicated by a line stamp and writing. From it are prepared duplicate slips, *off slips* (q.v.) and *signing slips* (q.v.).

Original terms
> A reinsurance expression signifying that the reinsurance is granted on the same conditions and at the same rate of premium as the original insurance.

Ostensible authority
> The apparent power of an agent to bind his principal, whether or not he has been granted that power.

Other insurance clause
> A clause in an insurance policy which restricts the right of the insured to effect other insurance on the risk or which seeks to provide how a claim shall be apportioned if other insurance has been effected.

Outstanding claims advance
> A reinsurance treaty may provide that if claims payable by the reinsurer exceed the reserve held by the original insurer for the payment of claims the reinsurer shall make an immediate payment, or advance, without waiting for the claims to appear in the periodic accounts.

Outstanding claims portfolio
> An amount payable by a cedent to a reinsurer in consideration of the reinsurer accepting liability arising under a

contract of reinsurance in respect of reinsurance claims incurred and arising prior to a fixed date.

Outstanding claims reserve
A reserve held by an insurer to meet claims notified but not yet paid.

Outturn
1. The amount or weight of the cargo discharged from a ship.
2. The condition of a cargo on discharge.

Outwards reinsurance
Business ceded by an insurer by way of reinsurance to other insurers or reinsurers.

Overage
1. Additional premium payable on a marine insurance open cover or policy when the insured goods are carried on a vessel which does not come within the scope of the Institute *Classification Clause* (q.v.), usually because it is too old.
2. The excess amount of a liquid cargo which weighs more when landed than the weight reported when shipped.

Overclosing
The (impermissible) act by a broker, when closing a placing, of allotting to an underwriter a larger line than the underwriter has written.

Overdue Market
A market for the reinsurance of a marine insurance where a ship is overdue or has suffered a serious casualty which may result in a total loss, and thus a means for original underwriters of quantifying, and possibly cutting, their loss.

Overheads
Fixed charges which do not vary proportionately with the amount of business done.

Over-insurance
Insuring property for more than its value. May be inadvertent or fraudulent.

Overlapping insurance
Insurance by two or more policies the cover of which is in part duplicated.

Over-line
An amount of insurance or reinsurance that exceeds the normal capacity of the insurer or reinsurer after allowing for automatic reinsurance facilities. An insurer who finds himself with more risk than he considers it prudent to bear is said to be overlined.

Overplacing
>The action of a broker in obtaining acceptances of lines on an insurance which exceed 100% of the insurance offered.

Overrider
>Same as *Overriding commission.*

Overriding commission
>A discount allowed to an agent or ceding insurer in addition to normal commission. In reinsurance it is commonly by way of contribution to the direct insurer's overheads. In direct insurance it may be payable to an employee or agent in respect of insurances written within his territory, even without his mediation.

Oversight clause
>A provision in a reinsurance treaty that either party may correct a failure to comply with the agreement due to oversight or misunderstanding.

Oversubscription
>In Lloyd's practice it is common for a broker to obtain subscriptions from underwriters for more than 100 per cent for a proposed insurance. The share of each syndicate in the insurance is then reduced proportionately.

Own damage
>In motor insurance, damage to the insured's own vehicle.

Own risk
>A risk that a person retains for himself, without insuring it.

Owners' clauses
>Clauses drafted by shipowners or large exporters or importers for use in their marine insurance policies.

Owner's liability
>Liability of the owner of a building (as distinct from an occupier) for claims in respect of bodily injury or damage to property. See also *Shipowner's liability.*

Owner's trading freight
>The addition to the cost of the goods of a shipowner (or a charterer) carried in the ship owned (or chartered) which he charges at the port of delivery as the price of carriage.

P

Package policy
>A policy that covers a number of different perils, e.g., a householder's policy.

Paid-up pension
A pension payable at some future date for which no further contributions have to be made.

Paid-up policy
A policy under which no further premiums are payable but some cover remains in force.

Paid-up share
A share in a limited company on which the face value has been paid up.

Pair and set clause
A clause in a property insurance policy which limits the insurer's liability for loss or damage to one constituent of a pair or set to the value of that constituent only.

Par value
Same as *Nominal value*.

Paramount clause
A clause in a contract that in the event of ambiguity overrides all other provisions of the contract.

Paramount War Clause (Cargo)
A clause in a marine cargo reinsurance contract which stipulates either that war risks cover is subject to terms and conditions no wider than those of the relevant London Institute War Clauses or that the reinsured shall apply the limitations of the U.K. Waterborne Agreement; and that war risks shall be cancellable at seven days' notice by either party.

Parent company
A company that owns another company.

Pari passu
Equally.

Parity clause
A clause in a marine insurance contract which is one of two or more such contracts and which provides that where there are differing rates of premium under them the lower rate shall prevail.

Part of
A reinsurance term used to make it clear that the reinsurer is accepting part only of the risk covered by the original insurance and that in the event of a *short closing* (q.v.) he will not be saddled with the whole risk.

Partial disablement
Reduction in one's ability to work, although one can do some work.

Partial indemnity clause
A clause in a *Knock-for-knock agreement* (q.v.) which applies

155

where one insurer does not cover the damage to his insured's vehicle or covers it subject to a large excess. In any such case the insurer concerned agrees to reimburse the other insurer one-half of his payment for damage to the vehicle he insures regardless of the question of legal liability for the accident that caused the damage.

Partial loss

A loss not amounting to a total loss.

Participating policy

An insurance policy the holder of which is entitled to a share of the insurer's surplus.

Participating preference share

A *preference share* (q.v.) which gives the holder, in addition to his right to a fixed dividend, a limited right to a share in the residual profits of the company.

Participation

1. There is said to be participation when a number of insurers each accept a portion of an insurance.
2. Sharing by a life assurance policyholder in the assurance company's surplus.
3. Belonging to the state pension scheme for earnings-related benefits.
4. Having a say in the running of a pension scheme.

Particular average

In marine insurance, partial loss of or damage to the subject-matter of insurance.

Particular charges

In marine insurance, expenses incurred by the insured or his agents to prevent or minimise a loss of the subject-matter insured from an insured peril. The term is customarily confined to charges incurred at destination.

Partnership assurance

Life assurance for partners an important object of which is to cope with the situation arising when the death of a partner gives rise to the need for paying off his share in the partnership.

Part-time agent

An agent who, as a subsidiary activity, introduces business to an insurer on which he receives a commission.

Party wall

A wall separating two buildings in respect of which the occupier on each side has a partial right.

Passenger liability

The limit of liability of a carrier to passengers for bodily injury

156

varies with the nature of the transportation. Liability to passengers in aircraft is restricted in amount by international conventions and legislation. A shipowner's liability to passengers is limited by legislation. The user of a motor vehicle may not contract out of his liability to passengers and must insure in respect of it without limit of amount.

Passing off
A person who passes off his goods so as to mislead people into thinking that they are the goods of another is subject to an action. He may insure in respect of his liability under a policy covering infringement of industrial property rights.

Past service benefit
Benefit under a pension scheme in respect of years before a person became a member of the scheme.

Past service pension
A right granted to an employee at the inception of a pension scheme, or when benefits are improved, to receive a pension on retirement related to his service before the scheme started.

Patent
A monopoly granted by the state to an inventor of a manner of new manufacture for a limited number of years in return for his disclosure of his invention.

Pauschal
A marine cargo insurance term (Dutch and German) relating to a provisional annual premium paid in advance.

Pay as may be paid
A reinsurance term providing that the reinsurer will not question payment of any claim for which the insurer is liable under the original insurance.

Pay as paid policy
A policy on livestock under which insurers agree to pay a supplement of a given percentage of compensation paid for slaughter of stock by the Department of Agriculture when slaughter is ordered to prevent the possible spread of a disease.

Pay-as-you-go system
The system of paying benefits such as retirement benefits as they accrue without making provision for their cost in future years.

Payment in lieu
A payment by a pension scheme to the state scheme whereby the pension scheme transfers to the state liability to pay a pension to a person contracted out of the state scheme.

Payment order
> An authority given by an insured to a broker to empower the broker to collect a claim on the insured's behalf.

Payroll basis
> Where business interruption insurance is arranged on a payroll basis the rate charged on salaries and wages is lower than that on gross profit.

Peak risk
> An exceptionally large insurance in a portfolio of smaller insurances.

Peak value clause
> A clause used in cargo insurance on cotton which provides that the sum insured shall be the peak value pertaining in the cotton market at the time of loss.

Penalty
> The maximum sum named in a bond as becoming payable by the surety in the event of default by the person guaranteed.

Pension
> A regular payment to a former employee or the like.

Pension administration
> The work of managing a pension fund and calculating and paying pensions.

Pension fraction
> Where in a pension scheme the premium depends on length of service or employment a given fraction of pay is used in calculating the pension due, e.g., 1/80 per annum.

Pension fund
> Assets earmarked for the payment of pensions.

Pension guarantee
> A guarantee that income payments under a pension scheme will be continued for a specified number of years even if the beneficiary dies during those years.

Pension mortgage
> A mortgage loan by a pensions insurer, repayable out of the lump sum available at maturity of the insurance.

Pension plan
> U.S. term for *Pension scheme* (q.v.).

Pension scheme
> A systematic provision for retirement pensions and associated benefits.

Pension transfer scheme
> An arrangement among groups of pension schemes or employers whereby a member of one pension scheme in the group may change to another without losing pension rights.

Pensionable salary
A definition in a pension scheme of what constitutes salary for the purpose of the scheme, e.g., whether overtime and commission are to be taken into account and how. (See *Final pensionable salary*.)

Pensionable service
A definition in a pension scheme of the nature and period of service to be taken into account in determining eligibility for membership of the scheme and the extent of pension entitlement.

Pensioneer trustee
A person approved by the Occupational Pensions Board as qualified to act to see that the conditions of a one-man pension scheme are observed.

Pensioner's rights premium
A payment to the state to ensure that members of a discontinued pension scheme who have reached state pension age receive from the state their *guaranteed minimum pension* (q.v.).

Pensions managed fund
1. A fund conducted by an insurance company for the provision of pensions, the investment profit being used for the benefit of the fund or of the employer. The insurance company may also administer the benefits.
2. A pensions arrangement where outside investment managers look after the fund.

Per capita
(Counting) by heads.

Per capita premium
A premium payable per head in respect of each of a number of persons.

Percentage adjustments
An increase (or decrease) by a percentage of fire insurance rates made to reflect changes in experience in the various classes.

Percentage of fire loss insurance
Insurance of consequential loss under which the sum payable is expressed as a percentage of the payment made for material damage.

Performance bond
A guarantee that a contract for construction will be carried out.

Peril
A possible cause of loss, such as fire.

Perils of the sea
The causes of fortuitous accidents or casualties of the seas, such as stranding, collision and heavy weather, but not the ordinary action of winds and waves which is in the nature of wear and tear.

Period policy
Same as *Time policy*.

Permanent disablement
Permanent loss of ability, in whole or in part, to work.

Permanent health insurance
Insurance against disablement by sickness or accident which is renewable at the insured's option up to a stated age. The insurers are bound to accept the renewal.

Perpetual insurance
A system of fire insurance whereby the insured makes a deposit, either in a lump sum or by instalments, representing a percentage of the value of property, the interest on the deposit being receivable by the insurer for payment of claims. The insured may terminate the insurance by withdrawing his deposit. Some schemes provide for a call on the policyholder if the insurance fund is depleted.

Perpetuity
An annuity payable without limit of time.

Persistency
A measure of the extent to which policyholders maintain their cover with an insurer by renewal of their policies.

Personal accident and sickness insurance
Insurance for fixed benefits in the event of death or loss of limbs or sight by accident and/or disablement by accident or sickness.

Personal accident insurance
Insurance for fixed benefits in the event of death or loss of limbs or sight by accident and/or disablement by accident.

Personal injury
Harm to the person, more safely referred to as bodily injury, since personal injury might be deemed to include damage to a person's reputation by defamation or the like.

Personal liability insurance
Insurance of an individual's liability to third parties, for injury or damage by negligent acts other than in connection with the use of a motor vehicle.

Personal pension plan
A fund created by an individual to buy a pension on retirement.

Personal property
The right or interest of a person in movable property as opposed to real property.

Personal reserve
A fund which an underwriting member of Lloyd's is obliged to accumulate as a reserve to meet potential liabilities under insurances written for his account. (Cf. *Special reserve*).

Personal surety
An individual who acts as guarantor to answer for the conduct of another who is referred to as the principal.

Personalty
Personal property. Pure personalty is property unconnected with land. Mixed personalty includes interests in land such as leaseholds.

PETA Plan
A combination of unit-linked pure endowment and term assurance.

Physical hazard
A physical feature that introduces or increases the possibility of a loss arising from a peril or one that may influence the extent of a loss.

Pilferage
Petty theft without breaking open cases.

Pirates
Persons attacking property at sea, including passengers who mutiny and rioters who attack a ship from the shore.

Placing
1. Effecting an insurance.
2. An insurance which has been effected.

Plain form of Policy
The standard marine insurance policy on an S.G. form with no clauses or special conditions attached.

Planned funding
A system of costing for pension schemes based on *controlled funding* (q.v.).

Plurality of risk
There is said to be plurality of risk where a fire insurance policy covers more than one location or set of property.

Pluvius insurance
Insurance in respect of loss arising from adverse weather conditions, notably heavy rainfall which causes the cancellation of an outdoor event.

Polarisation
Division of insurance intermediaries into two categories —

those placing business for one company only, and those free to place business with any insurer — without intermediate categories.

Policies incepting basis
A basis for a reinsurance treaty whereby the test of the reinsurer's liability is when the original insurance was effected — rather than whether the loss occurred or was notified during the reinsurance period.

Policies of Assurance Act 1867
An Act enabling assignees of life assurance policies to sue for the policy moneys in their own name.

Policy
A document setting out the terms of a contract to insure.

Policy conditions
The terms to which an insurance is subject.

Policy fee
A charge by an insurer for issuing a policy, as distinct from the premium.

Policy loan
A loan on the security of a long-term life assurance.

Policy owner
The person with proprietary rights in an insurance policy. The term is used in life assurance effected on the life of another to distinguish the owner of the policy from the person on whose life the assurance depends.

Policy proof of interest
A policy under which insurers agree to pay a claim without requiring the insured to prove that he has an insurable interest. By the Marine Insurance Act 1906, s.4(2), such a policy is deemed to be a gaming or wagering contract and is therefore unenforceable in a court.

Policy register
A record kept by an insurer of policies effected.

Policy reserves
Funds held by an insurer for the fulfilment of his obligations under policies.

Policy signing office
An office conducted jointly by a number of insurers, either Lloyd's underwriters or companies, where policies are signed on their behalf.

Policy year
The year that a policy runs, commencing with the inception date or the renewal date.

Policyholder (or Policy-holder)
The insured person.

Policyholders Protection Act 1975
An Act setting up the Policyholders Protection Board which is required to settle claims made by United Kingdom policy holders and third parties where the insurance company concerned is financially unable to meet them, the cost being met by a levy on other insurance companies and, in some cases, on intermediaries who placed life assurance with the insolvent company.

Policyholders' surplus
That part of the assets of an insurance company that is available for the benefit of policyholders.

Political risks
In credit or investment insurance, those risks that arise from political actions and are beyond the control of either party to the contract, such as currency transfer delays, moratoria, war, civil war or expropriation.

Pollution
Damage to air, water, land, property or the atmosphere by some noxious emanation.

Pool
A pool is created when a number of insurers agree that all insurances of a defined character shall be shared among them in specified proportions.

Pool schemes
Arrangements at Lloyd's whereby very small premium or claim payments are pooled rather than being accounted for individually.

Port risks insurance
Insurance of a vessel in port, the cover for collision liability and protection and indemnity risks being more extensive than that provided under a marine insurance hull time policy.

Port to Port
The period of cover given by a voyage insurance on a plain form of marine policy. For goods the cover runs from the loading of goods on the vessel until the goods are discharged on to the quay at destination or into the consignee's own craft. In hull insurance the risk attaches when the vessel sails and ceases when the vessel is moored in good safety at the port of destination.

Portability
The extent to which pension rights are transferable on a change of employer.

Portfolio
1. The totality of the business of an insurer or reinsurer.
2. A segment of the business of an insurer or a reinsurer, e.g., fire insurance business is called his fire portfolio.

Portfolio consideration
The premium payable for the reinsurance of a portfolio of insurance or reinsurance business to which may be added an extra payment to cover losses already outstanding or other charges.

Portfolio entry
At the outset of a reinsurance treaty a definition is necessary of the insurances to be included, viz., whether the treaty applies to business in force at its inception or only to subsequent insurances and renewals.

Portfolio mix
The constituents in an insurer's portfolio of insurance or reinsurance.

Portfolio premium
The premium payable for the reinsurance of a portfolio of insurance or reinsurance business.

Portfolio reinsurance
The cession by way of reinsurance of a *portfolio* (q.v.).

Portfolio return
Descriptive of the procedure when a reinsurance treaty is terminated and the reinsurer returns the proportion of premium relating to insurances in force and has no liability for claims thereunder.

Portfolio run-off
Descriptive of the procedure when a reinsurance treaty is terminated but continues to apply to premiums and further losses in respect of insurances in course.

Portfolio transfer
The transfer of the *portfolio* (q.v.) of one direct insurer to another.

Positions bond
A bond covering persons occupying stated offices.

Possible maximum loss
Same as *Maximum possible loss*.

Power of attorney
A written instrument empowering a person to act on behalf of another.

Preamble
Same as *Recital clause*.

Pre-Credit risk
In credit insurance, risks arising before the time for despatch of the goods to be sold.

Pre-existing condition
A state, usually of health, which existed before an insurance came into force.

Preference share
A share in the capital of a company which gives the holder preference over the holders of ordinary shares in the payment of dividends up to a stated amount, and in return of capital in a liquidation.

Preferred ordinary share
A share in the capital of a company which gives the holder the right to a fixed dividend, after payment of any dividend due to the holders of preference shares, in preference to the payment of dividend on other ordinary shares.

Premises
1. The beginning of an insurance policy or conveyance which sets forth the names of the parties and the consideration.
2. The subject of a conveyance, such as land or buildings, specified in the *premises* (1 supra) of the deed.
3. A building with its grounds and appurtenances, or that part occupied by the insured.

Premium
1. The consideration payable by the insured for an insurance.
2. The excess over the original value of a thing or over its par value.

Premium advice note
A note sent to an insurer or a policy signing office by an insurance broker when the broker's client is debited with the premium or credited with a return premium.

Premium base
See *Base premium.*

Premium earned
That part of a premium that relates to so much of the period of insurance as has already run.

Premium income
The income of an insurer from premiums.

Premium limit
The maximum total of premiums that may be accepted on behalf of an underwriting member of Lloyd's. The limit is governed by the underwriter's means and the amount of the premium deposit he has made.

Premium loading
 See *Loading*.
Premium rate
 The price per unit of insurance.
Premium receipt
 An acknowledgement that a premium has been received.
Premium receipt book
 A book held by the holder of industrial life assurance in which the collector notes the premiums paid.
Premium tax
 A tax on insurance premiums, applied in some countries.
Premium to be agreed
 See *Premium to be arranged*.
Premium to be arranged
 Phrase used when an insurer is asked to grant cover pending determination of the premium. By the Marine Insurance Act 1906, s.31, a reasonable premium is payable in such circumstances.
Premium transfer
 Method used at Lloyd's where a risk is insured for more than twelve months. The premium for the period in excess of twelve months is paid over, as an internal transaction, by the original syndicate to its successor syndicate as reconstituted for the ensuing year.
Premiums reducing
 In life assurance circumstances may arise where after a period premiums are payable at a reduced rate. For example, in a few cases, bonuses under with-profit policies are applied to reduce progressively the premiums payable rather than to augment the sum assured.
Premiums Trust Fund
 The fund into which premiums must be paid at Lloyd's, the money being held in trust for fulfilment of insurance contracts.
Prescription
 Creation (or extinguishment) of a legal right or obligation by the lapse of time.
Preservation
 Keeping a right to a future pension from a scheme one has left.
Preserved pension
 A deferred pension due to someone who has left a pension scheme. Since 1985 the rate of pension is increased annually to allow for inflation.

Prevention
It is the duty of the insured to take all reasonable steps to prevent or minimise a loss. See *Loss prevention.*

Primary carrier
An original insurer as distinct from a reinsurer (U.S.)

Primary exposure
Term used in aviation insurance to refer to risk arising from occurrences which although they may be serious have no catastrophic feature.

Primary insurance
Insurance of the initial layer of cover as distinct from excess insurance.

Primary reinsurance clause
A clause occasionally found in a policy, intended to make the reinsurers directly responsible to the original insured for the payment of losses.

Principal
1. One who uses an agent to perform some act on his behalf.
2. One whose obligations are guaranteed by a surety under a bond.

Principal office
In life reassurance, the ceding assurer.

Private health insurance
Insurance to pay the fees for private medical or hospital treatment.

Private insurance
Insurance transacted by private enterprise insurers.

Private wording scheme
Same as *Special wording scheme.*

Pro rata
In proportion.

Pro rata reinsurance
Same as *Proportional reinsurance.*

Probability
The likelihood of an occurrence.

Probable maximum loss
An estimate of the maximum loss that is likely to arise on the occurrence of a single event considered to be within the realms of probability, remote coincidences and possible but unlikely catastrophes being ignored.

Probate
Legal recognition that a will is valid.

Procuration fee
A fee paid to the introducer of an insurance.

Producer
1. One whose business it is to obtain insurances for an insurer.
2. The original broker who obtains a proposal for business effected at Lloyd's through a Lloyd's broker.

Products guarantee
Indemnity against claims arising out of the failure of a product to fulfil its intended function.

Products liability insurance
Insurance against the liability of a producer, supplier, tester or servicer of goods for injury to third parties or loss of or damage to their property caused by the goods.

Professional indemnity insurance
Indemnity to a professional man or firm against legal liability to compensate a third party who has sustained injury, loss or damage through breach of duty.

Professional reinsurer
A company that confines its business to reinsurance and does not undertake direct insurance.

Profit
See *With profits*.

Profit commission
A commission paid by an insurer in proportion to his profit on specified insurance business.

Profit-sharing
A system in group pensions and health insurance whereby if a scheme is profitable to insurers they will periodically return a proportion of the amount by which premiums exceed claims.

Profits insurance
Insurance against the loss of profits resulting from the occurrence of an untoward event such as a fire or machinery breakdown.

Proof of loss
1. A statement by the insured giving details of his loss.
2. In law the onus of proving that a loss has occurred and that it was caused by an insured peril rests with the insured.

Property damage insurance
Insurance covering damage to the physical property of third parties (U.S.).

Property insurance
Insurance of physical property belonging to the insured or for which he is responsible.

Property-linked policy
A life insurance policy the benefits of which are calculated

according to the value from time to time of specified properties.

Proportional reinsurance
Reinsurance of a part of an original insurance, premiums and losses being shared proportionately between reinsurer and insurer.

Proportional rule
The application of the *Average condition* (q.v.).

Proportionate benefits
Where, in permanent health insurance, the insured, while totally disabled from following his occupation, is able to earn something in another occupation, the insurance usually provides for payment of benefit proportionate to his loss of earnings compared with his previous average earnings.

Proposal
1. An application for insurance, often on a printed proposal form.
2. Formerly, the insurance company's prospectus, which set out the conditions on which insurance would be granted.

Proposal form
See *Proposal.*

Proprietary life company
A life assurance company owned by its shareholders.

Prosecution
1. Carrying on an activity with a view to accomplishing something.
2. Bringing someone before a court to face an accusation.

Prosecution clause
A clause in an insurance policy covering loss by dishonesty which obliges the insured, if so required by the insurer, to prosecute the person alleged to have caused the loss.

Prospect
One who is looked on as a potential policyholder.

Prospective rating
Basing a premium, in whole or in part, on the loss experience of a previous period.

Prospectus
1. A publication descriptive of services offered, e.g., a type of insurance.
2. A publication describing a proposed venture, e.g., inviting applications for shares in a company.

Protected rights
Rights under a pension scheme which a member retains despite a change in the scheme.

169

Protected risk
> Property subject to some special measure of protection, such as a burglar alarm.

Protection
> 1. Measure taken to guard against loss.
> 2. The financial safeguard given by the existence of insurance.

Protection and Indemnity club
> A mutual association of shipowners to protect themselves financially against certain marine risks. See *Protection and indemnity risks.*

Protection and indemnity risks
> Certain risks have in the past not always been readily insurable in the marine insurance market and shipowners have formed mutual associations (clubs) to cover them. Protection risks include quarantine expenses, liabilities to crews, and collision and impact damage, wreck removal expenses and liability under towage contracts, also liability for damage to other vessels apart from collision, etc. Indemnity risks include shipowners' liability for cargo lost or damaged, fines for inadvertent immigration or customs offences, etc.

Protest
> A declaration by the master of a vessel regarding damage to the vessel or its cargo.

Protracted default
> Credit insurance protects the creditor against non-payment of a sum due, whether the non-payment arises from insolvency on the part of the debtor or his failure to pay over a substantial period, usually 90 days after due date. This latter is called protracted default.

Provident fund
> A fund into which payments are made by individuals and their employers for the ultimate benefit of the individuals.

Provision
> 1. A term in a contract.
> 2. An amount retained or written off to provide for (a) depreciation or a fall in the value of assets or (b) a known liability even though its exact extent cannot as yet be determined. Often used interchangeably with *reserve* (q.v.).

Proviso
> A condition inserted in a contract on the observance of which the validity of the contract depends.

Proximate cause
>Every event is the outcome of a chain (or net) of previous events, but in the words of Bacon "It were infinite for the law to consider the causes of causes, and their impulsions one of another; therefore it contenteth itself with the immediate cause". This immediate or effective cause, not necessarily that closest in time to the event, is termed the proximate cause.

Pseudonym
>An abbreviation or combination of letters used in Lloyd's practice to identify a broker or underwriting syndicate.

Public adjuster
>One who negotiates settlement of a claim on behalf of the insured (U.S.).

Public Authority clause
>A clause in a fire insurance policy providing for the extra cost in rebuilding premises of meeting the requirements of public authorities.

Public liability insurance
>The insurance of liability for accidental bodily injury or damage to the property of third parties.

Public policy
>The courts may hold that an insurance is void because it is contrary to public policy, for example if it is an insurance for the benefit of an enemy alien in time of war.

Public Sector Transfer Club
>A *pension transfer scheme* (q.v.) that covers most public sector and nationalised industry schemes and some private ones.

Punitive damages
>1. In English law, damages awarded over and above what is required to compensate the plaintiff in respect of a limited number of torts, where either (a) there has been some abuse by the defendant in the exercise of a public function or (b) the defendant has obtained an advantage that outweighs any compensatory damages.
>2. In U.S. law, extra damages awarded by way of punishment or deterrence.

Purchased life annuity
>An annuity bought by an individual out of his own money as distinct from one provided under a pension scheme.

Pure burning cost
>Same as *Burning cost*.

171

Pure endowment
    A life assurance for a term of years providing for a sum of
    money to be paid only if the life assured survives to the end of
    the term. The premiums paid may or may not be returned in
    the event of earlier death, according to the terms of the
    contract.
Pure indemnity
    In marine insurance, indemnity as provided for by the Marine
    Insurance Act 1906 for unvalued policies, e.g., in the case of
    total loss of hull, the actual market value of the vessel. (In
    practice a *valued policy* (q.v.) is always issued.)
Pure loss cost
    The cost of paying claims expressed as a percentage of
    premiums.
Pure premium
    The amount required by an insurer to pay losses under an
    insurance without taking into account the insurer's general
    expenses.
Pure risks
    Risks inherent in the environment, such as fire or earthquake,
    as distinct from business risks or risks voluntarily undergone.
Pure salvage
    Same as *Salvage (1)*.

Q

Q.C. clause
    A clause in a professional indemnity policy providing that the
    insured shall not be obliged to contest any proceedings (with
    consequent undesirable publicity for the insured) unless a
    mutually agreed Queen's Counsel shall advise in favour of a
    contest.
Qualifying policy
    A life assurance policy approved by the Inland Revenue as
    eligible for favourable tax treatment.
Quantum (of damages)
    Damages expressed as a sum of money.
Quantum meruit
    As much as he has earned.
    When a contract comes to a premature end a person who has
    performed services under it may be entitled to a payment for
    what he has done (quantum meruit) even though his perform-
    ance under the contract has not been completed.

Quarter day
>Four days in the year on which rents and other engagements were commonly met and from one of which it was customary for fire insurances to run, viz. (in England, Wales and Northern Ireland):
>>Lady Day, 25 March
>>Midsummer, 24 June
>>Michaelmas, 29 September
>>Christmas, 25 December

Quay to Quay
>The period of cover given under a marine cargo policy which attaches as the goods are lifted from the quay at the port of loading and terminates when they are freed from the ship's tackle or landed from craft at the port of destination.

Quota share reinsurance
>Treaty reinsurance providing that the reinsurer shall accept a specified share of each risk.

Quota surplus reinsurance
>Reinsurance that combines *Quota share reinsurance* and *surplus reinsurance.*

Quotation
>Especially in life assurance, a statement by an assurer of the premium he will require for a particular assurance.

Quotation slip
>A slip on which an underwriter is asked to quote his terms for a proposed insurance for consideration by the proposer.

R

R/I Closing Form
>A form on which a direct insurer sets out closing details and which he sends the broker in order that the broker may close the reinsurance with the reinsurers.

R/I or direct
>Term used on a broker's slip when the broker has an order to place a risk but does not know whether it will be a direct insurance or a reinsurance.

R/I Order Form
>A form on which an insurer sets out details of a risk that he wishes to reinsure.

R/I Treaty Standard Slip
>A standard form for use by brokers in the placing of a reinsurance treaty.

Radioactive contamination
>The introduction of radioactivity through the escape of radiation from some radioactive substance.

Rain insurance
>Insurance against loss caused by a measured amount of rainfall occurring within a specified period.

Random sampling
>Selecting individual items from a large group in such a way that every individual item has the same chance of being included in the sample group.

Range
>The extent of classes of property covered by a policy or of the situation(s) at which it is covered.

Ransom insurance
>Same as *Kidnap and Ransom insurance.*

Rat(e)able contribution
>A proportionate contribution.

Rate
>The charge for insurance for each unit that is used as a basis for the calculation of premiums, e.g., per £100 of the value of property, or per capita for persons.

Rate guarantee
>An undertaking by an insurance company, as in an insured pension scheme, restricting the extent to which it will vary its rate of premium for a specified number of years.

Rate on line
>A rate of premium for a reinsurance which if applied to the liability accepted by the reinsurer will produce an annual premium sufficient to meet expected losses over a number of years.

Rated up
>Term applied to an insurance where the premium is higher than the norm.

Ratification
>Confirmation, as where a principal adopts as binding on him the act of another which was done on his behalf though without the principal's previous authority.

Rating
>1. The calculation of the premium applicable to an insurance.
>2. An assessment of standing (U.S.).

Rating bureau
>An organisation that collects statistics of losses and suggests to insurers what rates of premium appear to be indicated by the available facts (U.S.).

Ratio decidendi
>The principle of law on which a judgment in a lawsuit is based.

Realty
>All interests in land other than leasehold interests.

Reasonable despatch clause
>A clause in a marine insurance policy requiring that the insured shall act with reasonable despatch in all circumstances within his control.

Reasonable precautions clause
>A clause found in various classes of insurance policies that requires the insured to take reasonable precautions to guard against the occurrence of a loss.

Reassurance
>*Reinsurance* (q.v.) of life assurance.

Reassured
>Same as *Reinsured*.

Reassurer
>Same as *Reinsurer*.

Rebate
>A reduction or discount.

Rebating
>Reducing the premium as, for example, where the agent gives the insured all or part of the agency commission. This form of rebating is forbidden by law in some countries.

Recall of products insurance
>Insurance against the expense of recalling dangerous or defective products.

Receiver
>One appointed to manage property or receive the income of another.

Reciprocal exchange
>An unincorporated association for mutual insurance among members who pay premiums and share losses (U.S.).

Reciprocal insurance
>Insurance provided in a *reciprocal exchange* (q.v.).

Reciprocity
>The exchange of reinsurances between two reinsurers.

Recital clause
>The opening clause of a policy defining the parties.

Reconditioning charges
>Charges incurred by an insured to recondition damaged cargo and so minimise a loss.

Recourse indemnity
Indemnity to an exporter against the risk of a buyer failing to pay for plant and equipment on the ground of alleged failure or defects and to a lender against the risk of an exporter's insolvency.

Recovery
Money received by an insurer in respect of a loss, thus reducing the loss, by way of subrogation, salvage or reinsurance.

Recovery agent
One who pursues on an insurer's behalf a claim against a carrier of goods in respect of loss or damage to them, customarily on a "no cure, no pay" basis.

Rectification
The correction by the court of the wording of a written contract in order to give effect to what was the true agreement between the parties which the writing has failed to express.

Recurring endowment assurance
An endowment assurance under which capital sums are payable by the assurer to the assured at stated intervals during the currency of the assurance.

Red Line Clause
A clause printed in red in a marine cargo policy drawing the insured's attention to his obligation to preserve his right of recovery against a carrier or bailee for the benefit of the insurer.

Redemption
Paying off a loan and therefore recovering the security, such as a mortgage.

Redlining
Marking on a map an area within which one will not grant insurances (U.S.).

Reduced paid-up assurance
Where, under a long-term life assurance the assured wishes to cease paying premiums, the policy is said to become paid up, the sum assured being reduced.

Reduced premium policy
A life assurance policy where the premium in the first few years is lower than that for subsequent years.

Reducing option
An option in a pension scheme to accept a reduced pension in consideration of an increased pension for one's surviving spouse.

Reduction factor
A factor permitting the calculation of premiums or reserves for sickness insurance business from a table that relates to a particular period of indemnity.

Reduction of premium policy
A life policy for which the premium is progressively reduced in later years.

Rehabilitation
Helping a person who is under some handicap to resume a satisfactory life.

Rehabilitation of Offenders Act 1974
An Act that provides for certain offences, after a lapse of time, to be regarded as spent so that the offender will be treated in law as though he had not committed the offence. The Act is relevant to a proposer's discharge of the duty of disclosure.

Reinstatement
1. Making good. Where insured property is damaged, a policy may give the insurer the option to make it good rather than pay the loss in money. See also *Fires Prevention (Metropolis) Act 1774*.
2. The revival of an insurance or reinsurance by paying a premium to make good cover that has been depleted by payment of a loss.

Reinstatement clause
1. A clause in a fire insurance policy setting out the liability of the insurer if he elects or is legally obliged to reinstate the insured property in the event of a loss.
2. A clause in a reinsurance treaty that provides for a premium to be payable to replenish the sum insured after a loss.

Reinstatement Memorandum
Same as *Reinstatement clause* (1).

Reinstatement premium
Premium payable to restore the sum insured to its original level after it has been depleted by the occurrence of a loss.

Reinsurance
Transfer of all or part of the risk assumed by an insurer under one or more insurances to another insurer, called the reinsurer.

Reinsurance assumed
Reinsurance accepted from a reinsurer.

Reinsurance broker
A professional intermediary between insurers wishing to place reinsurance and those willing to accept it.

Reinsurance cover

A reinsurance cover is a contract whereby the reinsurer undertakes to grant reinsurance for a series of original insurances over a specified period. The period is usually short in comparison with that of a reinsurance treaty which is as a rule expected to last for a long period.

Reinsurance of common account

Marine reinsurance term applicable where an insurer has an obligation under one reinsurance contract to cede a proportion of a risk to one reinsurer and has subsequently entered into a long-term reinsurance contract with a second reinsurer to cede a fixed amount or proportion of all the insurances he (the insurer) accepts. He fulfils his obligation to cede under the second contract and reinsures on behalf of the first reinsurer such proportion of that cession as he is obliged by his prior obligation to place with the first reinsurer. This latter cession is known as reinsurance of common account, or reinsurance of joint account.

Reinsurance of joint account

Same as *Reinsurance of common account.*

Reinsurance reserve

A reserve to provide for the notional cost of reinsuring insurances that are in course so that part of the premiums are as yet unearned.

Reinsurance security

The financial strength of reinsurers.

Reinsurance to close

The method by which the underwriting account of a Lloyd's syndicate is closed by payment of a premium to cover outstanding liabilities into the underwriting account of a later year, or to other reinsurers.

Reinsurance treaty

A contract between two insurers whereby defined risks insured by one party are reinsured by the other to an extent specified by the contract.

Reinsurance waiver clause

A clause in a reinsurance contract whereby small adjustments to premiums on the original insurance are not made between the insurer and the reinsurer as it would be uneconomic to make them.

Reinsured

The reinsured is the insurer who cedes insurance by way of reinsurance.

Reinsurer
> An insurer who accepts reinsurance business from another insurer.

Rejection risk insurance
> Insurance against the risk that exports, such as frozen foods, will be refused admission under regulations applied by the importing country.

Relationship clause
> A clause sometimes found in liability policies excluding liability to members of the insured's family.

Release
> The surrender or discharge of some claim or interest; the document evidencing the surrender or discharge.

Release of reserve
> Where a company has reserved money for a particular purpose and the reserve (or part of it) is found not to be required for that purpose it is said to be released.

Remainder period
> The period, after the initial period, in a business interruption policy covering wages on a dual basis, during which some payment is made in respect of wages incurred, at less than the 100% provided for the initial period.

Remoteness of damage
> Where damage is only indirectly caused by an event giving rise to liability, or where the occurrence of the damage could not reasonably have been foreseen, it is said to be remote and is not recoverable.

Renewable term assurance
> Temporary life assurance which the assured is given an option to renew for a specified number of years.

Renewable term reassurance
> Expression sometimes used to describe a permanent risk premium life reassurance which runs for the life of the policy or any shorter term agreed at the outset.

Renewal
> Continuing an insurance after it has been current for a period.

Renewal agreement
> An undertaking by an insurer in a policy to renew the insurance upon the insured's tender of the premium.

Renewal notice
> A notice issued by an insurer of the forthcoming expiry of an insurance, containing a request for payment of the premium necessary for its continuation.

Renewal premium
The premium payable for the renewal of an insurance.

Repartition scheme
A pension scheme for a body of workers under which the cost of pensions payable to former members of the body is paid by the contributions of present members.

Replacement clause
A clause found in a marine cargo policy on machinery which provides that in the event of damage the insurer's liability shall be limited to the cost of replacing and fitting any damaged part.

Replacement cost insurance
Insurance of property for the cost of its replacement without deduction for depreciation, conditionally upon the sum insured being the replacement value.

Replacement in kind
In property insurance, the insurers often retain to themselves an option to pay for loss or damage or to replace it in kind.

Replacement value
The value of property expressed as the cost of replacing it.

Reporting excess of loss treaty
A facultative obligatory treaty, used principally for marine cargo reinsurance, which requires particulars of sums exposed on the cover to be notified to the reinsurer.

Reporting form basis
A basis for the insurance of property where values at risk fluctuate during the year. The insured periodically reports the value at risk. These are averaged and at the end of the year the premium is adjusted accordingly (U.S.).

Representation
A statement by a proposer about the facts relating to the risk proposed for insurance.

Request note
A document prepared by an insurer with particulars of a risk offered for facultative reinsurance.

Res ipsa loquitur
(The thing speaks for itself.) When in a legal action the onus of proof, e.g., of negligence, is on one party, he may sometimes discharge this onus by evidence of what has happened, if such a happening raises an inference of negligence.

Rescission
The setting aside of a contract.

Reserve
A fund set aside out of assets for general or specific purposes after provisions have been made. Often used interchangeably with *provision* (q.v.).

Reserve account
1. A fund set aside out of premiums retained temporarily by the reinsured to provide for the payment of claims that are ultimately the liability of the reinsurer under a reinsurance treaty.
2. A fund that an insurer may be required by a government to maintain in a country to provide for the payment of claims in that country.

Resident inspector
An employee of an insurance company who is responsible for the selling and servicing of the company's business in the area where he is situated.

Residual risks policy
A contract, supplementary to a contractors' all risks policy issued on a contract by contract basis, to cover minor works, including going back to work on a lapsed contract.

Residual value
In business interruption insurance expense incurred by the insured to minimise a loss may result in advantage continuing to the insured after the indemnity period covered by the policy. The value of this advantage is called the residual value.

Residual value insurance
Insurance against the contingency that property will not be of at least a given value at some future specified date.

Res judicata
The principle that once a competent court has adjudicated on a point the parties or their successors may not reopen the matter except by way of appeal.

Respondentia
A loan to the master of a vessel, on the security of its cargo, to enable the vessel to continue its voyage (Obs.).

Restraints
One of the perils covered by a plain form of marine policy is "arrest, restraints and detainments of all Kings, princes, and people". By the Marine Insurance Act 1906, First Schedule, rule 10, the term refers to political and executive acts, and does not include a loss caused by riot or by ordinary judicial process. An embargo is a restraint, but the anticipation of an embargo is not. "People" means the governing power, not the mob.

Restrictive covenant indemnity
> An indemnity against loss arising from acting in breach of a restrictive covenant on land, such as using the land in a way prohibited by such a covenant.

Retained benefits
> Rights under a pension scheme that an employee retains from employment which has earned them.

Retained line
> Same as *Retention* (1).

Retention
> 1. The net amount of risk that an insurer or reinsurer does not reinsure but keeps for his own account.
> 2. The amount of premium retained by an insurer after paying claims and expenses, viz., his profit (U.S.).

Retention bond
> In a construction contract where sums are payable by the principal to the contractor at various stages, the principal may be entitled to hold back a proportion as security. To enable the contractor to receive this he procures a retention bond from the insurer which protects the principal.

Retention limits
> The limits of amount up to which, in respect of various categories of insurance, the original insurer keeps the insurance for his own account and does not reinsure it.

Retention schedule method
> A profit-sharing arrangement between reassured and reassurer in life reassurance, whereby the parties share on an agreed basis in the profits from a scheme covering a large number of lives (U.S.).

Retroactive
> Same as *Retrospective*.

Retrocedant
> Same as *Retrocedent*.

Retrocedent
> A reinsurer who himself effects reinsurance in respect of some of the risk he has agreed to bear.

Retrocession
> A reinsurance of reinsurance.

Retrocessionaire
> A reinsurer who accepts reinsurance (as distinct from direct insurance) from another reinsurer.

Retrospective
> With effect from an earlier date; looking backward.

Retrospective rating
> The system of basing the premium for an insurance or reinsurance on the actual loss experience, with retrospective effect.

Retrospective reserve
> The reverse obtained by accumulating premiums received in the past from which is deducted the value of insurances granted.

Retrosurance
> There is said to be retrosurance when, after reinsurer A has retroceded all or part of his risk to reinsurer B, reinsurer B then further cedes all or part of his risk to a third reinsurer.

Return commission
> The commission returnable by an agent to an insurer upon the cancellation of an insurance.

Return for no claim
> A provision found in some policies that if no claim is made under an insurance, the insurer will return part of the premium.

Return period
> The period within which it is mathematically probable that a natural phenomenon such as an earthquake of given intensity will recur.

Return premium
> Premium returned to the insured for some reason, e.g., that the insurance never attached or that the risk was reduced in some way, for example, because an insured vessel was laid up for a time.

Revaluation
> Re-expressing an amount (e.g. of earnings), by use of an index, to reflect its real value.

Reversed onus of proof
> The law normally places on a party to a lawsuit the burden of proving certain facts. This onus of proof is sometimes shifted to another party either by statute or by contract.

Reversion
> 1. A right to succeed to property or a position.
> 2. The repossession of property after a lapse of time or the happening of an event.

Reversionary annuity
> An annuity payable only after the date of a specified event such as the death of some other person.

Reversionary bonus
> A sum added to the sum insured under a with-profits life

assurance, the sum becoming payable in full only when the policy matures or is terminated by death.

Revival
Bringing into force again an insurance after it has lapsed.

Rider
U.S. term for *Endorsement* (q.v.).

Rider policy
A motor cycle insurance policy issued to a rider to grant cover in respect of machines he is riding, as distinct from a policy covering a specified machine.

Riding Establishments Act 1970
An Act that requires those who conduct riding establishments to hold liability insurance indemnifying them and the hirer of any horse in respect of liability for:—
(a) injury to the hirer, and
(b) injury to any third party.

Riesco
At Lloyd's, a basis of allocating investment income in a calendar year over different years of account.

Riot
Riot, in law, has five elements:
(a) a number of persons, not less than three;
(b) a common purpose;
(c) execution or inception of the common purpose;
(d) an intent on the part of the persons to help one another by force, if necessary, against any persons who may oppose them;
(e) force or violence displayed so as to alarm at least one person of reasonable firmness and courage.

Riot (Damages) Act 1886
S.4(1) of the Act entitles persons whose property is damaged in a riot to obtain compensation from the police authority provided notice is given within fourteen days.

Rising cost method
Same as *Single premium method*.

Risk
Used in insurance in many senses, notably:
1. the subject matter of insurance;
2. uncertainty as to the outcome of an event;
3. probability of loss;
4. the peril insured against;
5. danger.

Risk assessment
Estimation of the extent of danger from a peril.

Risk assumption
Taking on oneself a chance of loss.
Risk avoidance
Taking steps to save oneself from exposure to a danger.
Risk index
An index of insurances issued.
Risk management
The systematic treatment of risk in order to preserve capital and income from financial loss arising from unfavourable events. This involves identifying, analysing and quantifying risks, taking measures to avoid or minimise loss, and deciding what financial treatment, such as hedging, insurance, and self insurance, is best calculated to minimise unavoidable losses.
Risk-premium reassurance
Life reassurance which reassures the risk of death by means of a series of one-year temporary assurances, so that the premium rate increases with age, while the sum reassured decreases by reason of the annual increase in the original assurer's reserves.
Risk prevention
Taking measures to prevent oneself from suffering loss from a peril.
Risk transfer
Transferring to another responsibility for a potential source of loss or for the financial consequences of any such loss that may occur.
Road risks insurance
Insurance of a motor trader in respect of vehicles on the road or in the course of a journey as distinct from internal risks insurance which applies to vehicles on his own premises.
Road Traffic Act 1972
An Act that requires the user of a motor vehicle to effect insurance of liability for bodily injury to third parties arising out of road accidents. As an alternative the user may deposit a sum of money or provide security.
Robbery
The offence of stealing accompanied at the time or immediately beforehand by force exercised against a person or by putting or seeking to put a person in fear of being subjected to force.
Room, The
The hall at Lloyd's in which underwriters sit to do business.
Rota Committee
A committee appointed at Lloyd's to interview candidates for

underwriting membership or for admission as a Lloyd's broker or underwriting agent.

Rotation clause

A clause in an open cover in which many insurers participate, to provide that in respect of a small declaration by the insured the proceeds shall not (for reasons of economy) be allocated among all the insurers but shall go only to one group of insurers, the proceeds of subsequent declarations going to another group and so on in rotation of all the groups concerned.

Rovers

Same as *Pirates*.

Rules for Construction of Policy

A set of twelve rules for the interpretation of a marine insurance policy where the context does not otherwise require. They are contained in the First Schedule of the Marine Insurance Act 1906.

Rules of Practice

Rules established by the Association of Average Adjusters as a guide to average adjusters in adjusting claims. They are in five sections:

(a) General rules
(b) General average
(c) York/Antwerp Rules
(d) Damage and repairs to ship
(e) Particular average on goods.

Running Down Clause

Same as *Collision Clause*.

Running off

Term applicable where an insurer has ceased to write an insurance or class of insurances but a liability remains under contracts already written which are said to be running off.

Run-off account

At Lloyd's, a year of account kept open after the date on which it would normally have been closed.

Run-off liability

Liability that remains to be met after insurance has terminated.

Run-off statement

A statement in respect of outstanding claims which compares the sums reserved for settlement of them with their actual cost.

S

Sabotage
  Malicious actions not committed by the insured which are aimed at preventing the normal functioning of a service or enterprise or of impending communications.

Sacrifice
  See *General average sacrifice*.

Sailing warranty
  There is an implied warranty in a voyage policy on a ship that the ship will sail within a reasonable time after the insurance has been accepted. An express warranty may specify the date by which the ship must sail.

Salary grade scheme
  Same as *Graded schedule scheme*.

Salvage
  1. The remuneration payable independently of contract to an outside party who takes part in a successful rescue operation to save life or property at sea.
  2. Property saved.
  3. Rescue of property.

Salvage agreement
  An express agreement, of which Lloyd's Form of Salvage Agreement is a standard, entered into by parties to a salvage operation. Agreements are usually on a "no cure-no pay" basis and provide either for payment of a fixed sum or for the sum to be decided by arbitration.

Salvage and Recovery clause
  A clause in a marine reinsurance treaty entitling the reinsurer to press for his share of any recovery obtained on the original insurance.

Salvage charges
  Charges recoverable under maritime law by a salvor independently of contracts.

Salvage Charges Clause
  A clause in a marine insurance hull policy which does not expressly refer to salvage charges. It limits the insured's right to expenses incurred under the *Suing and Labouring Clause* (q.v.) but gives him additional rights to recover the expenses of an unsuccessful salvage operation.

Salvage corps
  Bodies formerly maintained by fire insurance companies to protect property after the occurrence of a loss or when the property is threatened.

Salvage guarantee
An agreement whereby a guarantor agrees to meet a salvage award if the party responsible fails to pay it to the salvor. Such an agreement enables a salvor safely to release the maritime lien to which he is entitled on the salved property.

Salvage loss
Where goods insured under a marine policy are damaged and as a result of the damage are sold short of destination for less than their insured value there is said to be a salvage loss. The insurer must pay the difference between the insured value and the proceeds, after deduction of sale charges and survey fee, of the sale.

Salvor
One who salves property.

Sampling
Examining a small portion of a large group in order to draw conclusions about the group. See also *Random sampling*.

Schedule
1. That part of a policy in which the variable details are inserted.
2. Any itemised list, e.g., of premium rates for various trades.

Schedule policy
A policy that enumerates several hazards and the cover given in respect of each.

Schedule rating
Calculating the premium for a risk on the basis of its various features.

Scheme
A programme for the insurance of a group.

Scheme charge
A fixed charge that may be added to the basic premium for a group insurance.

School fees insurance
Assurance to provide sums for the payment of educational fees, either at the end of a fixed term or on the death of the life assured.

Scienter
Term used in pleading to indicate that a person had knowledge of a fact, e.g., that a domestic animal had dangerous propensities.

Scratching
Initialling an agreement.

Seasonal risk
1. A danger that arises at some particular time of year only.
2. An insurance subject to a danger at some particular time of year only.

Seaworthiness
The fitness of a vessel to encounter the ordinary perils of a voyage. There is an implied warranty in a voyage policy that the vessel is seaworthy in all respects including its equipment, stores and manning.

Seaworthiness admitted
There is an implied warranty in a marine cargo policy that the ship used for carriage is *seaworthy* (q.v.), and reasonably fit to carry the cargo to its destination. As the cargo owner can often not control the seaworthiness of a ship, insurers usually include a clause in the policy to modify the implied warranty.

Second leaving
A resubmission to a policy signing office by a broker of documents that have been queried on their first presentation.

Second loss insurance
Insurance that covers only a loss in excess of that covered by a *first loss insurance* (q.v.).

Second loss policy
Same as *Excess of loss policy*.

Second mortgage
A loan by way of mortgage on property that is already mortgaged to another person. The first mortgagee's rights have priority over those of a second mortgagee, a second mortgagee's rights over those of a third mortgagee, and so on.

Second surplus treaty
A reinsurance treaty under which the reinsurer accepts an amount of reinsurance for sums over those insured by the original insurer or reinsured under a *first surplus treaty* (q.v.).

Section 32 buy-out plan
Same as *Transfer pension scheme*.

Seen
Annotation by an insurer on a slip or other document submitted for his information to show that a matter has been brought to his attention.

Select mortality table
A mortality table based on lives that have undergone a previous selection process, e.g., by having been accepted for insurance, and therefore show, during a period known as the select period, the effect of selection.

Select period
> A period chosen for the study of lives selected at the outset of the period and included in a mortality table.

Selection
> The actions of an insurer in choosing what risks to insure and on what terms and in what proportions in order to achieve a balanced portfolio of insurances that benefits from the operation of the law of large numbers.

Selection against the insurer
> The observed phenomenon that under-average risks will be proffered more readily for insurance than above-average ones and that when an insured has an option in a policy he will tend to exercise it in the direction that is least favourable to the insurer.

Self-administered pension scheme
> A pension scheme administered by trustees.

Self-insurance
> The systematic provision of a fund by an organisation which does not effect insurance against a risk but hopes to be able to bear losses arising from the risk with the aid of the fund.

Self retention
> The portion of a risk that one keeps for one's own account and does not insure or reinsure.

Seller's interest
> The insurable interest of a seller, which ceases when the title in property passes to the buyer.

Sentimental loss
> The loss of property which has favourable associations (e.g., an engagement ring) may cause suffering disproportionate to the monetary value of the object lost. Conversely property with unfavourable associations (e.g. cargo which, though undamaged, has been involved in a shipwreck) may lose value as a result of such associations. Insurances are considered not to cover sentimental losses.

Separation of assets and liabilities
> Legal provision that the assets and liabilities of an insurance company transacting more than one class of insurance (e.g., life and fire) shall be earmarked in separate funds for each class, the assets being held for the benefit of the policyholders in the class and not available to meet liabilities arising in other classes.

Separation procedure
> Lloyd's procedure where the premium accounting entry is processed separately from the policy signing procedure.

Services rendered policy
  A policy insuring suppliers of services in respect of their credit risk.
Settled policy
  A policy that forms the subject of a trust.
Settlement
  1. The settling up of an account or claim.
  2. An agreement to resolve a difference of opinion.
  3. An instrument by which property is settled on a person or persons.
  4. A lateral movement, as opposed to *subsidence* (q.v.).
Settlement date
  The date specified in a market for the periodical settlement of accounts by brokers.
Settlement of Claims Abroad
  A scheme whereby a marine insurance may be endorsed to provide for claims to be settled by a settling agent at a named place abroad.
Settlement option
  An option in an insurance policy as to the form in which a claim may be settled. Thus, in property insurance, the insurer may commonly choose whether to pay, replace or make good, and in life assurance the assured sometimes has an option between taking the policy proceeds as a lump sum or in the form of an annuity.
Settlement policy
  A life policy expressed to be for the benefit of persons other than the life assured, e.g., a policy effected under the Married Women's Property Acts 1870–82 for the benefit of one's spouse or children.
Settlement rate
  See *Claims settlement rate*.
Settling agent
  A person authorised by an insurer to pay claims on the insurer's behalf.
Settlor
  One who settles property on another by means of a trust.
Seven day clause
  A *One disaster or casualty clause* (q.v.) providing for its application to a period of seven days.
Share
  The capital of a company may be divided into units known as shares in which dealings can take place. If not so divided capital in the form of stock may be dealt with in any amounts.

191

Share reinsurance
>Same as *Quota-share reinsurance.*

Shareholders' surplus
>That portion of the excess of assets over liabilities in an insurance fund to which the shareholders are entitled.

Ship
>By the Marine Insurance Act 1906, First Schedule, rule 15, "ship" includes the hull, materials and outfit, stores and provisions for the officers and crew, and in the case of vessels engaged in a special trade, the ordinary fittings requisite for the trade, and also, in the case of a steamship, the machinery, boilers and coals and engine stores, if owned by the insured.

Shipbroker
>A person acting as the agent for a shipowner in arranging charters and the carriage of cargo and passengers.

Shipowner's liability
>The liability of a shipowner for injury, loss or damage which may arise in tort or under contract, mostly covered by membership of a *Protection and Indemnity club* (q.v.).

Shock loss reinsurance
>Same as *Catastrophe reinsurance.*

Shopping
>The process whereby a life assurance company with a proposal for an impaired life approaches a number of reinsurers for competitive quotations.

Short closing
>The act of a broker when closing a line, in allotting to an underwriter less than the line he has written, either because more than 100% of the insurance has been subscribed, or because the insurance is for a smaller amount than was expected at the outset. Short closing, unlike overclosing, is permissible.

Short delivery
>There is said to be short delivery, as opposed to non-delivery, where a bulk cargo when unloaded is deficient compared with its shipped weight, or where part of a package fails to arrive. Cf. *Non-delivery* (q.v.).

Short form of indemnity
>A form of indemnity given by an insurer to a bonding company which has provided security to obtain the release of a vessel arrested by a U.S. court.

Short interest
>The part of the subject-matter of a marine insurance that has

never been at risk, e.g., the extent to which declarations under a floating policy fall short of the sum insured.

Short period rate
  The rate of premium for an insurance of less than one year, often appreciably higher than the annual rate.

Short rate
  Same as *Short period rate.*

Short-tail business
  Insurances where all claims are expected to be received during, or within a short time after expiry of, the insurance.

Short term
  In marine insurance, applied to insurances of less than twelve months.

Short term insurance
  1. Insurance that runs for one year or less, though the insurer may have an option whether to cease writing or to renew it.
  2. In marine insurance, an insurance of less than twelve months.

Short term rate
  Same as *Short period rate.*

Sickness insurance
  Insurance against disablement by sickness.

Sickness table
  Same as *Morbidity table.*

Signed line
  Same as *Closed line.*

Signer
  Same as *Signing slip.*

Signing A.P.
  An endorsement attached to a Lloyd's policy to add a new syndicate to an existing risk.

Signing indication
  An indication by an insurance broker of the effect of possible oversubscription on the line to be received by the underwriter.

Signing slip
  A broker's slip used for submitting details to Lloyd's Policy Signing Office. It may be the original slip, a certified copy, or a specially initialled slip.

Signing table
  The list of subscribing syndicates, lines and references, attached by Lloyd's Policy Signing Office to a Lloyd's policy.

Silent risk
> Premises in which no trade is carried on or no machinery is worked for manufacturing purposes.

Simple reversionary bonus
> A sum added to the sum assured under a life assurance, payable only when payment of the sum assured falls due and not compounded for the purpose of calculation of bonuses declared subsequently.

Simple risk
> A fire insurance, such as that on a private dwelling, that is not complex.

Simultaneous payments clause
> A clause in a reinsurance contract to provide that the reinsurer shall pay a claim at the same time as a claim is paid on the original insurance.

Single liability
> In the Admiralty Court, where two vessels, A and B, have been in collision and both were partly to blame, so that A is liable to B for part of B's damage and B is liable to A for part of A's damage, the court makes a single award to the party who has a net balance in his favour. Cf. *Cross liabilities* (1).

Single premium
> In life assurance, a single payment for the whole of the cover required however long the cover lasts.

Single premium method
> A method of calculating premiums under a pension scheme. Premiums are calculated separately in respect of the benefit earned in each year of membership.

Singleton policy
> A combined company policy form issued on behalf of a single insurer.

Sister Ship Clause
> A clause in a marine hull policy whereby the insurer agrees that where a ship is in collision with, or receives salvage services from, a ship in the same ownership, the insurer will settle claims for liability or salvage services as though the ships were in separate ownership.

Situation index
> An index kept by fire insurers of the location of risks insured.

Sliding scale commission
> Commission which rises in accordance with some factor, notably a commission whose rate rises with the profitability of a reinsurance treaty.

Sliding scale treaty
A reinsurance treaty under which the rate of premium in any year is calculated by reference to the claims experience over the previous x years.

Slip
A document submitted by a broker to underwriters and containing particulars of a risk proposed for insurance. The underwriter signifies his acceptance by initialling the slip and indicating on it the share of the insurance he will take.

Slip agreement
An agreement expressed by an underwriter on a broker's slip at a date subsequent to the original acceptance of the risk. Cf. *Honeycomb slip*.

Slip policy
In marine reinsurance and cargo insurance a slip may be treated as evidence of the contract. It is then termed a slip policy, a formal policy being prepared only if one is required for legal proceedings.

Small additional or return premiums clause
A clause in a policy providing the small adjustments of premium shall be waived, they being uneconomic to make.

Small Claims and Recoveries Pool Scheme
A scheme in Lloyd's market which provides that small entries for claims or adjusted premiums shall be paid into or out of a pool without being processed in respect of each insurance.

Smoke damage
If caused by fire is covered by a fire or marine insurance. Coverable in U.S. as an additional peril.

Social insurance
A scheme for the payment of benefits by a government or government agency, in respect of contingencies to which people generally are liable (e.g., old age, sickness, accidental injury, death or unemployment), the benefits being payable in whole or in part out of a fund of contributions by insured persons and/or their employers. Membership of the scheme is commonly compulsory.

Social security
The sum of measures taken by a government to protect the individual against shortfalls in income and to provide help at times of special need. One measure commonly employed is *social insurance* (q.v.).

SOLAS Convention
The International Convention for the Safety of Life at Sea, 1974.

SOLAS Protocol
A draft instrument of 1978 designed to enhance tanker safety for adoption by parties to the SOLAS Convention (q.v.).

Solicitor
1. A lawyer who prepares deeds, manages cases and acts as advocate in inferior courts.
2. A person authorised by an insurance agent to solicit and receive proposals for insurance (U.S.).

Solidarity
The principle underlying pay-as you-go pension systems that future contributors will pay what is necessary to meet pensions becoming due.

Solidarity fund
A reserve in an occupational pension fund into which profits (e.g. on withdrawal of a member) are paid so that pensions to other members may be augmented.

Solvency margin
The extent to which the realisable assets of an insurance company exceed its liabilities.

Sonic bangs
Pressure waves projected from the edges of an aircraft that is travelling at supersonic speed. Damage caused thereby is excluded from property insurance policies in the U.K.

Sound value
The value of goods at destination if they had arrived in sound condition.

Spare parts clause
A clause in a motor insurance policy limiting the insurer's liability for the cost of spare parts no longer available from the car manufacturer.

Special acceptance
The facultative extension of a reinsurance treaty to a risk not automatically included.

Special bonus
A bonus to life assurance with-profits policyholders that is out of the ordinary course and therefore unlikely to recur.

Special condition of average
Also known as the 75% condition of average. A condition in a fire insurance policy that provides for payment of a loss to be reduced proportionately if the sum insured is less that 75% of the value of the property insured.

Special damages
Compensation at law for specified and proved items of expense.

Special Drawing Right
A unit of value, based on a number of currencies, used to regulate limits of liability under international conventions.

Special peril
A peril customarily insured in conjunction with fire, such as explosion, riot, flood, storm and tempest, earthquake, subsidence, bursting or overflowing of water apparatus.

Special records clause
A clause in a reinsurance treaty providing that if the past experience figures alter materially the reinsurer can ask for a revised rate of premium with retroactive effect.

Special reserve
A fund that an underwriting member of Lloyd's may voluntarily accumulate, in addition to his *personal reserve* (q.v.), to meet potential liabilities under insurances written for his account.

Special settlement
A procedure available to brokers in the London market whereby signing or accounting procedures are given priority in a policy signing office and claims can be paid in advance of the normal monthly settlement.

Special wording scheme
A scheme operated by Lloyd's Policy Signing Office whereby special wordings agreed by leading underwriters are coded and printed for the use of brokers.

Specialty
A contract under seal.

Specie
1. A collective term for valuables such as gold or banknotes.
2. See *Loss of specie.*

Specific exclusion
An exclusion specified in a policy either by way of restricting the cover or of drawing attention to the fact that the policy does not provide the cover referred to.

Specific insurance
1. Where two insurances cover property and one has a narrower range it is said to be more specific.
2. An insurance covering a particular risk or property or class of property as opposed to one with a wider cover such as a blanket policy.

Specific reinsurance
Facultative reinsurance

Specification
> The description in a fire insurance polity of the property insured.

Speculative risk
> Risking a sum of money with the chance of gain as well as the chance of loss, e.g., putting risk capital into a business, or wagering.

Spes successionis
> The hope or expectation of succeeding to property.

Split annuity
> The combination of an annuity certain with a deferred annuity payable after the annuity certain terminates until the death of the annuitant.

Split risk
> When parts of the insurance on a given subject matter are placed with different insurers it is said to be a split risk. For example, the owner of a fleet of motor vehicles may insure the third party risk with one insurer and the own damage risk with another.

Spontaneous combustion
> Combustion that occurs without heat being applied externally, usually through the slow oxidation of a substance which progressively raises its temperature.

Spread loss reinsurance
> A form of excess loss reinsurance under which the premium rate is determined each year by the ceding company's excess losses in x preceding years.

Spread of risk
> Arranging one's affairs so that too much of one's fortune is not at stake from a peril at any given time or place.

Spreader clause
> A clause in an aviation passenger liability policy which provides that if more than the declared number of passengers is carried in an aircraft the limit of liability per passenger is automatically reduced.

Sprinkler insurance
> Insurance against damage to property caused by the leakage of sprinklers.

Stabilisation clause
> A clause in a reinsurance treaty providing for automatic adjustments in retentions according to fluctuations in an index of costs or prices.

Stability clause
> Same as *Stabilisation clause*.

Stamp (allocated) capacity
The aggregate of the premium limits of the members of a Lloyd's underwriting syndicate in any given year of account.

Stamp duty
A tax on a formal document such as an insurance policy that may be paid by affixing or impressing a stamp.

Standard construction
A building which conformed to Standard V (now abolished) of the Fire Offices' Committee was said to be of standard construction, as distinct from fireproof, fire-resisting or non-standard construction.

Standard deviation
A statistic summarising the variation in any series of numbers. The root mean square of the deviations of a set of numbers from their arithmetic mean.

Standard fire policy
A fire policy in the standard form devised by the Fire Offices' Committee.

Standard form
A policy in a form generally accepted by insurers in a market, such as the standard form of marine insurance policy.

Standard marine clauses
Same as *Institute clauses*.

Standard slip
A standardised form of broker's slip used by brokers for placing business with Lloyd's or insurance companies.

Standard turnover
In business interruption insurance the turnover of the insured business for the period during the twelve months before the date of material damage occurring, corresponding to the indemnity period which begins on that date.

Standards of construction
Five specifications of types of building construction devised by the Fire Offices' Committee for the classification of buildings in relation to fire risk. Now replaced by four grades of construction.

Standing charges
Expenses of an enterprise that have to be met even though turnover falls as the result of some misfortune.

Stare decisis
The doctrine that a court, subject to certain exceptions, is bound to follow a precedent set in previously decided cases on the same or closely related points.

Stationary condition
> The condition of a group where the number of lives and their age-distribution remain constant, increases in age and exits being exactly balanced by new entrants.

Statistical statement
> A standard form used at Lloyd's for the provision of statistical data when a long term reinsurance contract is under negotiation.

Statute of Frauds 1677
> An Act that requires a guarantee to answer for the debt, default or miscarriage of another person to be evidenced by a note or memorandum in writing.

Statutory declaration
> A declaration made under the Statutory Declarations Act 1835, viz. a written statement of fact signed and solemnly declared to be true before a commissioner of oaths or a magistrate.

Statutory exclusions
> Exclusions under a marine insurance policy stated in the Marine Insurance Act 1906, s.55: in particular, that the insurer is not liable for any loss attributable to the wilful misconduct of the insured or (unless the policy otherwise provides) for loss proximately caused by rats or vermin, or injury to machinery not proximately caused by maritime perils.

Statutory interest policy
> An industrial life assurance policy on the life of a parent, step-parent or grandparent, permitted up to £30, by the Industrial Assurance and Friendly Societies Acts 1948 and 1958.

Statutory liability
> Liability arising by virtue of statutory provisions or a breach of them.

Statutory notice before forfeiture
> A notice prescribed by the Industrial Assurance Act 1923 that must be served on an industrial assurance life policyholder in arrears with his premiums before the policy can be forfeited.

Stipulation
> A policy condition that does not go to the root of the contract so that a breach of it does not enable the insurer to escape his liability. The insurer's remedy is a suit for damages.

Stock
> 1. The goods held by a trader for sale.
> 2. A fund of capital or debt capable of being divided into

varying segments ownership of which is evidenced by a stock certificate.

Stock declaration policy

A fire insurance policy on stock, the insured being required to make monthly or quarterly declarations of the amount at risk, the premium being adjusted at the end of the year on the basis of the average of amounts declared.

Stock insurance company

An insurance company with capital in the form of stock, as opposed to a mutual insurance company (U.S.).

Stop loss reinsurance

A form of reinsurance under which the reinsurer pays the ceding company's losses in any year to the extent that they exceed a specified loss ratio or amount, subject as a rule to some specified limit.

Storm

Violent wind, usually accompanied by rain or hail or snow; not, therefore, simply a gust of wind or heavy or persistent rain by itself.

Street book

Same as *Situation index*.

Street works bond

A bond effected in favour of a highway authority to guarantee that the roads which a developer has undertaken to provide will be provided.

Strict liability

Liability imposed by law irrespective of fault on the part of the person made liable, though often subject to certain defences.

Sub-agent

One whose services are utilised by an agent in the course of the agent's activities on behalf of his principal.

Subject approval no risk

Phrase inserted in initial form (S.A.N.R.) on a slip when the insurer does not know whether the proposer will accept the insurer's terms and requires the proposer's confirmation which must be given without delay if the insurance is to attach.

Subject premium

The premium of a direct insurer on which the premium for reinsurance is calculated.

Subject to average

A provision in a non-marine property insurance that if at the time of a loss the value of the insured property is greater than the sum insured the insurer's liability for the loss will be reduced in proportion to the under-insurance.

Subject to survey

Phrase used to signify provisional acceptance of a fire insurance pending inspection by a fire insurance surveyor whose report will be required to determine the rate and provisos to be offered.

Subjective risk

The uncertainty of an event as perceived by an individual.

Subpoena

A legal summons to appear before a court to give evidence to (subpoena ad testificandum) or to produce a document (subpoena duces tecum).

Subrogation

The right of one such as an insurer, who has indemnified another in respect of a loss, to be put in the place of that other person with regard to all his other means of recouping the loss.

Subrogation clause

A clause in an insurance policy that is a contract of indemnity which sets out the insurer's rights to *subrogation* (q.v.) and frequently extends the right, e.g., by entitling the insurer to act in the insured's name against a third party even before settling the insured's claim.

Subrogation form

A standard form used in marine insurance by signing which the insured, when a claim has arisen, acknowledges the insurer's right to claim from a third party in the name of the insured.

Subscription

The extent to which an insurer is liable under a slip or policy signed on behalf of several insurers.

Subscription market

A market where a number of underwriters are available to consider and accept insurances offered for subscription by brokers.

Subsidence

Damage to buildings by subsidence is a peril covered by modern houseowners' policies. Subsidence is strictly a vertical downward movement but has been held to include settlement (a lateral movement).

Substandard

Term used to describe insurances that have some unfavourable feature making them unacceptable on standard terms for a class.

Substandard life

A life whose health is impaired.

Substitute

1. A person granted a ticket of admission to the Room at Lloyd's in order to conduct insurance business on behalf of an underwriting member, annual subscriber or associate, by whom he is employed.
2. An obsolete term for an *underwriting agent* (q.v.) at Lloyd's.

Substituted annuity

A pension bought with the proceeds of a pension policy on which the *open market option* (q.v.) has been exercised.

Substituted contracts

When a self-employed pension policy, effected under s.226 of the Finance Act 1956, matures the policyholder may employ the proceeds to effect a policy with another insurance company that offers a better pension than the original company. The contract with the new company is known as a substituted contract.

Substitution

The replacement of one insurer by another, as where the first ceases to underwrite.

Substitution of policies

By the Industrial Assurance Act 1923, s.25(1) where the owner of an industrial life policy agrees to accept a new policy in substitution for it, then unless the value of the new policy equals or exceeds the surrender value of the old the owner is entitled to the surrender value of the old policy or to an equivalent free policy.

Sudden and unforeseen damage

The wide form of words used in a modern engineering insurance policy to cover damage to the insured plant from both internal and external causes.

Sudden death clause

A clause in a reinsurance treaty providing for its automatic termination in the event of a change in control of the ceding company, its insolvency, etc.

Sue and Labour clause

A clause in a marine insurance policy whereby the insurer accepts liability for charges incurred by the insured in seeking to preserve his property from loss or to minimise a loss that would be covered by the policy. The insured is said to sue and labour for the protection of his property.

Suez Canal clause

A clause in a marine hull policy which provides that grounding in the Suez Canal, Panama Canal and other named locations shall not be deemed to be a stranding.

Sufferance bond

A bond given on behalf of the owners of a *sufferance wharf* (q.v.) as security for the payment of customs duty.

Sufferance wharf

A wharf where the Customs Authorities allow the loading and discharge of dutiable goods.

Sugging

Posing as a market researcher for the purpose of selling.

Suicide clause

A clause in a life policy whereby the assurers may refuse to meet a claim by the estate of the life assured arising out of his death by his own hand within a specified period after effecting the insurance.

Sum insured

The sum expressed in a policy as the amount payable on the occurrence of the event insured against in the case of a benefit policy, or as the maximum of the insurer's liability under a contract of indemnity.

Sums due policy

A credit insurance policy covering sums due for services rendered.

Super profit commission

An extra profit commission payable under a property reinsurance treaty over and above the ordinary profit commission.

Superannuation Funds Office

A department of the Inland Revenue responsible for examining pension schemes to see if they can be approved as qualifying for tax relief.

Supervision

The action of the state in overseeing the operations of insurers.

Supervisory authority

The government department or public authority charged with overseeing the operations of insurers in a country; in the U.K., the Department of Trade.

Supplementary accident insurance

The addition to a life assurance of special benefits in the case of accident.

Supplementary call

See *Call*.

Supplementary contract
In marine insurance the cover granted under the Sue and Labour clause is deemed by the Marine Insurance Act 1906 (s.78(1)) to be supplementary to the contract of insurance, so that the insured may recover his expenses under the clause even though the insured may have paid a total loss under the main contract. Other cover, such as that given by the Collision clause, is also considered as a supplementary contract.

Supplier default cover
Credit insurance cover against consequential loss arising from the insolvency of a supplier.

Supply bond
A guarantee that materials will be delivered and goods produced at the times required to enable a contract to be fulfilled.

Supra
Above.

Surety company
Same as *Bonding company*.

Surplus
The excess of the assets of an insurance fund over its liabilities on a given date, as actuarially calculated.

Surplus line
1. The amount of reinsurance required after the maximum line has been declared on a reinsurance treaty or cover.
2. A risk which a broker is unable to place with insurers in his own state and for which he must therefore seek cover outside the state (U.S.).

Surplus line reinsurance
Reinsurance of a risk in excess of the reinsured's retention, the reinsurer taking a line, or part of a line, of the business equal to the reinsured's retention limit.

Surplus reinsurance
Reinsurance of amounts over a specified amount of insurance, premiums and losses being shared proportionately between insurer and reinsurer.

Surplus treaty
A reinsurance treaty whereby one or more reinsurers agree to accept amounts of reinsurance, called lines, in a certain range of values over a specified amount (line) retained by the original insurer, the losses being shared proportionately by the original insurer and the reinsurer(s).

Surrender
> The giving up of an insurance policy by the insured to the insurer before the insurance has run its full course.

Surrender of bonuses
> Under a with-profits life assurance it may be possible to surrender the accrued bonuses while maintaining the policy in force. The discounted value of the bonuses is either paid to the assured or applied to reducing future premiums.

Surrender value
> The sum payable by an insurance company upon the surrender of a long-term policy (life or permanent health) before it has run its full course.

Survey
> 1. An inspection of premises or property proposed for insurance.
> 2. An inspection of a vessel, aircraft or cargo to ascertain the cause and extent of damage or the condition of insured property.

Surveyor
> A person qualified by knowledge and skill to make a report on the condition and value of property and the cause of damage to it.

Surveyor's report
> 1. In fire and accident insurance, a report of a survey relating to property or liability offered for insurance, made for the information of an insurer.
> 2. In marine insurance, a report as to the nature and extent of damage to a vessel or cargo for which a claim has been made, or the condition of a vessel or its cargo.

Survival certificate
> A certificate that an annuitant is still living.

Survivorship annuity
> An annuity payable during the lifetime of one who has survived another.

Sympathetic damage
> Damage to cargo by way of taint or the like arising from the proximity of other cargo.

Syndicate
> A group of underwriters on whose behalf insurances are accepted, each underwriter taking a proportion of the insurance for himself, without assuming liability for the proportions taken by the other members of the group.

Syndicate constitution
    A document detailing the members of, and their shares in, a Lloyd's underwriting syndicate.
Syndicate List
    A list of the syndicates subscribing a Lloyd's policy, showing each syndicate's signed line, pseudonym, syndicate number and reference.
Syndicate Sheet
    A large sheet showing the composition of each syndicate at Lloyd's.
Syndicate stamp
    Same as *Syndicate constitution*.
Synopsis sheet
    A document used in Lloyd's non-marine claims settlements.
System of check
    The precautions taken by an employer to reduce or eliminate the possibility of loss through the dishonesty of an employee.

T

Table
    1. A tabulation.
    2. A compact scheme of numerical information.
    3. In industrial life assurance a list of premium rates for a policy of a particular type.
Table of decrements
    A table, prepared on given assumptions, showing the expected numbers out of a group of lives who will leave the group for various reasons (death, lapse, surrender).
Table of definitive numbers
    A schedule of underwriters showing their participation in a Lloyd's policy.
Table of limits
    A guide for an underwriter showing the maximum sums that an insurance company is prepared to insure on various classes of property.
Tacit renewal clause
    A clause in a long term contract of insurance whereby annual renewal is automatic unless the insurer gives notice of specified length that he will not renew.
Taint
    Damage to cargo through stowage in close proximity to other cargo which affects it adversely.

Take down
Making an entry for accounting purposes in relation to a premium or claim.

Take note
A document prepared by a reinsurer to signify acceptance of a facultative reinsurance that has been offered in a *request note* (q.v.).

Tare
The weight of a container.

Target risk
1. A large, hazardous insurance.
2. A large insurance eagerly sought by brokers or insurers.

Tariff company
An insurance company that is a member of an association which prescribes minimum premium rates.

Tariff rate
The minimum rate of premium prescribed by a trade association for an insurance of a particular class.

Tax clause
A clause in an insurance policy which provides that in the event of a return of premium becoming due any tax allowed for by the insurer on the original premium shall be deducted from the return.

Tax paid clause
A clause in an insurance policy providing that the insurer will allow a deduction from the premium in respect of tax paid by the insured by reason of effecting the insurance.

Technical profit
Profit on underwriting calculated without allowance for interest on the insurer's funds.

Technical reserves
The reserves that an insurer must hold to enable him to discharge his eventual liabilities on the insurances he has issued.

Television insurance
Insurance of all-risks type on television sets.

Tempest
A severe *storm* (q.v.).

Temporary disablement
Inability to follow one's occupation in whole or in part for a limited period, for which benefits may be payable under a personal accident insurance.

Temporary importation bond
   A bond to secure the payment of duty on goods that have
   been temporarily imported if for any reason they are not
   exported again.
Temporary life annuity
   An annuity under which the insurer's payments cease on the
   death of the annuitant or at a specified date, whichever is the
   sooner.
Temporary life assurance
   Life assurance issued for a short period or for a term of years
   at the end of which the assurer is not bound to renew.
Temporary removal clause
   A clause in a property insurance policy covering property
   when temporarily removed from the location specified in the
   policy. This extension of cover, subject to various limitations,
   is found especially in household policies on contents.
Ten-to-one policy
   A form of group pensions policy, formerly popular, which
   provided deferred annuities and a death-in-service benefit of
   ten times the value of a deceased's expected pension.
Tenant's liability
   A tenant's liability as a private householder in respect of
   accidental injury or damage to the property of a third party
   may be covered by a household policy.
   A business tenant's liability for damage to property he rents is
   usually governed by an agreement with the landlord. A public
   liability policy may be extended to cover the tenant's liability
   to the landlord for damage to the property by negligence.
Tender bond
   Same as *Bid bond.*
Tender Clause
   A clause in a marine hull policy which provides for immediate
   notification of accident and gives the insurers various rights in
   connection with repairs, including one to take tenders for
   repairs.
Term
   1. A period of insurance.
   2. The time for which anything lasts.
   3. A word used in an understood or defined sense.
   4. A condition or stipulation in an contract.
Term assurance
   Same as *Temporary life assurance.*
Term-certain
   A fixed period.

Term policy
1. A *temporary life assurance* (q.v.) policy.
2. A non-life policy written for more than a year.

Terminal bonus
A bonus on a with-profits life assurance policy added to other bonuses when the sum assured becomes payable.

Terminal funding
A system whereby in a pension fund reserves are created in respect of an employee only when the employee attains retirement age.

Termination of adventure
Under a marine time policy, the time when the insurance expires. Under a marine voyage policy the time the vessel arrives at destination. Under a marine cargo policy, the time when the insurer's liability ceases because the goods have arrived at their destination or the cover is cut short by the terms of the policy.

Termination of Adventure clause
A clause in a cargo policy which continues the cover where the adventure is terminated short of destination in circumstances beyond the insured's control.

Terms of credit
The periods prescribed in an agreement with agents or brokers for the payment of their account.

Territorial limits
The geographical limits within which an insurance is stated to operate.

Theft
The dishonest appropriation of the property of another with the intention of permanently depriving the other of it.

Theft Act 1968
An Act that revised the law relating to theft and associated offences.

Theft insurance
Insurance of property against *theft* (q.v.). The insurance is often limited to theft accompanied by forcible entry to premises.

Thieves
By the Marine Insurance Act 1906 (rule 9 of Rules for Construction of Policy) the term "thieves" does not cover clandestine theft, or a theft committed by any one of the ship's company, whether crew or passengers. Pilferage must be expressly covered if cover is required.

Third Parties (Rights against Insurers) Act 1930
Where a third party is entitled to damages from a person who becomes insolvent and who is insured in respect of his liability to the third party, the Act transfers that person's right of indemnity from his insurer to the third party.

Third party
A person who is not a party to a contract such as a contract of insurance. As used in aviation insurance the term does not include passengers in the insured's own aircraft.

Third party insurance
Insurance of one's liability to another. In aviation insurance third party insurance is differentiated from insurance of liability to passengers in the insured's own aircraft.

Third party liability
Liability of the insured to persons who are not parties to the contract of insurance.

Third party only policy
In motor insurance a policy with cover limited to the insured's liability for injury to, or damage to the property of, third parties.

Third-party sharing agreements
Agreements between liability insurers that when their respective policyholders are involved in an occurrence giving rise to a third-party claim, any settlement will be shared between the insurers without apportionment of blameworthiness.

Thirds
See *New for old* (2).

Three-year accounting
A system of insurance accounting under which profits (or losses) for a given year are not determined until the end of three years.

"Three years' average" system
A system of basing profit commission on reinsurance treaties on the profits averaged over three years.

Threshold
Same as *Franchise* (1).

Ticket policy
An insurance issued by way of ticket or coupon giving personal accident benefits for a short duration or during a journey.

Time excess
A period immediately following an insured event in respect of which period the insured must bear his own loss.

Time on risk
> A period during which insurance has applied used for the calculation of premium when for some reason the insurance has been discontinued.

Time policy
> A marine insurance policy covering a period of time as distinct from a voyage.

Title
> The rights of ownership of property such as an insurance policy or other legal interest in it.

Title insurance
> Insurance in respect of loss arising from a defect in title to real property.

To pay as cargo
> A provision in a marine policy effected to supplement a cargo policy, as where a buyer wishes to cover himself for a higher value than that fixed in the seller's policy. When issuing the supplementary policy the insurers agree that where a loss is shown to be recoverable under the original policy they will not contest the higher value.

Top-slicing
> Where a payment under a life assurance contract results in a gain, for income tax purposes, to the policyholder, the whole gain is taxable but only at the rate that would apply to the total gain divided by the number of years the contract has been in force.

Tonner policy
> 1. A marine reinsurance under which the reinsurer undertakes to pay a fixed amount if a ship in excess of a specified tonnage becomes a total loss.
> 2. An aviation reinsurance under which the reinsurer undertakes to pay a fixed amount if an air crash results in a specified number of deaths.

Tontine
> A system whereby a number of persons contribute to a fund which at the end of a specified period is divided up among the survivors by way of payment of capital or an annuity.

Top Hat scheme
> A discretionary pension scheme usually provided by means of endowment assurance for high earners.

Tornado
> A violently rotating funnel cloud of small diameter. A violent squall blowing out of thunderstorms and dust storms.

Tort
    A civil wrong.

Tortfeasor
    One who is responsible for a civil wrong.

Total disablement
    Disablement which wholly prevents a person from performing his usual occupation.

Total loss
    1. A loss of the subject matter of insurance such that it is totally lost, destroyed or damaged beyond economic repair.
    2. A loss that gives rise to payment of the full sum insured.

Total loss of part
    A marine cargo policy may provide that a loss of a whole package in loading or discharge or the loss of a whole craft load shall be treated as a total loss of that part of the cargo and hence will not be subject to a franchise.

Total loss of vessel only
    A marine insurance policy on disbursements and the like may provide that the insurers shall pay only if the vessel is a total loss.

Total loss only
    A term used in marine hull insurance and reinsurance limiting cover to payment for a total loss. A clause is likely to define whether the cover is to include arranged or compromised total losses and whether sue and labour charges and salvage charges are recoverable.

Total loss only reinsurance clause
    See *Total loss only*.

Touch and stay
    An expression in a marine insurance policy which permits a vessel to call or stay at any unspecified customary ports on the vessel's route (without deviation).

Tourist floater
    A policy covering the baggage and personal effects of travellers (U.S.).

TOVALOP
    Tanker Owners' Voluntary Agreement Concerning Liability for Oil Pollution. An agreement by most tanker owners that, subject to a limit of liability, they will remove persistent oil discharged by their tanker and will reimburse any government for expense in cleaning up oil pollution resulting from the tanker owner's negligence.

Tow and Assist Clause
A clause in a marine insurance hull policy under which the insured warrants that the ship shall not be towed except where towing is customary or the ship is in need of assistance and that the ship shall not undertake towage or salvage services under a previously arranged contract.

Tracking
A process whereby an insurer follows the rates of other insurers (U.S.).

Trade losses
The losses recognised by a trade as those to which a commodity is naturally subject during the ordinary course of transit.

Trade mark
A distinctive mark or device on or accompanying an article intended for sale to indicate by whom it is made, selected or sold.

Trade risk
A risk inherent in a trade, such as occasional breakages in a china shop, which insurers do not normally cover.

Trading warranties
A set or warranties in a marine hull policy dealing mainly with prohibition of a vessel entering specified hazardous areas.

Trailer caravan insurance
Insurance of the structure and contents of trailer caravans whether in transit or on a site.

Transfer
Endorsement of a policy to substitute a different insured.

Transfer club
Where a pension scheme has agreed with one or more other schemes that members transferring from one to another will receive favourable terms, it is said to belong to a transfer club.

Transfer of portfolio
The substitution of a new insurer for the original one in respect of all insurance business of a particular class.

Transfer pension scheme
A scheme whereby a person leaving a pension scheme uses the transfer value (q.v.) to buy a pensions policy.

Transfer risk
In credit insurance the risk that a debtor though able and willing to pay is unable to transfer the money.

Transfer value
The estimated value of a person's rights under a pension scheme on transfer out of the fund.

Transferability
Where the rules of a pension scheme so allow, a sum of money to the credit of a member who leaves the fund may be paid over to another fund of which he is becoming a member.

Transit clause
A clause in marine and aviation cargo policies providing that the cover attaches from the departure from the place of storage at a place named in the policy until the cargo arrives at a place of storage at a named destination or at some alternative place.

Transparency
A risk proposed for insurance is said to be transparent when full information about it is available.

Transshipment bond
A customs bond in respect of goods to be transferred from one ship to another.

Trapping risks
The risks of a ship or cargo being trapped by war or similar perils.

Treasury stock
1. A British Government security.
2. Shares in a company that are owned by the company itself (U.S.).

Treaty
A contract providing for a number of reinsurances over a period.

Treaty balance
The sum due from a reinsurer to an original insurer, or vice versa, under an account of premium and claims payments relating to a reinsurance treaty.

Treaty reinsurance
Reinsurance under contracts (treaties) relating to specified classes of policies.

Trend
In business interruption insurance the policy provides that adjustments are to be made in calculating the rate of gross profit and the turnover to allow for the trend of the business.

Tret
Depreciation or allowance for wear and tear.

Triangulation
A table listing premiums earned in each of several under-

writing years showing claims paid year by year expressed as a percentage of premiums. The percentages form a triangle.

Tribunalisation

A financial vetting by an association of Lloyd's underwriters of someone to whom a Lloyd's syndicate contemplates issuing a binding authority.

Triennial valuation

Life assurance companies are required to provide a periodical actuarial valuation of their funds. The Companies Act 1967, s.79, reduced the maximum period between valuations from five years to three.

Trivial pension

A very small pension that the Inland Revenue will permit to be commuted for a lump sum.

True premium

A life assurance premium for a period of less than a year which is not an instalment of the annual premium and is not therefore payable if it does not fall due until after the death of the life assured, in contrast to an instalment of an annual premium.

Trust

A device of English law whereby the legal ownership of property is vested in persons known as trustees who hold it for the benefit of another (the cestui que trust).

Trust corporation

Defined by the Trustee Act 1925, s.68, as the Public Trustee, the Treasury Solicitor, the Official Solicitor, other officials prescribed by the Lord Chancellor, or a corporation either appointed by the court in any particular case to be a trustee, or entitled by rules made under the Public Trustee Act 1906, s.4(3), to act as custodian trustee.

Trust deed

A formal document creating a trust, stating its objects, naming trustees and defining their powers and duties.

Trustee

A person in whom the legal ownership of property is vested for the benefit of another (the cestui que trust).

Trustee security

A security in which trustees are empowered to invest trust funds with no restriction, unless the trust deed otherwise directs.

Trustees in general average

Two persons appointed by the shipowner and the cargo owners respectively to be trustees of a general average fund.

Tsunami
A swift sea wave of great height resulting from an earthquake.

Turnover
The trading receipts of a business

Twenty-four hours clause
A clause attached to a marine cargo policy, usually on refrigerated goods, where delay is an insured peril, including the risk of breakdown of machinery. The clause makes claims payable only where the breakdown lasts for 24 hours or more.

Twisting
Inducing a life assurance policyholder to lapse or cancel a policy in order to replace the policy with another to the detriment of the policyholder.

Two conditions of average
A provision found in floating fire insurances on merchandise in warehouses and the like. The insurance is made *subject to average* (q.v.) and in addition it is provided that if the property insured is the subject of a more specific insurance, that insurance shall be applied first, with the policy bearing the two conditions of average applying only to the uninsured balance.

Two plane warranty
A provision in an aviation excess of loss reinsurance which relieves the reinsurer of liability unless two or more aircraft are involved in the same loss occurrence.

Two rig warranty
A provision in a marine excess of loss reinsurance which relieves the reinsurer of liability unless two or more rigs are involved in the same loss occurrence.

Two risks warranty
A provision in a property reinsurance catastrophe treaty that the reinsurer will be liable only in respect of claims where at least two risks are involved in one event.

Two vessel warranty
A provision in a marine hull excess of loss reinsurance which relieves the reinsurer of liability unless two or more vessels are involved in the same loss occurrence.

Typhoon
A violent cyclonic wind in the North West Pacific and the China Seas; a hurricane.

U

Uberrima fides
Utmost good faith (q.v.).
(Uberrimae fidei = of the utmost good faith.)

Ullage
The natural loss of liquids in cargo.

Ultimate mortality table
A table showing the mortality experienced by lives who have survived at least a given number of years, known as the *select period* (q.v.).

Ultimate net loss
A ceding insurer's loss calculated for the purpose of a claim under an excess of loss reinsurance. Usually defined as the sum paid by the ceding insurer in settlement of the loss, less deductions for recoveries, salvage and claims on other reinsurances, and including adjustment expenses but not the ceding insurer's office expenses and employees' salaries.

Ultimate table
Same as *Ultimate mortality table.*

Ultra vires
Beyond the powers.

Umbrella arrangement
An arrangement between a Lloyd's broker and a non-Lloyd's broker whereby business is transacted at Lloyd's by the non-Lloyd's broker using the Lloyd's broker's slips. Also known colloquially as a piggy-back or flag of convenience arrangement.

Umbrella cover
1. Cover providing excess limits over the normal limits of liability policies and giving additional excess cover for perils not insured by the primary liability policies.
2. In reinsurance, cover against an accumulation of losses under one or more classes of insurance arising out of a single event.

Umbrella liability policy
A comprehensive liability policy.

Umpire
An arbitration clause in an insurance policy or reinsurance treaty often provides for the appointment of two arbitrators, one by each party to the dispute, and for the arbitrators to agree to appoint a third person, known as an umpire, who will reach a decision if the two arbitrators disagree.

Unauthorised insurance
Insurance by an insurer who has not been admitted to transact business in the state where the insured is situated.

Unbundled
When a policy, e.g., an engineering policy, provides services as well as insurance, and the insurer is willing to provide the services alone, they are said to be unbundled.

Under-average risk
A risk that is considered below the normal standard of its class for the purpose of insurance.

Under-insurance
Insurance that is not adequate in terms of the sum insured to provide for full payment of a loss.

Underlying insurance
1. The original insurance as distinct from an excess insurance.
2. In excess of loss reinsurance the insurance that is below the layer of cover under consideration.

Underlying premium
Same as *Base premium*.

Undervalued policy
A policy in which the value of the property insured is understated.

Underwriter
1. An insurer.
2. An individual who determines the acceptability of an insurance and specifies terms for it.
3. A person who solicits business on behalf of an insurer (U.S.).

Underwriting
Insuring.

Underwriting agent
1. A person authorised to accept insurances on behalf of an insurance company as its agent.
2. At Lloyd's a person who, without himself incurring any underwriting liability, (a) manages an underwriting syndicate (a managing agent) or (b) acts for an underwriting member in all respects other than managing an underwriting syndicate (a members' agent) or (c) acts as both a managing agent and a members' agent.

Underwriting and claims control clause
A clause in a reinsurance treaty reserving control of underwriting and claims negotiation to the reinsurer.

Underwriting cover
Same as *Working cover*.

Underwriting profit
> The profit derived from the transaction of insurance or reinsurance exclusive of interest on investments.

Unearned premium
> 1. Premium in respect of an insurance where the risk has never attached.
> 2. Where an insurance has attached, that part of the premium that relates to the period of insurance still to run.

Unearned premium insurance
> Insurance added to an aviation hull policy to provide for a return of part of the premium if the policy terminates prematurely on the occurrence of a total loss.

Unearned premium reserve
> A fund kept by a non-life insurer to provide for claims that may arise in the future under insurances that are still in course. It was formerly common to reserve 40% of premium income but in direct insurance more exact methods now prevail, e.g., the reservation of 1/365 of each premium for every day that the insurance has still to run.

Unemployment insurance
> Social insurance providing benefits for periods during which a person is unable to obtain work.

Unexpired risks reserve
> See *Unearned premium reserve*. It is not always sufficient to reserve a proportion of premiums based on the assumption that all insurances run for a year. Contingency insurances, for example, are paid for by a single premium to cover a claim whenever it may arise in the future.

Unfair calling cover
> Insurance against the risk that the principal under an unconditional bond will, without good cause, call on the surety to pay.

Unfunded scheme
> A scheme where pensions are paid out of current income.

Uninsurable risk
> A risk that no insurer will accept. This may be because the hazard is too great or cannot be quantified, or because it is a *business risk* (q.v.) or a *trade risk* (q.v.) which an entrepreneur is expected to bear himself.

Uninsured Standing Charges clause
> A provision in a business interruption policy that if any standing charges of a business are uninsured a proportionate reduction for a claim for increased cost of working shall be made in their respect.

Uninsured working expenses
Defined in a business interruption policy as purchases, carriage, packing and freight (other than the insured's own) and wages.

Unit-linked life assurance
Same as *Linked life assurance.*

United Kingdom limits
Small craft insurance is often confined to United Kingdom limits, namely, the territorial waters of the British Isles.

United Nations Convention on the Carriage of Goods by Sea 1978
This Convention recommended rules, to be known as the *Hamburg Rules* (q.v.) regulating shipowners' liabilities in respect of cargo.

Universal life plan
A flexible form of life assurance where the policyholder may vary from time to time both the premium and the allocation of premium between investment and death risk.

Unless caused by
A marine cargo insurance may provide that a franchise shall apply unless a loss is caused by the vessel and/or craft being stranded, sunk, on fire, in collision and/or contact with any substance, including ice but excluding water.

Unless General
Term used in a marine insurance policy to make it clear that the franchise does not apply to general average.

Unlicensed reinsurance
Reinsurance effected with a reinsurer not licensed to do business in the state concerned.

Unvalued policy
A property insurance policy where the sum insured has not been agreed by the insurer in advance as the actual value of the property. In the event of a loss, therefore, the value is open to discussion with a view to the insured being indemnified against his true loss up to the sum insured.

Up and Down Clause
Same as *Escalator Clause.*

Uplift
Increase in the value of benefits from a pension plan arising from a difference between guaranteed and current annuity rates.

Use and occupancy
A form of business interruption insurance (U.S.).

Utmost good faith
Insurance contracts are one of a limited class that requires the

parties (insurer and insured) to exercise the utmost good faith in their dealings with each other. Specifically the proposer of an insurance must disclose all material facts which would influence a prudent insurer in deciding whether to accept the insurance and if so on what terms.

V

Valuation Clause

A clause in a marine insurance hull policy which provides that in ascertaining whether a ship is a *constructive total loss* (q.v.) the insured value shall be taken as the repaired value and that no claim for constructive total loss based on the cost of recovery and/or repair shall be recoverable unless such cost would exceed the insured value.

Valuation linked scheme

A scheme for the calculation of premiums for the insurance of buildings whereby one rate is applied to the base value of the property and a lower rate to the additional value insured to provide against inflation.

Value

The premium for most property insurances is based on a value of the property estimated by the insured. In marine insurance it is customary to issue valued policies whereby the insurer accepts the insured's valuation in the absence of fraud. In fire insurance unvalued policies are the rule. Insurances on buildings are commonly for reinstatement value. Market value is the guide for other property unless the insurance is written on a reinstatement or new-for-old basis.

Value Added Tax cover

Credit insurance cover applying to the VAT element of sales invoices.

Valued as original

A marine reinsurance term making it clear that the reinsurance policy is a valued policy and that the value is the same as in the original policy though not all the cover is necessarily reinsured.

Valued policy

A policy under which the insurers agree in advance that the value of the property insured, as stated in the policy, shall be conclusively taken as the value, in the event of a total loss, barring fraud or, in the case of cargo, gross over-valuation.

Values at risk

The values of property insured or proposed for insurance.

Values policy
A form of marine reinsurance under which the reinsurer undertakes to pay a fixed amount if a ship in excess of a specified value becomes a total loss.

Variable annuity
An annuity the annual payment of which varies with the level of security prices.

Variance
The mean of the squares of the deviations from the mean of a number of observations.

Vending machine insurance
A form of all risks insurance on vending machines.

Vested rights
Provision in a pension scheme for an employee who leaves his employment before he is entitled to a pension to retain a right to a pension ultimately in respect of his pensionable service while a member of the scheme.

Vesting
Entitlement to a right, e.g., to a reversionary bonus under a life policy.

Violent and forcible means
Theft insurance cover may be restricted to theft following entry to premises by violent and forcible means. The sliding back of the latch of a lock by means of an instrument has been held to be a violent and forcible entry.

Vis major
Same as *Force majeure*.

Vocational Name
A member of Lloyd's who has signed an undertaking that he will make the business of Lloyd's his vocation.

Void
Without legal effect.

Voidable
Term used of a contract that may be avoided at the instance of a party to it but if not challenged is effective.

Volenti non fit injuria
The doctrine that a person who willingly takes a risk cannot complain if injury results from it. This defence has been removed in respect of claims by injured passengers in a motor vehicle by the Road Traffic Act 1972, s.148(3).

Voluntary excess
An *excess* (q.v.) which the insured agrees to bear in consideration of a reduction in premium.

Voyage policy
> A marine insurance policy covering a ship for a voyage, as distinct from a time policy.

W

Wafering
> Inserting a sheet of paper in a folded policy.

Wagering contract
> A policy of insurance where the insured has no bona fide insurable interest and no reasonable expectation of acquiring one. Such a policy is void.

Wages declaration
> A return by an insured of wages paid during a period of insurance, for the purpose of calculation of the appropriate premium.

Waiter
> A uniformed attendant at Lloyd's.

Waiting period
> 1. A period elapsing after the inception of an insurance during whch, if the event insured against occurs, the insurers will be under no liability for its occurrence.
> 2. A period of employment before an employee becomes eligible to join his employer's life assurance or pensions scheme.

Waiver
> The surrender or a right by express words or by the conduct of one who, after he has become aware of the right, fails to exercise it.

Waiver clause
> A clause in a marine insurance policy which preserves the respective rights of the insurer and the insured if either takes action to preserve the insured property from loss. The clause provides that any such action shall not be construed as a waiver or acceptance of abandonment.

Waiver of premium
> An agreement by an insurer to forgo a premium in certain circumstances, e.g., under a life assurance policy if the assured is totally disabled.

War
> The employment of force between governments or entities essentially like governments.

War (and Civil War) exclusion clause
> A clause in non-marine insurance policies, other than life,

excluding liability for losses consequent on war, invasion, act of foreign enemy, hostilities (whether war be declared or not), civil war, rebellion, revolution, insurrection, or military or usurped power.

War etc.
In marine insurance this term is taken to mean the perils of war, strikes, riots, civil commotions and malicious damage.

War perils
In marine insurance this term is taken to mean the perils of capture, seizure, arrest, restraint or detainment of princes or peoples, men of war, engines of war, mines, torpedoes or any hostile act.

War risk cancellation
War risk is often covered by marine insurance policies but they may contain a provision for cancellation of war risk cover after 7 (or 14) days' notice. Hull war clauses provide for instant termination of cover if a major war breaks out, viz., a war between any of five countries — the U.K., U.S.A., U.S.S.R., France and China. In aviation insurance war risk cover on cargo is subject to 7 days' notice of cancellation. On hulls cancellation is at 48 hours' notice or is immediate in the event of a major war.

War risk insurance
Not available for land risks on property or liability. It is presumed that in the event of war the Government will make provision. War risk is not at present excluded from life assurance policies in general. It can be covered in respect of marine and aviation.
Cf. *War risk cancellation.*

War risks agreement
An agreement among insurers not to insure property on land against war risks.

War Risks Insurance Act 1939
An Act empowering the Government to insure business stocks against war risks.

Warehouse bond
A bond issued to a warehouse keeper to secure the payment of duty on goods in store when they leave the warehouse.

Warehouse risk
The insurance of goods whilst in warehouse by a marine insurer. The risk is covered if within the ordinary course of transit. A marine insurance cargo policy may be extended to cover warehouse risk (often fire risk only) outside the marine policy cover, customarily for up to 30 days.

Warranted free from average (unless general)
Term applied to a marine insurance policy that does not cover partial loss (other than a general average loss).

Warranted free from particular average
Term applied to a marine insurance policy to make clear that the policy does not cover partial loss except a general average loss.

Warranty
1. In a contract of insurance, either (a) a promissory undertaking by the insured that some particular thing shall or shall not be done, or that some condition shall be fulfilled, or that a particular state of facts is affirmed or negatived. It must be exactly complied with. A breach entitles the insurer to deny liability; or (b) a requirement by the insurer as to some limitation of cover, e.g., "Warranted free of capture and seizure".
2. In a contract other than a contract of insurance, a collateral stipulation, the breach of which gives a right to claim damages but not to avoid the contract.

Water damage insurance
Insurance against damage caused by storm, flood or bursting or overflowing of water tanks, apparatus and pipes. Damage resulting from sprinkler leakage is separately insurable.

Waterborne Agreement
An agreement by marine insurers not to insure goods against war risk except when on board an ocean-going vessel with a time limit after arrival of port of destination.

Wear and tear
In property insurance damage by wear and tear is excluded.

Weather insurance
Insurance against loss caused by adverse weather conditions such as rainfall causing the cancellation of an outdoor sporting event or wind leading to the abandonment of ballooning or hang-gliding.

Weight and height table
A table used in life assurance underwriting showing the average weight of a man or woman of a given height. Appreciable overweight in particular increases the hazard and may lead to rating up.

Wet risks
A Lloyd's term for non-marine risks connected with the sea.

Whole account treaty
A reinsurance treaty covering all the insurances written in a section of the ceding insurer's business. Thus if an under-

writer had reinsured his marine account on a whole account basis the reinsurance would apply to *incidental non-marine business* (q.v.) written in his marine account.

Whole life assurance
Permanent life assurance under which the sum assured becomes payable only on the death of the life assured. The premium is usually payable annually throughout life but the policy may provide that it shall cease after a given number of years or at a given age. Alternatively a single premium may be charged.

Whole turnover insurance
Credit insurance may be effected either on the whole of the insured's business (whole turnover) or in respect of specified accounts only.

Widower's pension
A pension payable to a widower on the death of his wife who has been a member of a pension scheme.

Widow's annuity
An annuity payable to a married woman under a pension scheme after the death of her husband.

Widows' benefits
1. National insurance benefits for widows.
2. Benefits in pension arrangements for employed persons or the self-employed, providing pensions and lump sums for widows.

Widow's option
An option in many pension schemes for a male member to agree to accept a reduced pension in exchange for an increased pension to his widow.

Wilful misconduct
By the Marine Insurance Act 1906, s.55(2)(a), an insurer is not liable for any loss attributable to the wilful misconduct of the insured.

Winding up
The termination of a company by order of the court.

Windstorm
Cyclones, hurricanes and high winds (U.S.).

With average
Term used to describe a marine insurance which covers both total loss and partial loss from perils specified in the policy.

With profits
Term used to indicate that the policy to which it is applied is entitled to share in any surplus shown in a valuation of the insurer's relevant fund or funds.

227

With proportion

Term used to indicate that if an annuity is in course of payment and the annuitant dies before the next payment is due the assurers will make a proportionate payment in respect of the period during which he was alive.

Withdrawal option

A choice open to someone withdrawing from a pension scheme as to what should be done with the rights that have accrued to him under the scheme.

Withdrawal plan

A plan allowing for the assured under a single premium bond to make periodical withdrawals of money thereby reducing the value of the bond. For annual withdrawals up to 5% for 20 years income tax liability is deferred.

Without benefit salvage

By the Marine Insurance Act 1906 (s.4), a marine policy effected "without benefit of salvage to the insurer" is deemed to be a gaming or wagering contract. The issuing or effecting of such a policy is a criminal offence under the Marine Insurance (Gambling Policies) Act 1909.

Without prejudice

Term used in discussion and correspondence. Where there is a dispute or negotiations for a settlement and terms are offered "without prejudice" an offer so made or a letter so marked and subsequent letters in an unbroken chain cannot be admitted in evidence without the consent of both parties concerned.

Without profits

Term used in life assurance to denote that the policy is not entitled to share in the profits of the assurance company.

Without proportion

Term used to indicate that if an annuitant dies no payment is due to his estate in respect of the period elapsing between the last payment of the annuity and his death.

Work in progress cover

Credit insurance to protect a manufacturer who has to incur expense or enter into contracts with suppliers against the default of the prospective purchaser of the finished product.

Working cover

An excess of loss reinsurance with a stratum of cover in which frequent losses are expected as distinct from isolated exceptional losses.

Working layer
> A layer of excess of loss reinsurance in which frequent claims are likely to arise.

Working member (or Working Name)
> An underwriting member of Lloyd's who occupies himself principally with the conduct of business at Lloyd's by a broker or underwriting agent, or who, having retired, did so before his retirement.

Workmen's clause
> A clause in a fire insurance policy permitting the presence of outside contractors on the insured's premises.

World to World
> A provision in a marine insurance open cover permitting declarations from any place in the world to any destination.

Wrap-up insurance
> Same as *Omnibus insurance*.

Write
> Same as *Underwrite*.

Written line
> The amount of insurance that an insurer has agreed to accept when signing a slip. It may be more than the amount actually insured which is known as the *closed line* or *signed line*.

Written-paid basis
> An (unreliable) basis for calculating an insurer's loss ratio by comparing the premiums on insurances written during a period with the claims paid during the period.

Written premiums
> Total premiums received or due from all sources, including premiums for reinsurance assumed, during a period.

Y

Yacht insurance
> Insurance of yachts, usually comprising accidental loss or damage to the craft, salvage charges and sue and labour charges, and liability to third parties including passengers.

Year free of premium
> Some insurers offer insurance, especially household, under which every *x*th year's insurance is given free of premium.

Yearly renewable term assurance
> Temporary life assurance which the assurer agrees in advance may be renewed at the assured's option during a specified number of years.

Yield
> The rate of return on an investment or investments.

Yield to maturity
> The rate of return on a security that is held until it matures.

York-Antwerp Rules
> A set of rules applicable to the adjustment of general average. There are numbered rules and lettered rules. They stipulate that except as provided by the numbered rules general average shall be adjusted according to the lettered rules.

Z

Zillmerisation
> A process whereby in an actuarial valuation some acquisition costs of long-term business are not amortised but are set against mathematical reserves.

Zoning
> Dividing a territory into zones for the purpose of rating, e.g., earthquake insurance, or for the insurer's help in deciding how much insurance he can safely accept in a zone.

Institutions of Insurance

ASSOCIATION OF BRITISH INSURERS (1985)

The Association was set up in July 1985 to replace the British Insurance Association and a number of sectional trade associations, notably the Accident Offices Association, the Fire Offices' Committee, the Industrial Life Offices' Association, and the Life Offices' Association. Its objects are:-

(1) to protect and promote the interests of members in respect of all classes of insurance business and other related activities of members;

(2) to take concerted measures whenever the interests of members may be affected by the action of any government, body or other agency;

(3) to cooperate with any other association having similar objects.

The Association comprises about 400 insurance companies but not Lloyd's. The Institute of London Underwriters (marine insurers) and the Reinsurance Offices Association have retained a separate existence.

The Association has a Chairman, a board, and separate councils (the Life Insurance Council and the General Insurance Council) have been set up, each with its own chairman. Some subjects, such as investment and public affairs, are the responsibility of committees reporting directly to the board. Other subjects, such as taxation and legislation, are handled by committees that coordinate the interests of the two Councils.

ASSOCIATION OF INSURANCE TEACHERS (1984)

The Association was formed to aid the professional development of insurance teachers, encourage contact between them, and provide a channel of communication between insurance teachers, the insurance industry and its educational and professional organisations. Membership is open to part-time and full-time teachers. The Association publishes a bulletin and holds an annual conference on matters relating to insurance education.

AIDA

AIDA is the Association Internationale du Droit de l'Assurance (International Association of Insurance Law), founded in 1962 as the result of initiatives taken in Germany and Italy. It has numerous national chapters, of which the British Insurance Law Association is one, and organises every four years a world congress of insurance law.

ASSOCIATED SCOTTISH LIFE OFFICES (1841)

The centralisation of Scottish life assurance companies enabled the managers of the offices to meet regularly from an early date and resulted in the formation of the first trade association in life assurance. The membership comprises the chief officers of nine companies with head offices in Edinburgh or Glasgow.

The object of the Association is the advancement of the business of life assurance with special reference to the interest of Scottish offices by promoting uniformity of practice among the offices in matters of general administration, by watching over all legislative measures bearing on life assurance with a view to joint action in regard to them, and by affording opportunities for consultation and cooperation on all matters affecting the common interests of the offices.

In most matters the Association is able to make common cause with the Association of British Insurers (q.v.) established in London. The two associations therefore work closely together.

ASSOCIATION OF AVERAGE ADJUSTERS (1869)

The Association was formed to group experts in loss adjustments in marine insurance, particularly in regard to hulls and hull interests and with special reference to general average adjustments on behalf of shipowners. It has framed Rules of Practice under five heads, (A) General Rules, (B) General Average, (C) York/

Antwerp Rules, (D) Damage and Repairs to Ship, (E) Particular Average on Goods. In addition it adopts Uniformity Resolutions on matters of lesser importance on which uniformity of practice is desirable.

By the rules of the Association representative members (who are appointed by underwriting bodies as well as by shipowners, merchants and similar institutions) may propose resolutions intended to become Rules of Practice. If accepted by a majority at a general meeting a resolution becomes a probationary Rule which is kept under review by a committee of the Association and, if accepted by a two-thirds majority at the next general meeting, becomes a definitive Rule.

Adjusters generally follow the Rules of Practice. If they feel it advisable to deviate from them they are required to note this fact in their adjustment and explain why.

ASSOCIATION OF BURGLARY INSURANCE SURVEYORS (1953)

This Association of surveyors employed by insurers to survey premises from the point of view of security against theft has as its objects to seek to improve all aspects of security of premiums, property and persons; the collection, collation and dissemination of information concerning security equipment and services; and the promotion of occasional social events.

ASSOCIATION OF INSURANCE AND RISK MANAGERS IN INDUSTRY AND COMMERCE (1963)

The Association was founded as the Association of Insurance Managers in Industry and Commerce. "Risk Managers" was subsequently added to its title. The objects of the Association are to provide a forum for the exchange of views between those engaged in insurance and risk management in industry and commerce; to promote a better understanding of risk management and its techniques; and to form a representative body of opinion where necessary.

The Association is governed by a council of thirteen.

It is, in effect, a body representing corporate buyers of insurance who not only administer corporate insurance programmes but are prepared to use non-insurance techniques in the management of risk where it can be demonstrated that their use is advantageous.

ASSOCIATION OF CONSULTING ACTUARIES

This is a professional association of Fellows of either the Institute or the Faculty of Actuaries who are engaged in full-time consulting practice.

ASSOCIATION OF PROFESSIONAL, EXECUTIVE, CLERICAL AND COMPUTER STAFF

APEX, a trade union which had 150,000 members in 1979, counts some insurance staff among its membership.

ASSOCIATION OF SCIENTIFIC, TECHNICAL AND MANAGERIAL STAFFS (Insurance Staffs' Section) (1968)

ASTMS is a trade union which in 1970–71 absorbed in rapid succession the staff associations of the Prudential and the Royal and the Union of Insurance Staffs, formerly the Guild of Insurance Officials (1919). Its growth has been helped by the need felt by many small unions for central services which their resources cannot supply. In 1986 its insurance staffs' section had a membership of nearly 80,000. It negotiates pay and conditions in some 48 companies and institutions.

ASSOCIATION OF UNDERWRITERS AND INSURANCE BROKERS IN GLASGOW (1818)

This Association is composed of marine insurance companies and insurance brokers in Glasgow. It is carried on as a centre for marine insurance business and to protect the interests of underwriters and brokers.

ASSURANCE MEDICAL SOCIETY

The Society, which comprises medical advisers to insurance companies, exists for the discussion of the medical aspect of subjects connected with life and other forms of insurance with a view to obtaining increased information and greater unity of opinion.

The Society holds meetings and participates in periodical international congresses.

ASTIN (1957)

ASTIN (Actuarial Studies in Non-Life Insurance) is a section of the International Actuarial Association (q.v.) for the promotion of mathematical research in non-life insurance.

Membership is open, on payment of an additional subscription for registration, to all members of the International Actuarial Association.

ASTIN publishes a bulletin and holds periodical colloquia for members at which papers are presented.

AVIATION INSURANCE OFFICES ASSOCIATION (1949)

The Association is the trade association of companies transacting aviation insurance in the United Kingdom. Its objects are to constitute an official body representative of its members to promote and protect their interests, to promote joint action, to provide a medium of circulation of information among members, and to assist in the better conduct of aviation insurance.

The association works closely with Lloyd's Aviation Underwriters' Association. One of its first acts was to form a joint technical and clauses committee with that body.

BANKING INSURANCE AND FINANCE UNION

Formerly the National Union of Bank Employees this trade union was renamed in 1979 to mark the fact that it had been recruiting a number of members from insurance and other financial occupations in competition with the Association for Scientific, Technical and Managerial Staffs which had itself entered the banking field. BIFU's membership is still predominantly in banks but is also substantial in three large insurance groups.

BERNE UNION

See International Union of Investment and Credit Insurers.

BIPAR

BIPAR is the Bureau International des Producteurs d'Assurances et de Réassurances, or the International Association of Insurance and Reinsurance Producers, including both agents and brokers. It is thus an international trade association in which the British Insurance Brokers Association plays a part.

BRITISH INSURANCE (ATOMIC ENERGY) COMMITTEE (1957)

The Committee was constituted by insurance companies and Lloyd's underwriters to insure public liability and material damage risks of atomic installations. It operates pools for home, Canadian, German and general foreign risks, each company and Lloyd's syndicate designating what capacity it will allocate to the pool concerned.

BRITISH INSURANCE BROKERS ASSOCIATION (1978)

The Association is a trade association formed upon the merger of four previous associations, the Corporation of Insurance Brokers, the Association of Insurance Brokers, the Federation of Insurance Brokers, and Lloyd's Insurance Brokers' Association.

It is governed by a Council comprising some forty representatives elected from 23 regions. It has a network of specialist committees, among them the Insurance Brokers Reinsurance Committee, the United Kingdom Insurance Brokers' European Committee (U.K.I.B.E.C.), the United Kingdom Credit Insurance Brokers' Committee (U.K.C.I.B.C.) and a Smaller Brokers' Committee. Lloyd's Insurance Brokers' Committee maintains on an autonomous basis links with the Committee of Lloyd's in Lloyd's matters.

The Association publishes a monthly magazine, a technical bulletin and life and motor digests. It provides a forum for debate by members and through its regional organisation offers facilities for every broker to take part in its affairs.

Among the Association's programmes are ones for education and training, technical information and consumer relations.

The Association also exercises professional discipline over its members.

BRITISH INSURANCE LAW ASSOCIATION (1963)

The Association is the United Kingdom Chapter of the International Association for Insurance Law (AIDA). It was formed to consider and discuss matters of interest in the law relating to insurance, including social insurance. Membership is both corporate and individual.

The Association holds meetings and periodically forms study

groups. Its members participate in the quadrennial world congresses of insurance law, held each time in different cities, usually in Europe. A bulletin is published about four times a year. The Association has a Scottish branch in Edinburgh.

BRITISH INSURERS' INTERNATIONAL COMMITTEE (1966)

The Committee (until 1985 the British Insurers' European Committee) is the U.K. national association member of the European Insurance Committee (q.v.). On behalf of all British insurers it represents their interests in international organisations, including the E.E.C. and G.A.T.T. It expresses the views of British insurers on matters under discussion to the organisations and to government departments.

The Committee consists of a chairman and two deputies, appointed by the member organisations.

BRITISH LIFE ASSURANCE TRUST FOR HEALTH EDUCATION (1966)

This is a charity set up by the Life Offices' Association and the Associated Scottish Life Offices jointly with the British Medical Association. Its objects are to promote the use of educational technology for improved popular health education and medical and paramedical training through the setting of standards, the dissemination of information, and the organisation of research and development projects partly financed from other sources. A Centre for Individual Learning Materials was created in 1972.

BRITISH MARINE UNDERWRITERS' ASSOCIATION

A description used for Lloyd's Underwriters' Association and the Institute of London Underwriters when acting in concert as in the organisation of the annual conference of the International Union of Marine Insurance at Edinburgh in 1979.

CHARTERED INSTITUTE OF LOSS ADJUSTERS (1942)

The Institute was founded in 1942 as the Association of Fire Loss Adjusters. It received a Royal Charter in 1961.

CHARTERED INSURANCE INSTITUTE (1897)

The Chartered Insurance Institute is the educational and professional body for persons engaged or employed in insurance. It was formed as a federation of local insurance institutes which had earlier been established in various cities of the United Kingdom. The federation became the Insurance Institute of Great Britain and Ireland in 1908 and was incorporated by Royal Charter in 1912.

At the core of the Institute's work is the provision of examinations in insurance which lead to the award of diplomas of Associateship and subsequently of Fellowship to successful candidates who have worked for a specified period in insurance. In 1986 the Institute had 52,000 members, including 6,105 overseas. Of these 23,250 were Associates and 9,300 Fellows.

The Institute provides postal tuition for its examinations and encourages the provision of classes in institutions of further education. It has a College of Insurance which offers courses and conferences, including management courses.

It conducts a careers information service covering the whole of the insurance industry.

In furtherance of its educational work the Institute publishes a journal, issued three times a year. It offers prizes for papers by members on insurance topics.

The Institute maintains a large reference and lending library in London.

Members in the United Kingdom are also members of one of the Institute's 89 local insurance institutes, which arrange local educational and social programmes of their own. The largest, the Insurance Institute of London, forms many advanced study groups to consider and report on specific topics relating to insurance. The reports are published and circulated widely.

Outside the United Kingdom the Institute has six associated insurance institutes in the Republic of Ireland and over 40 affiliated institutes in other countries, principally in present or former Commonwealth countries.

The Institute is governed by a Council of over 100 members, appointed almost exclusively by local and associated institutes.

COMPANY OF INSURERS (1979)

The Company of Insurers is a society of individuals formed to be a City Guild (or Livery Company) of which there are now upwards of 90 in the City of London. Guilds were originally craft guilds with responsibilities for the conduct of members of their craft but nowadays only a few retain such responsibilities, such as the Goldsmiths' Company in respect of the hallmarking of goods made in precious metals. The name "livery company" is derived from the assumption of a distinctive dress or livery by guild members in the fourteenth century.

The Company has a Master, a Senior Warden, a Junior Warden and a Court of eighteen members. Its objects are social and charitable.

CRIMINAL INJURIES COMPENSATION BOARD (1964)

The Board administers the Criminal Injuries Compensation Scheme, set up by the Government to make payments of compensation to the victims of violent crime and to those injured in attempts to prevent crime or apprehend criminals. The Board consists of a chairman of wide legal experience and other legally qualified members appointed by the Home Secretary and the Secretary of State for Scotland after consultation with the Lord Chancellor. In 1986 it was decided to put the Board's work on a statutory basis.

DEPARTMENT OF TRADE AND INDUSTRY (INSURANCE DIVISION)

The Insurance Division exercises government supervision over insurance in Great Britain. It is headed by an Under Secretary and has a staff of some 80. It also uses the services of lawyers and accountants in the Department and of actuaries in the Government Actuary's Department.

The Division administers the Insurance Companies Acts. It considers plans of intended operation submitted by companies proposing to transact insurance business which must be controlled and managed by fit and proper persons. All insurers are required to submit periodic returns relating to their business. These are scrutinised with a view to ensuring as far as possible that each insurer will be able to discharge its liabilities. The Department has various powers, for example, it may call for information from an insurance company, inspect its books, direct that its investments be held by trustees, or forbid the company to accept further new business. In the last resort it may petition for the winding up of a company.

The Division drafts and administers regulations issued under the Acts which cover various aspects of consumer protection such as the allowance of a cooling-off period for life assurance proposers. It also monitors the Insurance Brokers Registration Council and the Policyholders Protection Board. It maintains liaison with supervisory authorities in the E.E.C. and takes a prominent part in negotiations on insurance matters within the E.E.C. and elsewhere.

EUROPEAN INSURANCE COMMITTEE

This is an association of insurers in Europe which takes an active part in negotiations with international bodies and in seeking to defend the right of insurance companies to carry on their business with a minimum of government intervention. The secretariat is in Paris.

EXPORT CREDITS GUARANTEE DEPARTMENT (1919)

This is a government department responsible to the Secretary of State for Trade, originally founded to facilitate exports to East European countries, but now world-wide in its scope. It operates under the Export Guarantees and Overseas Investment Act 1978 with an advisory council of businessmen.

Its principal object is to encourage British exports by making available export credit insurance to British firms selling overseas, to guarantee repayment to British banks and, in certain cases, to refinance a proportion of banks' medium and long-term credit advances. It also insures new British investments overseas against political risks such as war, expropriation and restrictions on remittances.

FACULTY OF ACTUARIES IN SCOTLAND (1856)

After supporting the formation of the Institute of Actuaries in London in 1848 the Scottish actuaries, a closely-knit body of men, decided that it would be desirable to have a professional institute of their own and set up the Faculty in Edinburgh in 1856.

The Faculty carries on activities similar to those of the Institute of Actuaries (q.v.) but has its own examination syllabus and conducts its own examinations. Fellowship of the Faculty is regarded as pari passu with Fellowship of the Institute. The Faculty does not grant the diploma of Associateship to persons who have not completed the whole of its qualifying examination.

The Faculty, like the Institute, has a large overseas membership.

The Faculty combines with the Institute in many activities such as the tuition service, the continuous mortality investigation and the appointment of liaison officers with universities. It took the lead in establishing the first chair of actuarial science in the United Kingdom at Heriot-Watt University.

The Faculty publishes its Transactions.

It is governed by a council of its Fellows.

FINANCIAL INTERMEDIARIES, MANAGERS AND BROKERS REGULATORY ASSOCIATION

See Securities and Investment Board.

FIRE MARK CIRCLE (1934)

This is a society with both corporate and individual membership. Its objects are to bring together persons interested in the origin and history of fire insurance offices, their fire marks and fire brigades, for the purpose of exchanging and recording information, and for the preservation of relics of the early days of fire insurance.

The Circle publishes a journal.

FIRE PROTECTION ASSOCIATION (1946)

The Association's objects are to advance the science of fire protection; to investigate the causes and spread of fire; to disseminate advice on fire protection and allied subjects; to propagate knowledge in connection with fire protection; and to cooperate with others interested in fire protection.

The Association was formed on the initiative of the Fire Offices' Committee but its membership has not been confined to the member-companies of that committee and its governing council contains, in addition to insurers, representatives of government departments, the Confederation of British Industries, the Industrial Fire Protection Association and others.

The Association provides to members, associate members and the public information and advice, training and conferences. Its many publications include a Journal. It acts as publisher to the Loss Prevention Council (q.v.), of which it is a subsidiary company.

FUEDI

FUEDI's full name is Fédération des Unions Professionnelles d'Experts en Dommages après Incendie et Risques Divers dans l'e cadre de la Communauté Européenne Économique, that is, the Federation of Professional Associations of Adjusters of Fire and other risks within the E.E.C.

It acts an an international trade association for adjusters, its membership including the Union of United Kingdom Loss Adjusters (q.v.)

GENEVA ASSOCIATION

See International Association for the Study of Insurance Economics.

GOVERNMENT ACTUARY'S DEPARTMENT

The Department is linked to the Treasury. It provides a consulting actuarial service for other government departments and has various statutory duties, for example, under the Social Security Acts.

HOME SERVICE INSURERS GROUP

This is a group of insurance companies and collecting societies who transact personal insurance of all kinds, (but principally industrial life insurance) through representatives calling at people's homes.

The Group exists to promote what is called the Home Service message. It comprises 14 insurance companies and collecting societies.

INCORPORATED ASSOCIATION OF ARCHITECTS AND SURVEYORS

This Association has a number of sections including one for fire surveyors which provides facilities for expanding the knowledge of members through lectures, discussion circles, conferences and association with other members. It issues a fire surveyors' magazine.

INDEPENDENT ADJUSTERS ASSOCIATION

An association of loss adjusters formed by firms outside the Chartered Institute of Loss Adjusters (q.v.). The two bodies are linked for international purposes in the Union of United Kingdom Loss Adjusters.

INDUSTRIAL ASSURANCE COMMISSIONER

See Registrar of Friendly Societies.

INDUSTRIAL INJURIES ADVISORY COUNCIL

The Council is constituted under the Social Security Act 1975 to consider and advise the Secretary of State on regulations and other questions relating to industrial injury benefit or its administration.

INSTITUTE OF ACTUARIES (1848)

The Institute is the professional association for actuaries in England and Wales. At its inception Scottish actuaries joined but broke away after six years to found the Faculty of Actuaries in Scotland (q.v.).

The Institute conducts examinations on which it awards diplomas of Associateship and Fellowship which now also requires an experience qualification. It provides tuition for its examinations through the Actuarial Tuition Service which is conducted jointly with the Faculty of Actuaries.

The Institute holds meetings at which papers are discussed. They are printed in its journal with a report of the discussion. Prizes and medals are awarded.

The Institute publishes a memorandum on professional conduct and practice and exercises disciplinary powers over its members.

It has a hall with a library in London. There is a students' society and local actuarial societies in Birmingham, Glasgow (for students), Manchester and Norwich, membership of which is open to members of both the Institute and the Faculty. Actuarial societies in some other countries such as Australia, India, New Zealand and South Africa, consist mainly of members of the Institute and the Faculty.

The Institute offers evidence on actuarial matters to government inquiries. It sponsors a bureau for continuous mortality investigation.

Management of the Institute's affairs is vested in a Council of thirty Fellows.

243

INSTITUTE OF ACTUARIES STUDENTS' SOCIETY (1910)

The Society was formed to assist junior members of the Institute of Actuaries to prepare for their examinations, to increase their professional knowledge, and to give them practice and confidence in public speaking. Any member of the Institute, and any member or student of the Faculty of Actuaries, is eligible for membership, also members of any other body of actuaries and university students studying actuarial subjects.

The Society holds regular meetings for the discussion of papers. It issues a journal and other publications. Its function of helping students in preparing for examinations is now discharged by the Actuarial Tuition Service run jointly by the Institute and Faculty of Actuaries.

INSTITUTE OF AUTOMOTIVE ENGINEER ASSESSORS

The Institute is a professional body for engineers who assess motor claims on behalf of insurers, whether as employees or as independent consultants.

INSTITUTE OF INSURANCE CONSULTANTS (1978)

The Institute was formed to enhance the status and ethical standards of insurance intermediaries for whom it maintains a code of conduct; to provide guidance and information to its members; and to arbitrate in disputes between members, companies and the public.

INSTITUTE OF LONDON UNDERWRITERS (1884)

The Institute was formed as a trade association for marine insurance companies active in the London market. Its membership of 20 companies at the outset has now grown to more than 100. In watching over the interests of its members the Institute acts in close cooperation with Lloyd's Underwriters Association and many other organisations.

The Institute is well-known for its specimen policy clauses which are drafted by the Technical and Clauses Committee, a joint committee of the Institute and Lloyd's. There is similar collaboration in the Joint Hull Committee (1910), the Joint Cargo Committee (1942) and other committees.

At frequent meetings of members current problems are kept under constant review. There are also weekly meetings of claims adjusters from both insurance companies and Lloyd's.

The Institute provides many services for its member companies, including the issue of policies since a Companies Combined Policy was first produced in 1942. The policy department notifies the details of risks signed on behalf of companies and of claims and returns of premiums. A central accounting scheme prepares statements for member companies and brokers and arranges settlements in major currencies.

The Institute is governed by an elected committee of 16 of whom three retire annually but are eligible for re-election. The committee elects a chairman and vice-chairman who usually hold office for two years.

INSTITUTION OF FIRE ENGINEERS (1918)

The Institution exists to promote, encourage and improve the science and practice of fire extinction, fire prevention and fire engineering.

INSURANCE BENEVOLENT FUND (1929)

The object of the Fund is to relieve necessitous circumstances arising from sickness, bereavement or personal or domestic misfortune from any cause among persons who are or have been wholly engaged or employed in insurance in the British Isles or the Republic of Ireland for not less than four years and among members or former members of the Chartered Insurance Institute or the Insurance Orphans' Fund. (The Orphans' Fund, now closed to new members, was a fund which provided for the orphans of its members in case of need.)

Benefit is paid discretionarily to persons eligible and their dependants.

Persons who subscribe a certain sum may support the Fund by becoming members but they do not have priority in receiving benefits.

The Fund is governed by a President and four other honorary officers and a committee.

INSURANCE BROKERS REGISTRATION COUNCIL (1977)

The Council was set up by the Insurance Brokers (Registration) Act 1977 for the purpose of establishing and maintaining a register of persons entitled by education and/or experience to designate themselves insurance (or reinsurance) brokers and a list of firms entitled to the designation.

The Council is empowered to approve educational institutions and qualifications for persons being educated as insurance brokers.

It must publish its register and list. It is required by the Act to draw up, and has drawn up, a code of conduct to guide the actions of insurance brokers.

The Council is also required to make rules for practising insurance brokers to ensure that they have the necessary minimum of capital and a margin of solvency and that they are not unduly dependent on any particular insurance company. Rules also govern brokers' accounting, professional indemnity insurance, and the making of grants to relieve or mitigate losses incurred through the negligence, fraud or other dishonesty of practising insurance brokers or their failure to account for money received. In this connection the Council may establish an indemnity fund or itself insure.

After due process in a disciplinary case the name of a broker who has been convicted of a criminal offence or has been adjudged by the Council to have been guilty of unprofessional conduct may be erased from the register or list.

The Council consists of twelve persons chosen to represent registered insurance brokers and five persons nominated by the Secretary of State for Trade and Industry.

INSURANCE INDUSTRY TRAINING COUNCIL (1968)

The Council is a voluntary body set up by the insurance industry:

(a) to make recommendations to employers on training in insurance, the further education to be associated with training and the standards to be attained;

(b) to encourage the provision of adequate facilities for training in insurance and associated further education.

Membership of the Council is drawn from persons nominated by organisations of employers and employees, and educationists.

The Council is financed by insurance employer organisations.

246

INSURANCE OMBUDSMAN BUREAU (1981)

The Bureau was established by 44 insurance companies to handle, investigate and resolve enquiries, complaints, disputes and claims between member companies and their personal policyholders in the United Kingdom. Although financed by insurance companies, the Bureau is an independent body, aiming at impartiality in adjudication. Of its council of eight members, only two are representatives of insurance companies. The number of member companies rose by 1985 to 163.

The Bureau has a small staff headed by the Insurance Ombudsman, a solicitor. In 1985 it dealt with over 3,000 enquiries.

The Ombudsman has power to see insurance company files and, where called on by a policyholder, to adjudicate and make an award which is binding on insurance companies up to £100,000, or £10,000 in health insurance cases. Policyholders do not lose their legal rights and can take action in the courts if they reject the Ombudsman's decision.

INTERNATIONAL MARITIME ORGANIZATION (1958)

Called until 1982 the Inter-Governmental Maritime Consultative Organization, this is a United Nations Specialised Agency established to provide means for cooperation and exchange of information among governments on technical matters relating to international shipping, especially with regard to safety at sea and marine pollution caused by ships. It is responsible for calling maritime conferences and drafting maritime agreements. It has produced technical codes relating to the construction and equipment of ships and the carriage of various types of cargo such as chemicals, ores and dangerous goods.

INTERNATIONAL ACTUARIAL ASSOCIATION

The first International Congress of Actuaries was held in Brussels in 1895. A score of congresses have been held since. The International Actuarial Association exists to cooperate with national organising committees in preparing the work of international congresses and the publication of their proceedings. It seeks to promote or conduct work or research of interest to the science or practice of the actuary and to publish a bulletin which brings together information relating to actuarial science and reviews works bearing on actuarial science. Sections formed by a number of members may be organised by the Association (cf. ASTIN).

Individual Actuaries may become Ordinary Members on payment of a subscription.

The Association appoints national correspondents in each country. Its headquarters are in Brussels.

INTERNATIONAL ASSOCIATION FOR THE STUDY OF INSURANCE ECONOMICS (1973)
(also called The Geneva Association)

The Association was formed by 22 insurance companies in 8 countries "to make an original contribution to the progress of insurance by objective studies on the interdependence between economics and insurance".

The Association has looked to areas in which insurance activities come into contact with activities of other economic sectors, for example, the state, industry, banking and consumers. It promotes the economic analysis of risk and insurance. Methods it has adopted in furtherance of its aims include conferences and lectures, the commissioning of research, the award of prizes and grants to writers and researchers and the publication of papers.

The Association is supported by contributions from its members. Its headquarters are at Geneva.

INTERNATIONAL CREDIT INSURANCE ASSOCIATION

This Association, with headquarters in Zurich, was formed by credit insurance companies to study questions relating to credit insurance and to facilitate the common action of members in the interests of their national and the international economy and of their insured and the safeguarding of their own position. (Cf. International Union of Investment and Credit Insurers.)

INTERNATIONAL UNION OF AVIATION INSURERS (1934)

The Union was set up by aviation insurers and reinsurers in various countries to speak on behalf of aviation insurance interests; to provide a central office for the circulation of information; and to assist in providing for the better understanding and conduct of international aviation insurance.

Its membership consists primarily of pools, groups or associations whose members are engaged in aviation insurance or reinsurance.

INTERNATIONAL UNION OF INVESTMENT AND CREDIT INSURERS
(also called the Berne Union)

The Union groups public bodies such as the Export Credits Guarantee Department in the U.K. to work for the international acceptance of sound principles of export credit insurance and for discipline in the terms of credit for international trade; also for international cooperation in fostering a favourable investment climate and developing foreign investment insurance on a sound basis.

INTERNATIONAL UNION OF MARINE INSURANCE (1874)

The Union, more than a century old, is the international trade association for marine insurance. It holds a conference every year in a different city. Many of the problems of marine insurance arise from international transit so the Union is involved in presenting the collective view of marine insurers on points that arise, especially in the legal field.

LIFE ASSURANCE LEGAL SOCIETY

The Society was formed for the exchange of information on legal topics of common interest to life assurance companies, the discussion of such matters and the making of recommendations. Membership is primarily corporate.

LIFE INSURANCE ASSOCIATION (1972)

The Association was formed to promote professionalism among all people involved full-time in selling life assurance. It has created an association that is recognised and consulted by government and other professional organisations in matters relating to life assurance. It seeks to encourage a continual improvement in technical knowledge by introducing educational courses, seminars and lectures, and to improve business standards by eliminating unprofessional practices.

Among its activities the Association organises a large conference each year.

LIFE ASSURANCE AND UNIT TRUST REGULATORY ORGANISATION

See Securities and Investment Board.

LINKED LIFE ASSURANCE GROUP (1972)

The Group is a trade association for companies specialising in linked life assurance. Its objects are to advance the interests of ordinary long-term life assurance business by ensuring high standards of professional conduct, to provide a forum for member companies and to represent them in discussion with government departments and other bodies.

Membership overlaps with that of the Association of British Insurers (q.v.).

LIVERPOOL UNDERWRITERS' ASSOCIATION (1802)

The Association was formed on the building of the Liverpool Royal Exchange at a time when marine underwriting was transacted primarily by individuals. It had a news room and an underwriters' room in the exchange. In the middle of the nineteenth century marine underwriters began to form insurance companies, which were admitted to membership, and by 1883 the Association had become predominantly a company organisation. Its objects are similar to those of the Institute of London Underwriters with which it collaborates.

A noteworthy feature of its annual report is its systematic analysis of merchant ship losses. Oil rigs and aviation losses are also dealt with.

Regular meetings of the membership ensure a useful exchange of information.

LLOYD'S (*c.*1688)

Lloyd's is a market-place for insurance which originated in Edward Lloyd's coffee house where underwriters and insurance brokers assembled. Then, as now, portions of risks offered for insurance were accepted by underwriters from insurance brokers acting on behalf of would-be policyholders. Each underwriting member is liable only for the portion of the risk that has been accepted on his behalf. Hence one is insured at Lloyd's, not insured by Lloyd's.

The underwriting room at Lloyd's is a hall in which sit over 300 active underwriters and members of their staff. The active underwriter accepts a share of any business offered to him on behalf of a group of underwriting members who have agreed to join the syndicate he represents and to accept personal liability for a specified fraction of the business written on behalf of the syndicate. Underwriting membership in itself therefore means only the provision of capital and the acceptance of a portion of risk.

Underwriters transact business only through approved insurance brokers, referred to as Lloyd's brokers, who are required to accept responsibility for payment of the premium to the underwriter even though the broker may not have received it from the insured.

Individuals are introduced to Lloyd's and proposed for membership by firms known as underwriting agencies which manage the business affairs of members or syndicates, or both. Applicants for membership must show satisfactory evidence of possessing substantial means and make a deposit as security for their underwriting. Their personal liability is unlimited.

Business transacted at Lloyd's was originally marine insurance. In modern times non-marine insurance exceeds the marine business in volume. Long-term life assurance is not transacted at Lloyd's.

Lloyd's is incorporated by Lloyd's Acts 1871–1982. Its governing body since 1982 is the Council, comprising members elected by underwriting members ('Names') who work in or around Lloyd's, members elected by the remaining underwriting members ('External Names') and persons, not being members of Lloyd's, who are nominated to the Council with the approval of the Governor of the Bank of England. The first-mentioned constitute the Committee of Lloyd's which meets weekly and supervises the day-to-day running of the market. The Council elects a chairman annually. It has powers to make bye-laws and to discipline members, brokers and underwriting agents. The Council is responsible for the organisation of the market. It holds the deposits made by members on trust and has a central reserve fund available to meet unpaid claims if any member should default. It also makes global returns to the Department of Trade and Industry on behalf of all Lloyd's underwriters. The affairs of underwriting syndicates are subjected to a strict audit by independent accountants reporting to the Council.

The Corporation has a staff of over 2,000. It provides centrally claims offices, shipping and intelligence publications, an aviation department, a policy signing office, data processing services, advisory and legislation departments and accounting services, as well as running the premises. Publications include a daily paper, Lloyd's List, reports of shipping movements, and a series of law reports on commercial and maritime cases.

Lloyd's maintains a network of firms, known as Lloyd's Agents, all over the world. They were originally appointed in 1811 to report shipping movements and other developments of interest to underwriters. They also carry out surveys of damaged ships and cargoes. They are not concerned with the placing of insurance business. Being a Lloyd's Agent carries no payment in itself but the Agent will receive fees for services he renders.

There are a number of trade associations within Lloyd's to look after the interests of specific groups, notably Lloyd's Underwriters' Association (1909) to deal with matters affecting marine underwriters, Lloyd's Underwriters' Non-Marine Association (1910), Lloyd's Motor Underwriters' Association (1931), Lloyd's Aviation Underwriters' Association (1935), and Lloyd's Underwriting Agents' Association. Lloyd's brokers formerly had Lloyd's Insurance Brokers' Association but the Association's members disbanded it on the formation of the British Insurance Brokers' Association of which Lloyd's Insurance Brokers' Committee now forms a partly autonomous section.

LLOYD'S REGISTER OF SHIPPING (1934)

A society for classifying ships which took over Lloyd's Register in 1834. It is governed by a committee which includes Lloyd's and insurance company underwriters, shipowners, shipbuilders, marine engineers and representatives of various shipbuilding and shipping organisations. It has a world-wide staff of surveyors numbering about 2,000 and many national committees outside the United Kingdom. It publishes annual registers of ships and yachts and keeps a file of all known sea-going merchant ships of 100 grt and over. Its consulting and investigating facilities are grouped into one department, Research and Technical Advisory Services (RATAS). It maintains a research laboratory at Crawley with facilities for engineering, metallurgical and photo-elastic research.

Among its activities Lloyd's Register is responsible for the certification and classification of all types of offshore installations. It carries out surveys of ships for the issue of statutory certificates required under international conventions. It supervises construction. It inspects cold stores and various land-based installations.

LOSS PREVENTION CERTIFICATION BOARD (1985)

The Board, part of the Loss Prevention Council (q.v.), was founded for the purpose of operating approval and certification schemes to replace those formerly provided by the Fire Offices' Committee, initially for

fire detection and alarm systems
halon and carbon dioxide systems
sprinkler and water spray systems
fire resisting doors and shutters.

The Board includes representatives of government departments, insurers, manufacturers' associations and user bodies, with no one interest predominating.

LOSS PREVENTION COUNCIL (1985)

The council was formed to provide an improved technical shield against fire and other major industrial disasters. After the winding up of the work undertaken by the Fire Offices' Committee and the salvage corps provided by insurers in London, Liverpool and Glasgow, insurers decided to rationalise their technical provision designed to minimise property losses.

The council operates three wholly-owned subsidiary companies: the Loss Prevention Technical Centre (LPTC), the Loss Prevention Certification Board (LPCB), both at Boreham Wood, and the Fire Protection Association, in London. (See separate entries for each.)

The aim is to provide a total fire and loss prevention service, including

rules, codes and recommendations for protection equipment and materials
approval and certification services
testing fire protection equipment and building materials
giving information and advice
training, education and documentation
research into new and developing hazards, including toxic exposure and industrial disease.

The council works with the Association of British Insurers and Lloyd's, and acts as an approvals body on their behalf, but many of its operations are independent, for example, certification.

LOSS PREVENTION TECHNICAL CENTRE (1985)

The centre operates in three divisions.

The Standards Division, based on the resources of the former Fire Offices' Committee (Technical) Department maintains the F.O.C.'s former activities in approving appliances until they are superseded by the Loss Prevention Certification Board (q.v.), and is open to undertake other work commissioned by insurers.

The Testing Division, based initially on the resources of the Fire Insurance Research and Training Organisation at Boreham Wood seeks to exploit commercially the opportunities provided by new schemes for testing fire protection equipment, building materials and structures.

The Research Division offers advice on hazards and losses likely to arise from technological developments and new industrial processes.

MANCHESTER MARINE INSURANCE ASSOCIATION (1904)

The Association is a trade association of insurance companies transacting marine insurance in Manchester. Its objects are as widely expressed as those of the Institute of London Underwriters though in practice marine insurance in Manchester is primarily a cargo insurance market and member companies are likely to be members at head office level of the London Institute.

The Association holds formal monthly meetings and brief informal weekly meetings.

MARKET LIAISON COMMITTEE FOR REINSURANCE EDUCATION AND TRAINING

See Reinsurance Offices Association.

MOTOR CONFERENCE

The Motor Conference is the name given to the standing joint committee of the Association of British Insurers and Lloyd's Motor Underwriters' Association. This meets to discuss questions affecting motor insurance.

MOTOR INSURANCE REPAIR RESEARCH CENTRE (1969)

The Centre, known colloquially as Thatcham, from its location, was formed by the British Insurance Association and Lloyd's to control the cost and improve the standard of motor vehicle repairs.

The Centre undertakes repair work on cars and applies work study to calculate times and to recommend repair methods. It produces a parts guide, with prices, which is regularly updated. It follows new developments in car manufacture and is able to suggest to manufacturers modifications or arrangements that will result in economy of repair. It disseminates information and recommendations based on research. It provides courses for motor engineer assessors to acquaint them with the latest repair and painting methods and fosters a systematic approach to estimating.

The Centre is financed by contributions from motor insurers.

MOTOR INSURERS BUREAU (1946)

The Bureau is a company formed by insurance companies and Lloyd's underwriters transacting motor insurance in the United Kingdom to provide machinery for the implementation of an undertaking by motor insurers to the government that third parties injured in road accidents would not be deprived of damages because a motorist lacked the statutorily required third party insurance.

The Bureau is supported by contributions from motor insurers.

MUTUAL INSURANCE COMPANIES ASSOCIATION (1942)

The Association is a trade association of mutual insurance companies active in the non-life field. Its objects are the consideration of matters connected with the business of its members and the taking of measures considered expedient for the protection or furtherance of the interests of members.

NATIONAL ASSOCIATION OF PENSION FUNDS (1923)

The Association provides an advisory and information service for its members and organises conferences on pension matters. It has a wide membership including trustees of pension schemes, representatives from insurance companies, pension consultants, consulting actuaries and trade unions, as well as those concerned with statutory schemes.

255

NATIONAL SUPERVISORY COUNCIL FOR INTRUDER ALARMS LIMITED (1971)

The principal aims of the Council are to ensure a high standard of ethics, service and equipment and maintenance of installations of intruder alarm systems, to maintain a roll of approved installers; to carry out inspections of installations; and to investigate complaints. The Council seeks to make it increasingly difficult for breaking and entry while at the same time reducing the high rate of false alarms.

The Council has established a roll of approved installers of intruder alarm systems and takes disciplinary action against installers who fail to conform to standards or to the Council's rules and regulations. The Council also polices through an inspectorate the British Standards applicable to intruder alarm systems.

NATIONAL UNION OF INSURANCE WORKERS

This trade union provides for the agents or field workers of a number of industrial assurance offices.

OCCUPATIONAL PENSIONS BOARD (1973)

The Occupational Pensions Board was set up by the Social Security Act 1973. A main function is to advise the administrators of pension schemes whether scheme rules conform with statutory requirements for the preservation of benefits for scheme members who leave before normal pension age, to advise on amendments of rules proposed or needed to secure conformity and, where necessary, to make a determination as to whether rules conform.

The Board has power in certain circumstances to authorise or make modifications to scheme rules, or to direct that a scheme be wound up, if the scheme administrators do not possess the powers necessary so to act or if they can act only through procedures that would be excessively cumbersome.

The Board has a duty to advise the Secretary of State for Social Security on proposals to make regulations under social security legislation which affect occupational pension schemes. It may also advise the Secretary of State, when invited to do so, on general questions affecting occupational pensions schemes.

OFFICE OF FAIR TRADING

The Office is a government department responsible for the administration of the Fair Trading Act 1973, the Consumer Credit Act 1974 and the Restrictive Trade Practices Act 1976. Under its head, the Director General of Fair Trading, it keeps under review commercial activities in the United Kingdom, seeking to protect the consumer against unfair practices and to encourage competition. It has divisions for consumer affairs, competition policy, consumer credit and legal matters.

ONE-FIFTY ASSOCIATION (1921)

The Association was formed to advance knowledge of and interest in loss of profits insurance and the interchange of views of those knowledgeable in the subject. The title derives from the name often given to loss of profits (or business interruption) insurance, namely Consequential Loss, shortened to CL which is 150 in Roman numerals.

PERSONAL INSURANCE ARBITRATION SERVICE

A scheme supported by 26 insurance companies or groups for the settlement by arbitration of claims up to £25,000 under personal insurances including household, holiday, life and motor insurance. Consent to arbitration is required from both parties. Arbitration is free of charge to the claimant. A decision is binding on both parties.

POLICYHOLDERS PROTECTION BOARD (1976)

The Board was established by the Policyholders Protection Act 1975 to compensate policyholders and injured third parties in the United Kingdom who suffer loss because of the inability of insurance companies to meet their financial obligations and to impose levies on insurance companies and, in some cases, intermediaries to finance the operations of the Board.

The Board consists of five persons appointed by the Secretary of State for Trade and Industry.

POLICY SIGNING AND ACCOUNTING CENTRE LIMITED (1976)

The Centre provides a centralised checking and signing facility for various classes of non-marine insurance and reinsurance, thus simplifying procedures and accounting where more than one member company is involved in a risk.

The Centre has over 120 member companies.

REGISTRAR OF FRIENDLY SOCIETIES (1846)

The Chief Registrar of Friendly Societies certifies the rules of friendly societies that apply for registration. He exercises numerous functions, including a surveillance of the accounts of friendly societies, under the Friendly Societies Acts, the Building Societies Acts and other statutes.

Under the Industrial Assurance Acts and the Insurance Companies Acts the Chief Registrar, styled for this purpose the Industrial Assurance Commissioner, is charged with various functions in relation to industrial assurance companies and collecting societies. Among other powers he receives and may reject accounts and returns, awards payment of a surrender value when there is doubt as to the continued existence of the life assured, and adjudicates in disputes.

REINSURANCE OFFICES ASSOCIATION (1968)

The Association was established as a trade association for companies transacting reinsurance business to facilitate and encourage cooperation between such companies on technical matters of general interest and the study and development of reinsurance.

The Association is a trade association for companies transacting reinsurance business. Its objects are to bring such companies together, to facilitate and encourage cooperation on technical matters of general interest, and the study and development of reinsurance; also to consult with and make representations to the government in connection with transaction of reinsurance by its member companies in the U.K.

In 1985 the Association had 112 companies as members and a further 241 as correspondent members.

The Association is governed by an executive committee of ten, plus a chairman and deputy chairman. It has four standing committees — education and training, legal, taxation and finance. The Association helped to form the Market Liaison Committee for Reinsurance Education and Training (M.A.L.I.C.) which has encouraged improved facilities for education and training in reinsurance and membership of which is not confined to representatives of companies.

Member companies are brought together at the annual general meeting and at periodical forums and discussion meetings. The Association also holds a biennial international reinsurance seminar.

Technical subjects such as earthquake risks have been studied in depth and a number of published reports have resulted. The Association also publishes a bulletin which digests articles in the world press on insurance and reinsurance internationally. In addition it monitors proposed legislative measures which could affect reinsurance.

SALVAGE ASSOCIATION (1856)

The objects of the Salvage Association are to protect interests, notably those relating to insurance, in respect of shipping and cargoes and other property that is the subject of insurance. The principal function of the Association is the investigation of casualties in which insurers have an interest. Surveys are conducted to establish the nature, cause and extent of damage to property and to recommend to the parties concerned what steps should be taken about repair or otherwise. The Association will, if required, take charge of salvage operations.

Among other activities the Association will issue certificates of approval for towage and voyages. It will inspect sites proposed for the lay-up of vessels and approve arrangements proposed for mooring, etc. It also surveys shipbuilding and repair yards, and reports on the fitness for particular voyages of vessels proposed for insurance, including yachts and motor cruisers. It assists in the assessment of projects to recover oil from the sea and surveys rigs, platforms and pipelines. It protects the interest of insurers, shipowners and cargo owners when there are casualties or the danger of loss. It may draw up and negotiate salvage contracts and supervise recovery operations and the disposal of salved cargo.

The Association maintains records in respect of sunken ships and cargo since 1860. It maintains an information retrieval department.

Surveys are also conducted on nuclear and conventional power plant, boilers, electrical plant and equipment, dock installations, machinery and underwater cables.

The Association is governed by a committee half the members of which are appointed on behalf of Lloyd's and half on behalf of insurance companies.

SECURITIES AND INVESTMENT BOARD

The Financial Services Act 1986 provided for the setting up of the Securities and Investment Board (SIB) which has the ultimate responsibility for overseeing and regulating all investment business of which life assurance is considered a part. The Board delegates powers to a number of self-regulatory organisations (SROs) including, for life assurers, the Life Assurance and Unit Trust Regulatory Organisation (LAUTRO), and, for brokers and other intermediaries, the Financial Intermediaries, Managers and Brokers Regulatory Organisation (FIMBRA). The SIB will take under its umbrella recognised professional bodies (RPBs) so that professional persons such as solicitors and accountants who conduct investment activities may be subjected to comparable regulation. Other organisations such as an Investment Management Regulatory Organisation (IMRO) and an Investment Ombudsman are in contemplation in 1987.

The 1986 Act is concerned primarily with investment matters so that it affects life assurance rather than general insurance. In early 1987 it is not yet clear how the operations of the Insurance Brokers' Registration Council and the Insurance Ombudsman Bureau which deal with both life and general insurance, will be affected.

SOCIAL SECURITY ADVISORY COMMITTEE

The Committee is constituted under the Social Security Act 1980 to advise the Secretary of State for Social Services on all social security matters except those relating to benefits for industrial injuries and diseases and occupational pensions. It scrutinises preliminary draft regulations under the Act, and representations made on them.

UNION OF UNITED KINGDOM LOSS ADJUSTERS

This is an association formed jointly by the Chartered Institute of Loss Adjusters and the Independent Adjusters Association to deal with international matters affecting loss adjusters.

UNITED KINGDOM CREDIT INSURANCE BROKERS COMMITTEE

See British Insurance Brokers Association.

UNITED KINGDOM INSURANCE BROKERS EUROPEAN COMMITTEE

See British Insurance Brokers Association.